TARGETING
TRANSITIONS

TARGETING TRANSITIONS

Marketing to Consumers During Life Changes

PAULA MERGENHAGEN

AMERICAN DEMOGRAPHICS BOOKS

AMERICAN DEMOGRAPHICS BOOKS.

A Division of American Demographics, Inc.
127 West State Street, Ithaca, NY 14850
Telephone: 607-273-6343

Executive Editor: Diane Crispell
Associate Editor: Shannon Dortch
Publisher: Wade Leftwich
Associate Publisher: James Madden
Marketing Associate: Matthew Klein

This publication is designed to provide accurate and authoritative information in regard to the subject matter covered. It is sold with the understanding that the publisher is not engaged in rendering legal, accounting, or other professional services. If legal advice or other expert assistance is required, the services of a competent professional should be sought.

Library of Congress Catalog Number: 94-790-022

Cataloging In Publication Data
Mergenhagen, Paula 1957–
Targeting transitions

Hardcover: ISBN 0-936889-29-2
Paperback: ISBN 0-936889-30-6

Book design and composition: Paperwork

Contents

DEDICATED to my husband, D. Paul DeWitt,
and to the memory of my grandmother, Mary Mergenhagen.

Foreword

MARKETING MAY BE a dynamic art, but marketers often look at consumers in a static way. They think of people as they are right now—married or single, parents or not, homemakers or paid employees, and so on. This ignores the fact that people are a combination of what they have been, what they are, and what they will become.

Take income, for instance. Marketers are sometimes puzzled by affluent people who act differently from one another. Some carefully watch money; others cheerfully spend it. Taking individuals' histories and psychologies into account makes these differences more understandable. People who had to be careful with money in the past may have a very different attitude toward spending than those who have never worried about paying the bills. Likewise, many homemakers have not always been home, and many plan to return to the paid work force in the future. Addressing them as people who have been and will always stay home can be a real mistake.

Transitions are especially relevant now because the rate of societal change has accelerated. The life cycle is far less stable and predictable than it was a few decades ago. People can and do marry at any age; many do so more than once. The same goes for having children and changing jobs. No longer is childbearing limited to women under 40 or retirement to men over 65.

Some life transitions are joyous, while others are painful. Most, however, share a degree of stress, demanding adjustments in attitudes, self-image, and lifestyle. From the marketer's point of view, most transitions also create a need for products and services. Becoming a parent for the first time is perhaps the most obvious example. People who lived a (relatively) carefree life suddenly decide it's time to buy a "sensible" Volvo, get life insurance, find a bigger house, and, of course, buy lots of baby products.

This book examines the crossroads of people's lives and spells out the opportunities they offer to business. In doing so, it points to the well-traveled roads we think we understand, as well as the increasing number of obscure sidepaths we need to understand better.

JUDITH LANGER
President, Langer Associates
New York, NY
August 1994

Acknowledgments

THERE ARE A NUMBER of individuals and organizations I would like to thank for making this book possible, either directly or indirectly:

First, I am very grateful to everyone I've worked with at *American Demographics*, especially Brad Edmondson, who accepted my first unsolicited article, and Diane Crispell, who did such a wonderful job editing the book.

I am also very grateful to Dorothea Heiden and Claudia Shoro at the United Way of Middle Tennessee. Because they gave me a part-time work schedule, I was able to continue working there as research director while writing the book. Cheryl Scutt, my former boss at United Way, played a major role in this as well. Their kindness and support helped me tremendously during a very busy and stressful time.

Many individuals from many organizations provided me with data and/or allowed me to interview them. Their contributions are felt throughout the book and are truly appreciated.

Nancy Hendrix of Demographic Data Consultants in Nashville first piqued my interest in market research almost ten years ago and gave me my first opportunity to moderate focus groups. Many thanks.

I owe a great deal to Vanderbilt University and the colleagues, professors, and students there who taught me how to be a sociologist and a researcher.

I would also like to acknowledge the influence of the American Association for the Advancement of Science. After participating in its Mass Media Science and Engineering Fellows Program back in 1983, I got the idea that I could somehow combine social science and journalism. In this book, I've tried to do that.

Through the years, my parents always encouraged my academic endeavors, something for which I am very grateful.

Finally, I want to thank my husband for many, many things, but most of all, for being there.

LIFE TRANSITIONS
Past, Present, and Future

IN THE 1989 movie *Parenthood,* the final scene depicts the birth of a baby. As relatives anxiously wait for news, the audience is led to believe that the woman giving birth is a newly married teenager. It turns out to be her newly remarried mother.

Marriage. Parenthood. Graduation. Retirement. We often think of these life events as happening at a certain time and in a certain order. But that was never really true, and it's less true all the time. A linear view of the life cycle is no longer on target. Americans now marry more often. They have children before, during, between, and after marriages. The school-to-work transition has also blurred as people pursue education throughout their worklives and beyond. Even the retirement transition is not black-and-white.

Millions of Americans go through life-changing transitions each year, virtually all of which necessitate purchases of various kinds. People in transition buy products ranging from wedding gowns to cribs, and services such as those provided by divorce attorneys and funeral directors. Some of these markets are on-the-spot opportunities, lasting only as long as the wedding champagne holds out. But the transitional customer can become a lifetime customer, too. Young adults establishing their first independent households make potentially long-lasting brand choices about everything from shampoo to cars. Couples buying their first home may require the services of a realtor again when they divorce a few years later.

Transitions often happen simultaneously. Marriage and parenthood can occur at or around the same time. Some brave souls make a move right before or after they have a child; others face the organizational nightmare of getting married and buying a house at the same time. Other transitions prompt moves, too, including getting a job, getting divorced, and retiring. Getting divorced may also initiate a career change or return to school. People who care for an infant or elderly parent may change jobs, cut down on their hours, or leave the work force altogether. Those who face multiple transitions are among the most stressed of all; they are also the neediest customers.

The vast majority of Americans marry and have children; most work and retire; and virtually everyone moves at least once. Some transitions are less common or seem less momentous to society at large, but are nonetheless critical turning-points in the lives of those who experience them—the person who becomes disabled, the stay-at-home parent whose youngest child starts school. Each is an opportunity to get people through an experience that may be joyful or sorrowful, but is in any case stressful.

WHY TRANSITIONS HAVE CHANGED

Why has the timing and frequency of life transitions changed? Three of the most important reasons are the impact of the baby boom, shifts in the workplace, and advances in technology.

The Baby Boom

The baby-boom generation born between 1946 and 1964 is better-educated than any preceding generation of Americans. This is especially true for women. Just 38 percent of women in the high school class of 1960 enrolled in college immediately after graduation. For the class of 1968, the share was 49 percent.

Extended education sets off a lifetime of postponement. Boomers began by putting off the family-related transitions their parents had typically made by their early 20s—namely, marriage and parenthood. The changing social environment also meant that they didn't always make these two transitions in that particular order. Out-of-wedlock childbearing became increasingly common, and so did that antecedent/alternative to marriage—living together.

Baby-boom women used their educations to make headway in the labor force, which further postponed marriage and parenthood. Paid jobs made women less dependent on their husbands, making divorce a more viable economic and increasingly socially acceptable option. As divorce became common, remarriage followed suit.

The Changing Workplace

As marketplace competition has become more global, corporations have responded by shedding layers of middle management. During one recent five-year period, almost six million people with three or more years of tenure with their employers were laid off. Almost one-fourth were managers and professionals. Formerly secure positions have become tenuous, causing individuals to rethink original career choices. Early retirement packages mean people can opt out of the labor force sooner. Out of desire or necessity, they often return to work at least part-time.

Although downsizing seems to imply that companies have become less concerned with workers' lives, the general trend has been for employers to become more involved in the work- and family-related issues and transitions their employees face. New parents usually receive at least some paid time off, as well as health benefits to help cover the costs of having a baby. Adult children frequently receive help from employers in locating elder care for aging parents. Employees facing job changes are sent to outplacement firms, retraining programs, or relocation counselors. Companies are very clear about their goal: keeping valued employees productive in times of personal stress. They often turn to outside vendors to provide such support to their workers.

Technology and Society

Technological advances, whether they take place in medicine or office automation, have profound effects on the timing and frequency of life transitions. Advances in the treatment of chronic conditions mean that individuals will live longer, although not necessarily better, increasing the likelihood that a middle-aged child will be called upon to care for an elderly parent. The limits of biology have expanded in other ways as well, as new reproductive technologies permit women in their 40s, 50s, and even 60s to become mothers.

Technology can also render whole job categories obsolete. Machines sometimes take over tasks previously performed by clerical and factory workers. These displaced workers can benefit from retraining and retooling. This has created a marked spread in the age distribution of college students, for whom graduation may come at age 30, 40, or beyond.

FINDING OPPORTUNITY IN TRANSITION

To make the most of the marketing opportunities that transitions offer, businesses need to understand people in transition, how they have changed, and how they may change in the future. This book sets out to do just that.

Part I (chapters 2 through 5) covers major family-related transitions. Part II (chapters 6 through 8) looks at job-related transitions, and Part III discusses the transition linked with so many others—moving—followed by a wrap-up of ten overall transition trends. Each chapter discusses past, present, and future trends in the marketplace, as well as examples of businesses that are successfully serving these markets. Each chapter ends with a summary list of the product/service opportunities for the transition, followed by a comprehensive source listing. The index offers a quick-find reference for specific product and service categories, demographic and consumer topics, as well as companies and studies mentioned in the text.

The following chapter summaries provide a taste of the book's contents:

Marriage and Remarriage

In 1960, it was common for couples to marry in their teens and early 20s. Remarriage was relatively rare because divorce rates were low. In the 1990s, median age at first marriage has risen to the mid-20s, and almost half of weddings are remarriages for one or both spouses.

Even so, three in four brides and grooms are under age 35, and the number of adults in this age group will decline about 5 percent between 1994 and 2000. Marriage rates have also dropped as more Americans choose to remain single. Those who serve this market will face increasing competition for the business of newlyweds. On the bright side, a growing share of older brides and grooms means consumers with more money to spend.

Parenthood

Just as people are marrying later, they are becoming parents at later ages, too. Still, most women give birth to their first child while in their 20s. Since this is a declining age group in the U.S. right now, demographers expect fewer babies during the late 1990s, although annual totals may hover around the four-million mark.

As with marriages, lack of market growth means increased competition for businesses that serve newborns and their parents—from hospitals and maternity shops to makers of baby food and diapers. But as with newlyweds, new parents who are older are usually more affluent. More than half of new mothers are working in the paid labor force within a year of their baby's birth, creating many dual-income households with more money, less time, and a definite need for day care.

Divorce

Divorce rates began their steady rise in 1970, the year that no-fault divorce became legal in California. During the mid-1980s, rates leveled off, and the annual number of divorces has been about 1.2 million since then. Still, four in ten marriages are expected to end in divorce, and a return to pre-1970 levels isn't likely.

The majority of people who end their marriages are young, with no children to argue over and few assets to divide. They may only require some education about the process and a little legal help. But a growing minority of divorces involve couples who have been married many years and have both children and significant amounts of property in common. These people need help from professionals ranging from divorce attorneys and accountants to pension analysts and psychologists.

Caregiving and Death

Caregiving is a "new" transition in that, for the first time in history, large numbers of middle-aged people are being called upon to care for aging relatives. Because of improvements in medical technology, the number of Americans most at risk of becoming incapacitated—those aged 85 and older—should nearly double in the 1990s. More than five million chronically disabled Americans aged 65 and older were living outside of institutions in 1989.

About three-fourths of caregivers are women. Most are in their 40s and 50s. Baby boomers are rapidly aging into this group, and as they do, the number of caregivers will increase. Since most boomer women work outside the home, their need for home-health-care and homemaking services will increase. So will their need for employer assistance in locating services for aging relatives.

Caregivers will eventually be faced with the loss of their loved one through death. At that time, the services of funeral homes, counselors, and lawyers become important. Although not all individuals who die are elderly, almost three-quarters are.

Graduation

The number of young Americans aged 18 to 24 declined 13 percent between 1980 and 1994, but the number of people entering institutions of higher education continued to increase. Why? Partly because a larger share of high school graduates (more than six in ten) now go directly to college. In 1992, that amounted to 1.5 million college-bound graduates. But the college market is also growing because of the large number of people aged 25 and older who are returning to campus.

Many of these nontraditional students are women who attend school part-time. They are likely to hold down jobs and raise families at the same time that they study for tests. Their needs are very different from those of 18-year-old freshmen. Still, young undergraduates remain extremely important to marketers because they are first-time users of so many products; so are the the noncollege youth who set up their own households.

Career Change

In spite of media attention to baby boomers in midlife crisis, American working men are actually somewhat less likely to change occupations today than they were in the mid-1960s. On the other hand, they are increasingly likely to seek out services that help them manage their careers and investigate alternatives to their current positions. Because of corporate restructuring and layoffs, they are also more likely to need outplacement or other job-search assistance.

Women are the true "career changers" of the 1990s. Their rates of occupational mobility have been on the rise over the past 30 years. As society's idea of appropriate careers for women has changed, women have been more than willing to make major switches in their life's work. They also frequently seek the advice of career counselors. Altogether, in 1991, 10 percent of American workers aged 16 and older—about ten million men and women—were in a different occupation than a year earlier. They have benefited from increases in corporate-sponsored education and on-the-job training. So have the businesses of independent consultants who supply much of that training.

Retirement

Over the past 40 years, new retirees have become more youthful. In the early 1950s, average retirement age in the U.S. was 67. By the late 1980s, it had dropped to 63. No one knows whether this trend will continue, because it's unclear whether baby boomers will have the financial means to retire early. On one hand, the share of women eligible for retirement benefits will grow dramatically. On the other hand, boomers are not known for thrifty behavior. Furthermore, those who delayed childbearing may face the "sandwich" dilemma of raising kids and caring for elderly parents at the same time. In either case, the retiree population will begin to grow after the turn of the century, and it will keep growing for nearly two decades.

Moving

A fast-paced society is not necessarily a more mobile society. Americans today are actually less likely to move than they were in the 1960s. Increased numbers of dual-earner couples may constrain some households from moving, but most moves are local, anyway. The real reason that America is less mobile is because it's older. The good news is that older people are more likely than average to buy moving services. When baby boomers were young, they borrowed trucks, enlisted the aid of friends, and made the move themselves. But boomers no longer have that kind of time or energy; neither do their friends.

Most moves are to rental units, and renters, especially those with children, have special needs. The one-fourth of moving households that do buy homes are a good market for many industries in addition to real-estate and mortgage banking. While they don't usually make major renovations the first year or two after they move in, people quickly begin to customize and furnish their new abodes.

TEN TRANSITION TRENDS

Chapter 10 recasts the findings of the previous eight chapters in a different light. Rather than cover a particular type of transition, it discusses ten overall trends in the way Americans make life transitions:

1) Transitions previously considered one-time events now occur more than once.

2) Ages at which "transitions of youth" occur have shifted upward.

3) Markets for "transitions of youth" will (temporarily) decline.

4) Markets for "transitions of maturity" will grow.

5) Women have been affected more than men by changes in life transitions, and women more often make the buying decisions surrounding transitions.

6) Transitions occur over a period of time and often have two or three different stages.

7) Consumers are often highly stressed during periods of transition.

8) Consumers often lack the time to handle transition-related tasks.

9) Consumer transitions provide business-to-business opportunities, too.

10) Businesses can use transitions to develop lifelong relationships with customers.

HOW TO REACH PEOPLE IN TRANSITION

Knowing about people in transition isn't enough, of course; you have to be able to find them, too. One of the best ways to reach those in the midst of life transitions iS through direct mail. Numerous businesses sell mailing lists of such individuals. But how can you find these companies?

A good place to start is the *Direct Marketing List Source* from SRDS (formerly known as Standard Rate and Data Service). This periodical has information on a large number of direct-mail lists, both consumer and business. Many list categories deal with transitions, including: "Babies" (new parents), "Brides" (newlyweds), "College and Alumni" (recent graduates), "Education and Self-Improvement" (potential career changers), "Occupant and Resident" (recent movers), "Senior Citizens" (retirees, elders living with children), and "Teenagers" (high school students).

Entries include the name, address, and phone number of the list manager, description and source of the list, and rental rates. The bimonthly publication is available for $354 a year from SRDS, 3004 Glenview Road, Wilmette, IL 60091.

PART I

FAMILY MATTERS

CHAPTER 2

MAKING
A MATCH
The Marriage/Remarriage Transition

WHEN DAVID EARNHARDT and Patricia Sommers wed in 1992, it was a remarriage for both. They wanted something different than a traditional wedding and finally settled on a Jamaican theme. After finding an outdoor location, they hired a reggae band and a Caribbean caterer. Earnhardt and Sommers paid for the 80-guest reception themselves, something common among remarrying couples. Both 38 years old and working, the couple "really didn't have any problem paying for it," says Sommers. "We had the money."

According to the National Center For Health Statistics (NCHS), remarriage is common these days. Almost half of the 2.4 million marriages in 1988 were remarriages for the bride, the groom, or both, up from about one-third in 1970. As the number of divorces has increased over the years, so has the number of remarriages—from 700,000 in 1970 to 1.1 million in 1988. Although the share of divorced people who remarry has decreased since 1970, there are almost four times as many divorced people now as there were then.

Even so, a slim majority of marriages, 54 percent, still take place between two people who have never been married. In 1988, that amounted to 1.3 million weddings. But numbers of first marriages reached a peak in the early 1970s and have fluctuated somewhat since then, gradually declining. Some, but not all, of this decline can be explained by the movement of baby boomers out of their early adult years. It is also the case that fewer single people are marrying today, and they are doing so at later ages.

Marriage Trends

Remarriages now account for nearly half of all weddings in a given year.

(thousands of marriages, percent that are remarriages, and marriage rate per 1,000 population, 1970–92)

	marriages	percent that are remarriages	marriage rate
1992	2,362	N/A	9.3
1991	2,371	N/A	9.4
1990	2,448	N/A	9.8
1989	2,404	N/A	9.7
1988	2,396	46%	9.7
1986	2,407	46	10.0
1984	2,477	45	10.5
1982	2,456	45	10.6
1980	2,390	44	10.6
1978	2,282	43	10.3
1976	2,155	41	9.9
1974	2,230	37	10.5
1972	2,282	33	10.9
1970	2,159	31	10.6

Source: National Center for Health Statistics

The wedding market is much more segmented than in the past. Young couples entering their first marriage have different needs than older consumers who are remarrying. Close to half of first-time brides have formal weddings, and these are expensive affairs. *Modern Bride* magazine estimates that they cost an average of $17,500 in 1993. Remarrying couples spend less than first-timers, but they are also indulging in more elaborate celebrations now that second marriages are no longer considered taboo.

In 1993, the entire newlywed market accounted for nearly $35 billion in U.S. retail sales. Newlywed households are far more likely than the average household to purchase or be given tableware, jewelry, cookware, appliances, linens, household accessories, and many other items. In addition to traditional items, couples are increasingly likely to want nontraditional gifts, like tools, patio furniture, camping equipment, and electronics.

Because people are marrying at later ages and more are remarrying, many newlyweds already have the basics. As a result, some hardware stores and home centers now offer gift registries. Even mortgage companies are getting into the act. Once primarily the bride's domain, grooms are more likely to get involved with wedding gifts, hoping to receive items like power tools and sports equipment.

Once the honeymoon ends, a couple's consumer needs have only just begun. The biggest part of young newlyweds' budgets goes to housing and home furnishings, and young childless couples are more likely than other households to buy new automobiles. This may also be their last chance to enjoy their freedom before children arrive. They spend a disproportionately high share of their food bill on eating out.

But many newlyweds don't have the luxury of starting out their married lives unencumbered. Half of divorcing couples have children, so many people entering second unions bring children with them into the new marriage. It is estimated that over half of all Americans will at some time in their lives be part of a stepfamily. Stepfamilies have many unique needs. They offer a wide variety of business opportunities, from travel to insurance.

TRENDS IN THE MARKET

There were nearly 2.4 million marriages in the U.S. in 1992, according to the NCHS. This represents a slight decrease after several years of increase during the 1980s. The marriage rate—the number of marriages per 1,000 population—also began falling in the late 1980s.

Both trends are partly due to the aging of the baby boom. Although more people are marrying at later ages than ever before, marriage is largely a transition of the young. Seventy-seven percent of those who married in 1988 were under the age of 35, 14 percent were aged 35 to 44, and just 9 percent were aged 45 and older. During the late 1990s and into the 2000s, the number and rate of marriages should continue to decline as baby boomers move into their 40s and 50s. In the mid-1990s, two-thirds of the adult population is aged 35 and older. By 2010, the share will be 70 percent. Likewise, the number of childless married couples under age 35 could decline from 3.8 million to 2.8 million during the 1990s, according to projections by *American Demographics* magazine.

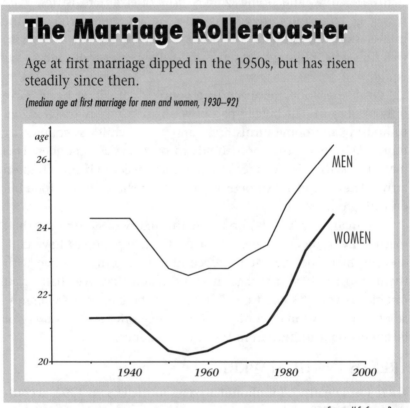

The Marriage Rollercoaster

Age at first marriage dipped in the 1950s, but has risen steadily since then.

(median age at first marriage for men and women, 1930–92)

Source: U.S. Census Bureau

Americans have been increasingly likely to delay their first marriage. Between 1970 and 1992, median age at first marriage rose from 23 years to 27 years for men and from 21 years to 24 years for women, according to the Census Bureau. Education accounts for much of the delay. The most highly educated men and women wait longest to get married, and today's young adults are better-educated than previous generations. According to the NCHS, the average age at first marriage for high school graduates in 1988 was 23 years for women and 25 years for men. The average age for college graduates was 27 years for women and 28 years for men.

While the majority of people put off marriage but eventually wed, the chances that some will never make this transition have increased. The share of unmarried individuals who wed each year has been declining for more than 20 years. Paul Glick, a former Census Bureau demographer, says more couples are now living together outside of marriage, which is partially responsible for the drop. "It doesn't mean [unmarried] people aren't mating," he notes. Indeed, the number of cohabiting couples more than doubled between 1980 and 1992, from 1.6 million to 3.3 million. In contrast, the number of married couples increased just 8 percent, according to the Census Bureau.

According to demographers Robert Schoen and Robin M. Weinick, about 96 percent of men and 97 percent of women who had survived to age 15 in 1970 were expected to marry at some time in their lives. By 1988, these expectations had declined to 84 percent and 88 percent, respectively. "The fact that women have independent incomes and are more highly educated has made them much more selective," says researcher Judith Langer of Langer Associates in New York City. "There's less pressure to marry today."

Remarriages

But once married, many Americans prefer the arrangement, even if they pursue it with someone other than their original spouse. An increasing share of marriages are remarriages. "Remarriage in the United States has become a relatively common life-course event," say Census Bureau researchers Arthur J. Norton and Louisa F. Miller.

Forty percent of remarriages in 1988 united two divorced persons. Half were not first marriages for just one of the partners, evenly split between remarrying brides and remarrying grooms. In 11 percent of remarriages, one or both spouses were widowed.

Three in ten divorced people remarry within 12 months of their divorce, according to the NCHS. The average divorced woman who

Who Remarries Whom

The most common type of remarriage unites two divorced people.

(marriages involving at least one previously married partner, by previous marital status of each partner, 1988)

GROOMS		BRIDES			
		Never-Married	Divorced	Widowed	Total
	Never-Married	None	261,600	12,000	273,600
	Divorced	257,100	455,600	32,500	745,200
	Widowed	8,700	30,800	32,100	71,600
	Total	265,800	748,000	76,600	1,090,400

Source: Barbara Foley Wilson and Sally Cunningham Clarke, "Remarriages: A Demographic Profile," Journal of Family Issues, June 1992

remarries is 35 years old and has been divorced for 3.9 years. The average man is 39 and has waited 3.6 years. The interval between marriages lengthens with age. While divorced grooms aged 20 to 24 wait an average of only 1.3 years before remarrying, those aged 65 and older wait 7.1 years. Total remarriage rates for the divorced are also highest among young adults, but the number of remarriages peaks among older age groups because there are more divorced people at those ages.

In 1970, 86 percent of ever-divorced men and 80 percent of ever-divorced women were expected to remarry at some point in their lives, according to demographers Robert Schoen and Robin M. Weinick. By 1988, those proportions had dropped to 78 percent and

72 percent, respectively. Even so, "remarriage will still be relatively widespread, resulting in, among other things, a continued increase in the number of reconstituted, blended, and/or stepfamilies," according to Norton and Miller of the Census Bureau.

THE BIG DAY (AND THE NIGHTS THAT FOLLOW)

Marriages that are firsts for both bride and groom are often expensive affairs. In the 1991 movie *Father of the Bride,* an upper-middle-class father played by Steve Martin holds the reception at his home and still ends up with a tab exceeding $50,000. And that's just for the reception. But Martin's experience is unusual. In 1993, *Modern Bride* magazine estimates that the total cost of a formal wedding for first-time brides—from the ring to the reception—was $17,500. Almost half of all first-time brides have formal weddings.

It wasn't always the case, but June has become the traditional time to get married, possibly because it's a pleasant time of year in most parts of the country. "The weather is good in June," says Annie Thurow of *Modern Bride.* "Many people do outdoor receptions, and they take pictures outside." On the other hand, June is not as popular as it was when more people married right out of high school or college, she notes. August is the second most popular month for weddings, followed by May and July.

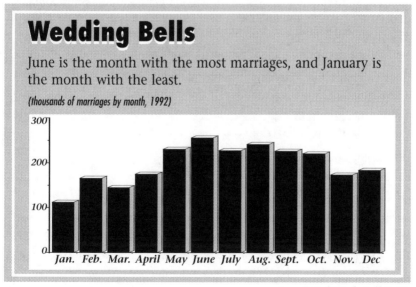

Wedding Bells

June is the month with the most marriages, and January is the month with the least.

(thousands of marriages by month, 1992)

Jan. Feb. Mar. April May June July Aug. Sept. Oct. Nov. Dec

Source: National Center for Health Statistics

Most first-time brides wear traditional long white gowns with trains, says Diana Tran, owner of Diana's Couture and Bridal in Washington, D.C. Tran is a custom dressmaker who frequently alters and restores wedding gowns originally worn by mothers and grand-mothers. Restorations and alterations account for one-third of her bridal business. Brides wear these gowns for sentimental reasons, notes Tran, but economy also plays a role. Most remarrying brides will choose an ivory gown or suit, she says, "usually with a simple design."

Formal weddings average almost 200 guests, according to *Modern Bride*. Sixty percent hold receptions in the evening. Sixty-one percent hold receptions in a catering hall, club, or restaurant; 17 percent at a hotel; 17 percent at a church or temple; and 5 percent at a private home.

Wedding Bills

Forty percent of the cost of a formal wedding is for the reception.

(average cost of a formal wedding, 1993)

Reception	$7,000
Music	600
Photography	1,090
Videography	480
Flowers	860
Limousine	300
Invitations/announcements	340
Clergy/church or synagogue	220
Bridal party gifts	250
Engagement ring	2,760
Bride's wedding ring	710
Groom's wedding ring	400
Bride's shoes	50
Wedding gown	850
Headpiece/veil	170
Groom's formalwear	110
Attendants' attire	750
Men's formalwear rentals	530
Total	$17,470

Source: Modern Bride/Cahners Publishing

About one-fifth of second-timers also have formal weddings. Wedding industry sources estimate that 25 to 30 percent of their business comes from remarriages. Among younger couples, it is often a remarriage for one of the parties but not the other. In 1988, one in four remarriages included a divorced bride and never-married groom. Another fourth involved a never-married bride and divorced groom.

How do the receptions of first- and second-time brides differ? According to *Modern Bride*, a reception for a formal wedding costs an average of $7,000. But that's just for the reception hall, food, and beverages. Music and flowers add another $1,460. Because second weddings are less likely to be formal, about 35 percent as much is spent on receptions for remarriages as for first marriages.

Like Earnhardt and Sommers, the couple introduced at the beginning of this chapter, remarrying couples typically foot some or all of the bill for their own wedding. This gives them more control over the format it will take. Second-time brides tend to have smaller weddings, with perhaps 50 to 100 guests, say industry experts. "It generally includes the extended family and wider circle this couple has acquired through more than one marriage," says Julia Davidson, a wedding florist and owner of the Tulip Tree in Nashville, Tennessee. Second-time brides are also more likely to be nontraditional in their tastes. Earnhardt and Sommers served up jerk chicken with beans and rice. The reception was held in an outdoor pavilion, decorated with paper lanterns and neon lights. Vows were taken outdoors by a lake, with guests reciting philosophical quotes concerning the nature of marriage.

Wedding parties are larger when first-time brides are involved. For a formal wedding, they average ten attendants—five male, five female—according to *Modern Bride*. Second-timers usually have a smaller wedding party. They rarely include more than four attendants, says florist Julia Davidson.

Photography packages also tend to be different for first- and second-timers. "In first weddings, you show the bride doing everything, like having the garter removed," says Mindy Orman of Orman and Orman Photographers in Nashville, Tennessee. For second weddings, there's less focus on the bride; "they choose more pictures of family and close friends," says Orman. Wedding photography for a formal wedding costs an average of $1,100, according to *Modern Bride*. Couples who want a video of the big day can expect to add another $500 to the tab.

If second marriages are an expanding market niche for the wedding industry, so are ethnic celebrations. According to a *Wall Street Journal* article about African-style weddings, "competition is minimal and consumer interest in the concept is high at a time when *Brides Today* magazine reports that black couples are spending a total of $3.2 billion a year on their weddings." Products with increasing sales include custom-designed invitations, special clothing and wedding bands, as well as brooms used for the African wedding tradition of broom jumping. "The whole business of Afro-centric goods is a growing industry," says Nancy Flake of Howard University. "There are lots of entrepreneurial opportunities that spin off of that."

Honeymoons

Regardless of what the wedding is like, most newlywed couples go on honeymoons. But their destination is not likely to be the stereotypical trip to Niagara Falls. Honeymoons are now more likely to be taken outside the continental U.S. than in the past. "People used to go to the Poconos. Now they go to Hawaii," notes *Modern Bride's* Thurow. Older brides and grooms who both work can more easily afford overseas travel.

In 1990–91, two-thirds of newlyweds honeymooned outside the continental U.S., according to a survey of *Modern Bride* readers. They spent an average of $3,900 on their trip, up 39 percent from 1986–87. Hawaii, Mexico, Jamaica, U.S. Virgin Islands, and the Bahamas were the most frequent destinations.

Almost half (46 percent) of newlyweds honeymooned within the continental U.S., spending an average of $2,400, almost twice as much as in 1986–87. Their most popular destinations were Florida, California, Pennsylvania, South Carolina, Virginia, Tennessee, New York, and Nevada. Some made stops in both foreign and domestic locations.

The average honeymoon lasts nine days, although 17 percent of newlyweds spend two weeks or more. Seventy-five percent of honeymooners travel by air; 16 percent take cruises. Seven in ten make use of a travel agent or travel service. Nine in ten destinations are joint decisions of the bride and groom.

COUNTING UP THE GIFTS AND SETTLING INTO MARRIED LIFE

When people think of bridal registries, traditional housewares such as crystal, silver, and china usually come to mind. Rarely do people think of the home itself. But in 1992, ARBOR National Mortgage of Uniondale, New York, set up a money-market account through Chase Manhattan Bank permitting wedding guests to contribute to a couple's downpayment on a house. Thus, the ARBOR Home Bridal Registry was born.

Over two-thirds of all ARBOR's retail home loans go to first-time buyers, and the company specializes in that area, says Nancy Boles, senior vice president, marketing. "Part of our strategy in putting together the bridal registry was trying to attract newlyweds to let them know we have very affordable loan programs."

Boles came up with the registry idea after attending employees' weddings. Many of the couples were already living together and had basic household necessities. But they were usually renting, and what they really needed was the downpayment for a home. "If [newlyweds] can get a couple thousand dollars in their account to start them off, it becomes a psychological base," says Boles. The program has received more than 2,000 inquiries in the two years, and three dozen couples have signed up, mostly dual-career professionals in their late 20s.

ARBOR has the right idea. According to *Modern Bride,* the newlywed market accounted for $5 billion in mortgage downpayments in 1993. Although it may take couples several years to actually make a purchase, attracting their attention early will help mortgage companies gain their business.

Newlyweds in their 20s often look for condominiums rather than single-family homes, says Alice Moore Weaver, a Nashville, Tennessee, real-estate agent. "They're not thinking about starting a family yet," she notes. Some are in graduate or professional school and "thinking in terms of finishing their education and building equity." Older couples are more likely to have been working for a while, and one or both may already own condominiums at the time of the marriage. Their next step will probably be a single-family home, says Weaver.

Although newlywed households accounted for just under 3 percent of all U.S. households, they accounted for 5 percent of sales of furniture and home accessories in 1989, according to *Modern Bride*. But only couples who move into another residence after they marry are likely to buy much furniture, says Britt Beemer, chairman of America's Research Group in Charleston, South Carolina. "Our research suggests that two out of three people today who are getting married are moving into one of the two households they already have, if they were not already living together to begin with." But all newlyweds buy lots of home accessories, says Beemer.

Newlywed couples who do move into new homes spend an average of $3,500 to $3,800 on furniture, not including other home accessories, says Beemer. Ready-to-assemble furniture is a particular favorite. "It's a 7-to-1 leader over any other category from a unit perspective," says Beemer. "It's styled toward a younger consumer. It fits with their lifestyle." Casual dining groups is the number-two furniture item purchased by newlyweds, followed by sleeper sofas, mattresses, and freestanding wall units for home-entertainment centers.

Nontraditional Gifts

Newlyweds need lots of things to start their new lives, many of them nontraditional. "We're seeing an increase in such items as camping equipment, patio furniture, gas grills, and tools," says Laura Walther, director of gift registry services for Service Merchandise, a catalog showroom based in Brentwood, Tennessee, with stores in 37 states.

Walther says that grooms have become much more involved in the whole process surrounding weddings and wedding gifts. "No longer do you have strictly lingerie and kitchen showers. You're having showers that involve two people rather than just the bride. Now you have 'tool time' and 'sports' showers." When grooms get involved, the ticket price increases, says Walther. "Brides tend to be more laid-back. But the grooms say, 'Come on, this is a wish list.'"

All types of electronics—from fax machines to telephones, camcorders, and VCRs—are very popular, according to Debra Remington, gift registry manager for the department-store division of the Minneapolis-based Dayton Hudson Corporation. Electronics are frequently given as group gifts. Newlyweds accounted for 7 percent of sales of telephones in 1989, higher than the 3 percent of all households they represented, according to *Modern Bride*. They accounted for 6 percent of audio equipment sales and 4 percent of video equipment sales.

Group wedding gifts are also popular at Home Depot, a major home-center chain that started a bridal registry in 1992. Brides and grooms can "pick a new $300 door for their home, and four or five friends will go in on it," says Home Depot spokeswoman Jenifer Swearingen. Friends may also chip in to buy appliances—newlyweds are twice as likely as others to get refrigerators or microwave ovens, and three times as likely to get clothes dryers, according to *Modern Bride*.

Couples who wait until their late 20s or 30s to marry may exercise more control over their registry choices, notes Service Merchandise's Walther. In the past, brides "thought they had to register for china and the things their mother wanted them to have. Now, it's 'What do I need?'"

Nevertheless, brides and grooms are still buying and receiving lots of traditional items. In 1993, newlywed households accounted for an estimated $1.6 billion in retail sales of tableware and tableware accessories and $500 million in linens, domestics, and accessories, according to *Modern Bride*. Although newlywed households made up 3 percent of U.S. households in 1989, they accounted for 75 percent of retail sales of fine china dinnerware, 46 percent of fine crystal stemware, 29 percent of tableware and accessories, and 21 percent of jewelry and watches. They also represented 16 percent of bath towel sales, 12 percent of nonelectric cookware and bakeware, 12 percent of small appliances, and 11 percent of linens and domestics.

Traditional or not, brides and grooms are busy people, and so are their guests. Some department stores are trying to make the registry

Wedding Shopping

Newly married couples are likely to buy or receive as gifts a wide variety of products, including jewelry, household furnishings, tableware, and video equipment.

(bridal market retail sales, in millions of dollars, by major product categories, 1993)

	sales
Tableware	$1,240.3
Tableware accessories	404.3
Linens, domestics, and accessories	494.1
Nonelectric cookware and bakeware	240.4
Small kitchen appliances	226.6
Household appliances	879.6
Furniture and household furnishings	2,173.1
Jewelry and watches	2,979.8
Luggage	61.3
Cameras	70.0
Audio equipment	118.9
Video equipment	303.3
Telephones	48.3
Personal computers	89.9
Automobiles	5,217.8
Bridal party gifts	241.7
Wedding gowns	604.5
Reception services	6,655.3
Honeymoon travel	3,587.9
Housing down payments	5,044.3
Home improvements	249.8
Investments	3,583.0
Beauty care	139.0
Trousseau	320.1
Total	$34,973.3

Source: Modern Bride/Cahners Publishing

process as easy as possible. The Dayton Hudson Corporation started a nationwide 800 number for bridal gifts in 1992. It meets the needs of out-of-town wedding guests, as well as those who just can't make it into a store to do their shopping. "A lot of people don't have a lot of time," says Debra Remington of Dayton Hudson. "They can just pick up the phone at work and order a gift."

Monogrammed towels may seem like perfect wedding gifts, and they probably are—for 90 percent of newly married couples. But for the rest, this selection could prove embarrassing. That's because 10 percent of married women in the U.S. don't use their husband's last name, or don't use it exclusively. According to a 1993 survey conducted for *American Demographics* by NFO Research, 5 percent of married women use hyphenated names and 2 percent use their maiden name exclusively. The other 3 percent use different variations, such as using their maiden name as a middle name or for social and legal, but not professional, purposes.

Younger, better-educated, and higher-income couples are more likely to have a wife who doesn't use her husband's last name. Fourteen percent of married women under age 40, 10 percent of those in their 40s, and 5 percent of those aged 50 and older do not use their husband's last name exclusively. This is also true of 15 percent of women with bachelor's degrees, 21 percent with post-graduate degrees, but less than 5 percent of those without a college education. Thirteen percent of married women with household incomes of $60,000 or more, but just 7 percent of those with incomes between $13,000 and $40,000, use a nontraditional last name.

Their homes and the things in them are not all that newlyweds have on their minds. In an analysis of the government's Consumer Expenditure Survey, demographer Margaret Ambry finds that young childless couples spend 72 percent more than the average household on new cars. According to *Modern Bride,* newlyweds spend $5.2 billion a year on new cars.

And newlyweds are going places in those cars. The first years of marriage may be the last chance to get out of the house and kitchen before another big transition comes their way—parenthood. More than half of young childless couples' food dollars are spent in restaurants and on carry-out items, and they spend considerably more than others on alcohol—more than 1 percent of their total annual expenditures.

READY-MADE FAMILIES

Some newlywed couples don't have the luxury of freedom before the kids come along. Many bring children from a previous union into

their new marriage. Stepfamilies have seen tremendous growth over
the years, according to the Census Bureau.

In 1990, the U.S. had 5.3 million married-couple stepfamily
households containing 7.3 million stepchildren under age 18. This
represents 21 percent of all married-couple families with children, a
5-percentage-point increase over 1980. Almost half of these households (47 percent) included both step- and biological children.

Complex Family Ties

The number of married couples with biological children
only increased 1 percent in the 1980s, while the number
with stepchildren grew 35 percent.

(thousands of married-couple households with children under age 18 by type of relationship, 1980 and 1990)

	1990	1980
total	25,314	24,091
biological children only	19,253	19,037
adoptive only	345	429
biological mother-stepfather	2,619	1,818
biological father-stepmother	152	171
joint biological-step	2,475	1,862
joint biological-adoptive	324	429
joint step-adoptive	8	12
joint bio-step-adoptive	0	25
unknown	137	309

Source: U.S. Census Bureau

The vast majority of stepchildren in these families (92 percent)
live with their biological mother and stepfather. Between 1980 and
1990, the number of children living with both biological parents
declined 6 percent. In contrast, the number living with stepparents
increased 19 percent. This rise was entirely due to a 24 percent increase in children living with biological mothers and stepfathers.

The number living with biological fathers and stepmothers actually declined 16 percent.

Because children in stepfamilies often shuttle between homes in different places, they may travel more than other children. Patricia Schiff Estess, author of *Remarriage and Your Money*, suggests that airlines or car manufacturers could use this situation to good advantage by acknowledging the presence of stepfamilies in their advertising.

Stepfamilies are also more likely than intact families to need certain financial and legal services, Estess notes, because their financial responsibilities are more complex. Remarried couples frequently have three bank accounts—one joint and two separate, she says. "They feel more comfortable doing this, especially in the first ten years of a marriage."

Stepfamilies also make good prospects for life insurance companies. "A stepfamily often utilizes life insurance as a major estate-planning tool," says Estess. They need more insurance than the average person to cover children from a previous marriage. Stepparents also want to make sure that their assets will be distributed according to their wishes. Washington, D.C. attorney Susan Friedman frequently helps stepfamilies do just that. "In a second marriage, people are concerned that their biological children have their rights protected in case they die," she says. Friedman says the interests of the children are a priority for the biological parent, but may not have quite the same importance for the stepparent.

As with intact families, stepfamilies are "concerned about their retirement savings and children's educations," says Barry Clark, a financial consultant with Merrill Lynch in Wichita, Kansas. Half of the families he works with are stepfamilies, a share that has increased steadily since he started consulting in 1983. Stepfamilies become interested in financial planning once their expenses from blending households have stabilized, about one to three years after marriage, says Clark.

But financial goals may be more difficult to achieve in stepfamilies than in intact families because their incomes are often lower and spread over more people. Forty-five percent of intact families have household incomes of $50,000 or more, compared with 37 percent of stepfamilies, according to demographer Paul Glick. Just

29 percent of intact families have incomes below than $30,000 a year, compared with 39 percent of stepfamilies. "Poor people are more likely to divorce, so they're more likely to remarry," says Glick.

Along with financial issues, issues of childrearing cause major concern in newly formed stepfamilies, says Margorie Engel, author of *Weddings for Complicated Families*. Many stepfamilies seek counseling on these issues, says Nashville psychologist Ruth Arbitman Smith. Differing styles of discipline and differing expectations for children's behavior often create problems, she says.

When families blend, two sets of potentially incompatible family traditions must also blend. "Maybe one family opened gifts on Christmas morning. The other one always did it Christmas Eve," says Engel. "Now what do they do?" Children do not always welcome the changes a stepfamily brings, changes that may include giving up a private bedroom and sharing with a stepsibling. Even the Brady Bunch, that ideal blended TV family, had trouble adjusting.

Becoming a stepparent can be an especially difficult adjustment for someone who's never been a parent at all. When David Earnhardt married Patricia Sommers, he had no children, but she had a small son. "Suddenly you're an instant parent to a 4-year-old," he says. Counseling helped him to build a satisfying relationship with the boy.

Earnhardt is not alone. An increasing number of men have found themselves in his shoes over the last decade. But the numbers of remarriages and stepfamilies will probably not grow during the 1990s as they did during the 1980s. The marriage rate continues to decline, and the divorce rate has been leveling off. Nevertheless, stepfamilies will continue to be an important consumer segment because so many people are involved in them at one time or another.

PRODUCTS AND SERVICES FOR
The Marriage/Remarriage Transition

The Wedding Day

Catering
Flowers
Photography and
  videography
Reception halls/hotels
Music
Limousine service
Printing
Jewelry
Bridal and formalwear
  (rented and purchased)
Honeymoons
Airlines
Cruises
Car rental
Resorts
Travel agents

The Gift and Newlywed Market

Real-estate agents and
  home builders
Mortgages
Apartments
Furniture

Carpeting
Appliances
Home accessories
Electronics
Tableware
Linens and domestics
China
Crystal
Cookware
Small appliances
New cars

Nontraditional Gifts/ Purchases

Sports and camping
  equipment
Patio furniture and
  outdoor items
Tools
Home decorating
  products and services

Blended Families

Banking services
Life insurance
Financial planning
Family counseling

SOURCES

Alexander, Suzanne. **"Firms Cater to African-Style Weddings."** *The Wall Street Journal,* August 24, 1993, pp. B1–2.

Ambry, Margaret K. **"Receipts from a Marriage."** *American Demographics,* Ithaca, NY, February 1993, pp. 30–37.

Brightman, Joan. **"Why Hillary Chooses Rodham Clinton."** *American Demographics,* Ithaca, NY, March 1994, pp. 9–11.

Day, Jennifer Cheeseman. *Population Projections of the United States, by Age, Sex, Race, and Hispanic Origin: 1993 to 2050.* Washington, DC: U.S. Bureau of the Census, 1993.

Editors of American Demographics. **"The Future of Households."** *American Demographics,* Ithaca, NY, December 1993, pp. 27–40.

Engel, Margorie. *Weddings for Complicated Families: The New Etiquette.* Boston, MA: Mt. Ivy Press, 1993.

Estess, Patricia Schiff. *Remarriage and Your Money: Once Again, For Richer or Poorer.* Boston, MA: Little, Brown and Company, 1992.

Glick, Paul C. and Barbara Larney. **"Parents with Young Stepchildren and With Adult Stepchildren: A Demographic Profile."** Paper presented at the annual meeting of the Stepfamily Association of America, Lincoln, NE, October 4, 1991.

Larson, Jan. **"Understanding Stepfamilies."** *American Demographics,* Ithaca, NY, July 1992, pp. 36–40.

Mergenhagen DeWitt, Paula. "**The Second Time Around.**" *American Demographics,* Ithaca, NY, November 1992, pp. 60–63.

Modern Bride/Cahners Publishing. **Bridal Market Retail Spending Study, 1993 Updates.** New York, NY: Cahners Publishing, 1993.

Modern Bride/Cahners Publishing. **Honeymoon Market Report 1991.** New York, NY: Cahners Publishing, 1992.

National Center for Health Statistics. **Advance Report of Final Marriage Statistics, 1988, Monthly Vital Statistics Report**, Vol. 40, No. 4, Suppl., Public Health Service, Hyattsville, MD, 1991.

National Center for Health Statistics. **Annual Summary of Births, Marriages, Divorces, and Deaths: United States, 1992, Monthly Vital Statistics Report**, Vol. 41, No. 13, Public Health Service, Hyattsville, MD, 1993.

Norton, Arthur J. and Louisa F. Miller. **Marriage, Divorce, and Remarriage in the 1990s.** Washington, DC: U.S. Bureau of the Census, 1992.

Saluter, Arlene F. **Marital Status and Living Arrangements: March 1992.** Washington, DC: U.S. Bureau of the Census, 1992.

Schoen, Robert and Robin M. Weinick. "**The Slowing Metabolism of Marriage: Figures from 1988 U.S. Marital Status Life Tables.**" *Demography,* Vol. 30, No. 4, November 1993, pp. 737–746.

Waldrop, Judith. "**Here Come the Brides.**" *American Demographics,* Ithaca, NY, June 1990, p. 4.

Waldrop, Judith. "**The Honeymoon Isn't Over.**" *American Demographics,* Ithaca, NY, August 1992, pp. 14, 17.

Waldrop, Judith. **The Seasons of Business: The Marketer's Guide to Consumer Behavior.** Ithaca, NY: American Demographics Books, 1992.

Wilson, Barbara Foley and Sally Cunningham Clarke. **"Remarriages: A Demographic Profile."** *Journal of Family Issues,* Vol. 13, No. 2, June 1992, pp. 123–141.

OTHER RESOURCES

Coleman, Marilyn and Lawrence H. Ganong. **"Remarriage and Stepfamily Research in the 1980s: Increased Interest in an Old Family Form."** *Journal of Marriage and the Family,* Vol. 52, November 1990, pp. 925–940.

Journal of Family Issues. Vol. 13, No. 2, June 1992. [The entire issue is devoted to remarriage.]

South, Scott J. and Stewart E. Tolnay (eds.). *The Changing American Family: Sociological and Demographic Perspectives.* Boulder, CO: Westview Press, 1992.

CHAPTER 3

BUYING BOTTLES AND BOOTIES
The Parenthood Transition

PAULA AND JAN JENNINGS were aged 36 and 47, respectively, when their first child, Callie, was born in 1989. Son Ryan appeared on the scene three years later, by which time the Jennings—both professionals with long work histories—had built a large new home to accommodate their offspring.

Paula Jennings represents a minority of new mothers because most first births occur to women under age 30. But she represents a minority that has grown over the past decade. During the 1980s, birth rates for women over the age of 30, particularly those aged 35 and older, rose sharply. The share of these births that are first births has also grown. Both trends are good news for those who market to new parents because older parents spend more than younger parents, and first-time parents spend more than those who've done it before.

The not-so-good news is that the large group of baby-boom women that fueled the baby boomlet of the 1980s and early 1990s is reaching the end of its childbearing years. The youngest boomers turned 30 in 1994 and the oldest turned 48. This means that births in the U.S., which peaked at almost 4.2 million in 1990, will probably decline during the rest of the 1990s and into the early 2000s. In 1993, births totaled 4.0 million.

Fewer births will mean increased competition for a wide variety of businesses that cater to newborns, from obstetric services to baby food and nursery furniture. Knowing what parents want and need will be especially important in the coming years.

What new parents want is heavily influenced by their age. Older mothers are more likely to be employed, which means they are often short on time but have considerable income. They can afford the upscale baby products carried by specialty catalogs and stores that evolved over the past decade. Working parents are also willing to pay for convenience; finding quality day care is a high priority.

People who wait longer to become parents tend to be highly educated. Acquiring those educations is one of the reasons they put off parenthood. Education is also a primary determinant of interest in childbirth preparation classes, information about childbirth and parenting, and the use of nontraditional options such as birthing centers.

When parents have their first child, they need everything associated with baby care all at once. About four in ten births in 1991 were first births, up from 26 percent in 1960. Although the share of first births among women in their 30s and 40s increased between 1980 and 1991, more than three-fourths of first births are to women under age 30. Younger parents may not spend as much in upscale specialty stores, but they are good customers for retail discounters. And of course, all new parents, regardless of age, income, or whether the child is a first or fourth, have to buy things like diapers.

The desire to make the transition into parenthood also gives rise to other types of businesses—infertility treatment and adoption services. Adoption as a path to parenthood has declined over the past two decades. On the other hand, more people are now seeking treatment for infertility. Although age-specific infertility rates have not risen over the past two decades, the delaying of parenthood and aging of the baby boom means that a larger number of couples are having problems conceiving. An entire industry focused on infertility treatment has evolved to help them become parents.

TRENDS IN THE MARKET

The baby boomlet that began in the late 1970s is finally winding down. Between 1989 and 1990, the number of births increased 3 percent, to 4.2 million, according to the National Center for Health Statistics (NCHS). This was the largest number seen since 1962, and it was probably the boomlet's peak. Births fell 1 percent in 1991, slightly less than 1 percent in 1992, and just over 1 percent in 1993, although they remained just over the four-million mark.

The Census Bureau has plotted three alternatives for the future of births. According to its low-fertility series, the U.S. will see 3.6 to 3.9 million births a year for the rest of the decade. This scenario assumes that women will average 1.8 children. The bureau's high-fertility series projects that births will continue to top 4.1 million a year for the rest of the 1990s and reach 4.3 million in 1999. This series assumes that women will have an average of 2.5 children. The middle series, considered most likely, expects births to rise slightly to nearly 4.1 million in 2000 and assumes that women will have an average of 2.1 children.

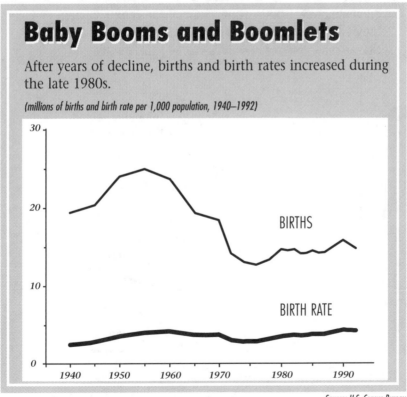

Baby Booms and Boomlets

After years of decline, births and birth rates increased during the late 1980s.

(millions of births and birth rate per 1,000 population, 1940–1992)

BIRTHS

BIRTH RATE

Source: U.S. Census Bureau

Indeed, two children is the number that women want, according to a 1992 Census Bureau survey. This ideal holds for teenagers as well as women in their 30s. About 48 percent of women aged 18 to 34 expect to have two children, 14 percent expect to have one child, and 29 percent want (or already have) more than two. Just 9 percent plan to remain childless.

The two-child ideal has been in force since the late 1970s. But as recently as 1967, women wanted (or had) an average of three children. Today, "a woman wants to finish her education, get into the labor force, and get economically stabilized" before becoming a parent, says Census Bureau demographer Amara Bachu. "Once she gets older, she doesn't have the time or energy to take care of more than one or two kids."

How do expectations compare with reality? Actual family size is

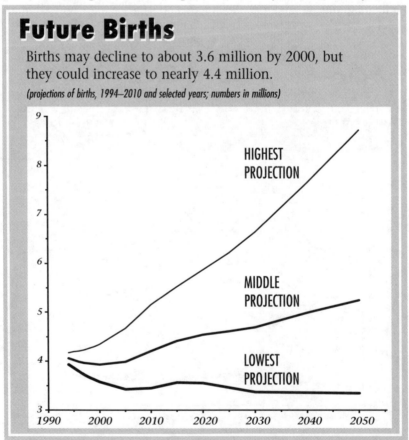

Future Births

Births may decline to about 3.6 million by 2000, but they could increase to nearly 4.4 million.

(projections of births, 1994–2010 and selected years; numbers in millions)

Source: U.S. Census Bureau

usually a little lower, says Bachu. The group of women who have just ended their childbearing years expected to average 2.2 children, but ended up with an average closer to 2.0. Bachu says that women currently in their 20s will probably have families no larger than the women who have just completed their childbearing. "It will stay around two children on average, not more than that."

But some feel that today's young women may have more children than their predecessors. "I think we're going to see bigger families," says Irma Zandl of The Zandl Group, a New York City–based firm that tracks the attitudes of youths. For young women today, "the idea of staying home with a baby is not considered a waste of time," she says. This attitude may be a reaction to their own childhoods. "They were brought up as latchkey children," says Zandl.

Although the youngest baby boomers are 30 years old in 1994, they still strongly influence the ranks of new mothers. These women married and began their childbearing relatively late. What's more, they are continuing to bear children after demographers expected them to slow down.

Between 1980 and 1991, the share of births to women in their 30s increased from 19 percent to 30 percent. This was partly because

Aging Mothers

In the 1980s, the share of mothers under age 25 declined, the share in their late 20s remained stable, and the share over age 30 grew.

(number of live births and percent distribution by age of mother, 1980 and 1991)

	1980	1991
total births	3,612,258	4,110,907
age of mother:		
under 20	16%	13%
20 to 24	34	27
25 to 29	31	30
30 to 34	15	22
35 to 39	4	8
40 and older	1	1

Source: National Center for Health Statistics

the overall share of women who were in their 30s increased, from 19 percent in 1980 to 22 percent in 1991. But the annual birth rate for this age group—the number of babies per 1,000 women aged 30 to 39—also increased. The birth rate for women aged 30 to 34 increased 31 percent between 1980 and 1990, and that for women aged 35 to 39 grew even faster, 60 percent. The birth rate also grew 41 percent for women aged 40 to 44; even so, they account for only 1 percent of all births.

Between 1990 and 1991, however, the birth rate for women in their late 30s increased just 1 percent. "It may be that we've reached a peak in the proportion of women who want to postpone marriage and childbearing," says NCHS analyst Stephanie Ventura. "But it's going to stay high. I don't think we're ever going to return to a point where everyone has children in their 20s."

Both numbers and rates of births dropped slightly for women in their 20s and early 30s between 1990 and 1991. Baby boomers have now passed out of their 20s and have been replaced by the smaller baby-bust generation, which accounts for the declining numbers. But it isn't entirely clear why rates dropped, says Ventura. Although the decline was small, ranging from 1 percent to 2 percent, it had a large impact because more than three-fourths of all births are to women in their 20s and early 30s.

Teenagers' birth rates have continued to increase substantially since the mid-1980s. However, because the share of teenagers in the population has been declining, teenage births were a smaller percentage of births in 1991 (13 percent) than in 1980 (16 percent). The share of teenagers will be increasing in the late 1990s, however, so they could represent a growing share of new parents. Teen parents are of dubious importance to some marketers because they are likely to be poor, but they are important for those who aim at a downscale market.

About one-fourth of women who give birth in the U.S. today are unmarried at the time. But not all are never-married teenagers. As the stigma of unwed motherhood has declined, older and better-educated women have come to see this as a viable route to parenthood. Even so, TV's Murphy Brown is still in the minority. Almost two-thirds of unmarried women who gave birth between July 1991 and June 1992 were under age 25, compared with the one-fourth share held by married women that age.

Unwed Mothers

Two-thirds of births to teenagers are out of wedlock, compared with 12 percent of those to women aged 30 and older.

(thousands of births to unmarried women and as percent of total births, by age of mother, July 1991 to June 1992)

	births to unwed women	percent of births in age group
women aged 15 to 44	893	24%
15 to 19	203	65
20 to 24	357	38
25 to 29	167	15
30 to 44	166	12

Source: U.S. Census Bureau

New parents have lower-than-average incomes, mostly because they haven't reached their peak earning years. About 19 percent of births that occurred between July 1991 and June 1992 were to women with family incomes of $50,000 or more, compared with 33 percent of all families in 1992. Thirty-six percent of babies arrived in families with incomes below $20,000, versus 25 percent of all families with incomes this low.

PURSUING PREGNANCY

Most couples want to become parents, but this is easier said than done for some. Couples who find it difficult to conceive and bear children have several options these days. The traditional choice has been adoption. However, the number of adoptions in the U.S. declined from 180,000 to 120,000 between 1970 and 1990, says Paul Denhalter at the National Council for Adoption. Stepparents often adopt their spouse's natural children, but at least half of all adoptions involve children unrelated to the adoptive parents.

For those who go this route, it can be an expensive proposition that typically involves attorneys, social workers, and adoption agencies. These services can run from $5,000 to $11,000 for a domestic adoption and $8,000 to $20,000 for an international adoption, an attorney told the Gannett News Service in 1993. One in ten unrelated adopted children is foreign, according to a study by the NCHS. It is not surprising that households with incomes of $35,000 or more are almost five times as likely as those with incomes of $15,000 or less to adopt an unrelated child.

But today, many couples are taking a different route to achieve parenthood. An increasing number are visiting infertility clinics in hopes of having their own biological baby. The number of people seeking help for infertility problems rose from 1.1 million in 1981 to 1.4 million in 1987, according to the NCHS.

In 1988, 11 percent of married couples with a wife aged 15 to 44 had problems conceiving or carrying a pregnancy to term. This amounted to 3.1 million couples with problems. About 1.1 million were childless; the other 2 million already had at least one child. The number and rate of couples with such problems conceiving or carrying babies hardly changed between 1982 and 1988. But since 1976, the number of childless couples with a wife aged 35 to 44 experiencing difficulties has grown 37 percent.

Eighty-five to 90 percent of infertile couples seeking treatment could benefit from low-tech remedies such as surgery and drugs, according to the U.S. Office of Technology Assessment. But for 10 to 15 percent, conventional treatments do not work. Not all will pursue high-tech treatments like in-vitro fertilization (IVF, or "test-tube" conception), but an increasing number do. The number of U.S. infertility clinics performing high-tech procedures increased from 84 in 1985 to more than 300 in 1993, according to Joyce Zeitz at the American Fertility Society in Birmingham, Alabama.

Many people try to educate themselves about new infertility treatments, which has created a large and growing market for self-help books. "There are more infertility titles now than ever before," says Susan Arnold at Waldenbooks in Stamford, Connecticut. Bestsellers include *How to Be a Successful Fertility Patient* and *How to Get Pregnant with the New Technology.*

In 1992, 21,722 IVF procedures were performed in the U.S., nearly three times the number in 1987, according to Zeitz. Not all are performed on aging baby boomers racing to beat the biological clock. Women over age 35 are more likely to be infertile, but younger women are more likely to be treated. "The bulk of procedures are done on people under age 35," says Zeitz.

High-tech infertility treatments are not cheap—the average procedure costs $7,000, and prices range from $4,000 to $11,000 per try.

American Infertility

Childless wives aged 35 to 44 are most likely to have problems having babies.

(thousands of married women and percent with impaired fecundity*, by age of woman and presence of children, 1976, 1982, and 1988)

	married women			percent with impaired fecundity		
	1988	1982	1976	1988	1982	1976
all women:	29,147	28,231	27,488	10.7%	10.8%	15.7%
(with and without children)						
15 to 24	3,337	4,741	6,020	7.6%	8.8%	10.8%
25 to 34	13,646	12,924	12,179	10.9	9.7	15.5
35 to 44	12,163	10,566	9,288	11.4	13.1	19.1
with no children:						
(total age 15 to 44)	5,533	5,098	5,235	20.5%	21.7%	21.4%
15 to 24	1,404	1,989	2,738	8.4	11.1	10.6
25 to 34	2,979	2,256	1,931	20.0	21.1	27.3
35 to 44	1,149	853	565	36.4	47.8	53.9
with one or more children:						
(total age 15 to 44)	23,614	23,134	22,254	8.4%	8.4%	14.3%
15 to 24	1,932	2,752	3,282	7.1	7.2	11.1
25 to 34	10,668	10,668	10,248	8.3	7.3	13.2
35 to 44	11,014	9,713	8,723	8.8	10.0	16.8

* Impaired fecundity includes women unable to conceive and those unable to carry a pregnancy to term.

Source: National Center for Health Statistics

At least ten states require some type of coverage for infertility treatment, but this does not necessarily include expensive procedures such as IVF. President Clinton's proposed national health-care plan specifically excludes IVF, which could affect the industry's future growth.

DEALING WITH PREGNANCY

Whether it's through medical technology, their own persistence, or both, most women do eventually become pregnant. But if hospitals want their maternity business, they can't afford to wait until this point to start attracting women. "Women choose where they're going to have a baby at least two years before they ever become pregnant," notes Sally Rynne, president of Women's Healthcare Consultants in Evanston, Illinois. Hospitals and their affiliated physicians need to attract women with good gynecological care first, says Rynne.

As the U.S. moves into a more managed health-care environment, hospitals will be increasingly likely to market not only to consumers, but to employers and insurers as well. Many hospitals already offer cost-effective packages that appeal to those paying the bill as well as those receiving the services. St. John West Shore Hospital in Westlake, Ohio has a maternity package for low-risk pregnancies, complete with prenatal care, childbirth classes, ultrasound testing, delivery, a candlelight dinner, and a follow-up home visit. The cost of the package is considerably less than the total cost of those services individually, says hospital spokesman Tom Hitchcock. "Package pricing is a trend in health care," he says.

"If there's one service that the business world is paying a lot of attention to, it is prenatal care," says Rynne of Women's Healthcare Consultants. "They're very interested in good packages that have incentives to get women into prenatal care early. The costs of pre-term and low-birth-weight babies are so high."

The use of ultrasound testing has become a routine way of checking for fetal abnormalities. But parents-to-be have found other reasons to value the procedure. As a 1993 *Wall Street Journal* article notes: "All over the country, expectant Moms and Dads are paying as much as $150 a pop for prenatal videos filmed by companies with ultrasound equipment and cute names like 'A Womb's Eye View.' Others are hounding their doctors to make video copies of their ultrasound tests." They want to get a headstart on documenting the important milestones in their child's life.

But couples are not interested in entertainment alone when it comes to pregnancy. They want to be educated about all facets of childbirth and childrearing. This is especially true for older and better-educated parents. At the same time, they have less time to acquire the knowledge. "Women were flocking to seminars and workshops ten years ago," says Rynne of Women's Healthcare Consultants. Today, she says, they are receiving more direct mail from health-care providers—pamphlets, booklets, and videos, as well as telephone information lines.

Expectant parents can't learn everything from books, however. Childbirth preparation classes are extremely popular with first-time mothers and fathers. The most popular form of childbirth preparation is Lamaze, a method dating back to the 1960s. About 1.6 million couples enroll for Lamaze-certified classes and another 1 million for similar classes each year, according to a 1993 *Wall Street Journal* article. This amounts to 95 percent of all first-time parents above the poverty line. Parents typically attend classes over a 6-to-8-week period at hospitals, community centers, and homes around the country.

Some entrepreneurs have added a new twist to the training scene. Joyful Expectations of Northport, New York offers weekend childbirth courses for busy professionals. Couples stay overnight at a hotel and receive a total of ten hours of instruction on Saturday and Sunday. Director Iris Jumper hosted four couples for her first class in April 1992. By 1994, she was teaching at least two dozen couples a month in two locations outside of New York City. "I have hundreds of doctors now who refer clients to me, and hospitals too," says Jumper. Couples come from all over the eastern U.S. to attend the classes. One couple even flew in from Bermuda. Most are professionals with busy schedules.

Meanwhile, Lamaze's name recognition has allowed that organization to branch into other areas. "Thirty years of heavy breathing have given Lamaze the awareness and goodwill that cost brand-name advertisers hundreds of millions of dollars," notes *The Wall Street Journal.* ASPO/Lamaze, the certifying organization for instructors, recently licensed a line of maternity clothes under the "Lamaze by A.M.I." label.

Ninety-four percent of expectant mothers purchase maternity clothes, according to a 1993 reader survey by *American Baby* magazine.* About four in ten purchase maternity clothes during the first trimester, eight in ten during the second trimester, and half during the third trimester. Mothers who already have children are just as likely as first-timers to buy maternity clothes. "A lot of women give away their maternity clothes, not expecting to have any more children," says Jodi Baer, manager of a Mothers Work Maternity store in New York City. Styles change between pregnancies, too.

Women are less self-conscious about showing their pregnancies today, says Baer. They want clothes similar to what they wear when they're not pregnant. *American Baby* found that shirts and pants were the two most commonly purchased items, bought by nine in ten expectant mothers. Half bought dresses. Just one in ten bought a bathing suit, and despite their working status, only one in ten bought maternity suits.

PREPARING THE NURSERY

While buying clothes for themselves, mothers-to-be frequently start searching for things to fill a baby nursery. Although this process continues after the baby is born, new parents need at least some items— like clothes and a crib or bassinet—to welcome their new arrival.

Almost half of new and expectant mothers (44 percent) purchase baby furniture in mid-priced department stores, according to *American Baby's* 1993 reader survey. Thirty-six percent buy furniture at discount department stores like Kmart, 28 percent at catalog showrooms, 26 percent at infant/child specialty stores, and 23 percent at toy stores. Those with household incomes of $35,000 or more are more likely than others to buy things at catalog showrooms and specialty stores and less likely to shop at discount department stores.

Sales of baby furniture and related items reached $3.3 billion in

---

* *Subscribers to* American Baby *are older, better-educated, and more likely to work than the general population of expectant mothers.*

1992, a 3 percent increase over 1991, according to Deborah Albert at the Juvenile Products Manufacturers Association. This was a slow-down from the tremendous 31 percent increase that occurred be-tween 1990 and 1991. First-time parents probably account for about three-fourths of those sales, says Robert Barbato, owner of the USA Baby franchise in Rochester, New York. Dividing three-fourths of 1992 sales by the number of first births in the U.S. yields an average of nearly $1,500 apiece, a number that Barbato feels is an accurate estimate.

But some parents spend much more than that to fully furnish and coordinate a nursery. These are the parents who interest Cooky Hoffman. She and her husband own Treasure's Island, Inc., a family-run baby-store business in Minneapolis. Their customers are usually in the late 20s and early-to-mid-30s, says Hoffman. "They have a lot more money [than younger parents]. They're a lot more interested in coordinating a nursery."

Baby furniture and bedding has become "very trendy" in the past ten years, notes Hoffman, and parents can find a much greater selection of materials and patterns than in the past. Over half of Treasure's Island customers sign up for its baby registry. Strollers are the most requested item, even for those on a second or third preg-nancy. "Very few strollers survive past one or two children," says Hoffman. Car seats are popular, too. Many working couples buy two, adds Hoffman, so one parent can drop off the baby at day care and the other can pick up the child.

A whole branch of the baby-products industry is concerned with nothing but safety products, such as cabinet latches and gates for doorways and stairs. Many parents buy these at baby specialty stores, but others order them through numerous mail-order catalogs. Many of these purchases are one-time buys. "Parents stock up on safety products" for the first baby, says Eric Schultz of Boston's First Step, ltd. which markets a variety of baby products through its "hand in hand" catalog. "You buy the lid lock for the toilet seat and make sure your light switches and outlets are protected. But you only do that once."

Catalog customers, like baby-store customers in general, are pri-marily female. Although fathers are becoming more involved in childrearing these days, mom usually buys baby items. Women do 88 percent of the shopping for baby furniture, says Britt Beemer, chairman of America's Research Group in Charleston, South Carolina. That's about 20 percent higher than for other types of furniture, he says. Catalog shoppers are also likely to be women who juggle responsibilities. They "probably have a little less time and a little more money, and they're willing to spend it for the convenience," says Schultz.

The number-one baby item parents order from catalogs is clothing. Just 6 percent of new and expectant mothers purchased baby furniture from catalogs, according to *American Baby*'s 1993 reader survey, but 26 percent bought clothes. Those with household incomes of $35,000 or more are nearly twice as likely as others to do so.

Still, mothers usually buy baby clothing at stores, the survey found. Regardless of income, stores like Kmart and Wal-Mart are popular. Three-fourths of *American Baby*'s readers buy baby clothes at discount department stores, 72 percent at mid-priced department stores, 37 percent at children's value price stores, 35 percent at infant/child specialty stores, and 29 percent at upscale department stores.

Enthusiastic as they may be, few women expecting their first child buy absolutely everything they need before the baby arrives. "Overall, new mothers were much more likely than expectant mothers to have purchased clothing or shoes for their baby," notes the *American Baby* study. "First-time mothers (both new and expectant) were slightly more likely to buy new clothes for their baby than mothers who already had a child."

Today, baby showers are almost as common as bridal showers. They are frequently held in offices and schools as well as homes. As baby showers have increased in popularity, so too have the number of infant gift registries, says Laura Walther, director of gift registry services for Service Merchandise, a catalog showroom based in Brentwood, Tennessee. Most women who register do so at more than one store, she believes. "They want to make it more convenient for their friends."

First-time mothers are more likely than others to register for gifts. So are those who have had at least five years between births, says Walther. "Either they have given everything away, thinking they're not ever going to have another baby, or there have been dramatic changes in products."

Expectant and new parents are more likely to receive certain items as gifts than buy them themselves, according to *American Baby*'s survey. Over one-third of playpen owners received the item as a gift; just two in ten purchased it new themselves. Four in ten owners of bassinets/baby cradles received the item as a gift; only two in ten bought it themselves. Seven in ten stuffed-toy owners received them as gifts while four in ten made their own purchases. Although new mothers are more likely to buy baby clothes than receive them as gifts, almost half receive sleepwear, four in ten get stretch suits, and one-third each get infant gowns, socks, and jogging suits as presents.

CHILDBIRTH CHANGES

Hospitals have been Americans' place of choice to have babies since the early 20th century. But new parents are demanding changes in the types of hospital rooms where births take place. In 1988, separate labor and delivery rooms were used for two-thirds of all births, according to a survey by Inforum Inc., a health-care information company in Nashville. By 1993, that share had dropped to 38 percent. Most births now take place in a single room used for some combination of labor, delivery, recovery, and postpartum care.

In 1992, just 21 percent of hospitals had a traditional maternity unit that offered only separate labor and delivery rooms, according to the American Hospital Association, down from 26 percent in 1989. "Even in small towns and outlying areas, the conversion to single-room maternity care is prevalent," says Sally Rynne of Women's Healthcare Consultants. Women like birthing rooms because they have homelike amenities. The birth experience becomes less medical and more personal.

Single-room care is also cost-effective, says Elizabeth Hamilton of Phillips and Fenwick, a consulting firm in Scotts Valley, California. This will be increasingly important in a managed-care environment. Indeed, insurers now play an important role in determining where women go for maternity care. About 14 percent of mothers with newborns say their insurance plan was the primary influence in their hospital choice, according to Inforum's 1993 survey.

A small number of women opt to have their babies at birthing centers. Just 14,200 babies were born in birthing centers in 1991, according to the NCHS. They accounted for one-third of non-hospital births, or less than one-half of one percent of all births. (Another 0.7 percent of women had their babies at home in 1991, usually for religious reasons.) These facilities are used only for low-risk deliveries because they have no high-tech equipment. According to a national study of birthing centers published in the *New England Journal of Medicine,* women who deliver at birth centers are less likely than average to be unmarried, poor, teenaged, black, or to smoke or drink. They are more likely to have finished college.

Birthing centers primarily rely on certified nurse-midwives to deliver patient care. These practitioners, most of whom are women, are registered nurses with additional training in labor, delivery, and maternity care. They maintain affiliations with physicians who serve as backup support if complications arise. The number of certified nurse-midwives in the U.S. has risen from about 500 in the mid-1970s to more than 4,000 today, according to the American College of Nurse-Midwives.

In 1981, nurse-midwives attended 55,500 births. By 1991, the number had risen to 167,700. But just 4 percent of midwife deliveries occur at birthing centers, and 2 percent occur in homes. The vast majority—94 percent—occur in hospitals.

Many midwives are mothers themselves. They have personally experienced pregnancy and birth. Patients feel comforted by their common experience. But consumer preference is not the only reason why the use of nurse-midwives will grow in the future. They are also a cost-effective way to deal with uncomplicated pregnancies. "The system is going to be much friendlier to [midwives] than it has been in the past because the dollars are going to come in a different manner," says Sally Rynne of Women's Healthcare Consultants. Female physicians are also favorites with pregnant women. About one-fourth of ob-gyns are women, but surveys by Women's Healthcare Consultants find that 30 percent to 60 percent of women prefer a female doctor.

Birth Options

Almost 40 percent of women give birth in separate labor and delivery rooms, but just 19 percent prefer this option.

(percent distribution of women who gave birth in the past 12 months by preferred and actual type of delivery option, 1993)

	percent preferred	percent actually used
separate labor and delivery rooms	19%	38%
one room for labor and delivery	18	29
one room for labor, delivery, and recovery	21	17
one room for labor, delivery, recovery, and post-partum care	33	13
none of these	2	2
no response	8	2

Totals do not add exactly to 100 due to rounding.

Source: © Inforum Inc., Nashville, TN

HELPING NEW PARENTS

Women's increased labor force presence and men's increased involvement in family life has forced employers to face the facts: workers are often parents, too. Under the Family and Medical Leave Act that took effect August 1993, organizations with 50 or more employees are required to provide up to 12 weeks of unpaid leave for new parents, including those who adopt children. Even before the act passed, however, the number of employers offering help to new parents was on the rise.

In 1992, 63 percent of large employers offered formal parental leave beyond the time employees took as disability and accumulated vacation or sick days, according to a survey of 1,026 major U.S. companies conducted by Hewitt Associates of Lincolnshire, Illinois. Over 90 percent of the companies have 1,000 employees or more. Ninety-seven percent offered unpaid leave, while 3 percent offered paid leave or a combination of paid and unpaid time off.

Such benefits are less common when the universe includes medium-sized organizations, according to a 1991 Bureau of Labor Statistics (BLS) survey. Policies also discriminate against new fathers. Thirty-seven percent of full-time employees in companies with 100 or more employees could take unpaid maternity leave, but just 26 percent could take unpaid paternity leave.

Formal policies are even less likely to cover employees in small organizations. Only 18 percent of full-time workers in establishments with fewer than 100 employees had unpaid maternity leave benefits in 1992, according to the BLS, and 8 percent had paternity leave. But small companies often arrange informal leaves for valuable workers, says Ken McDonnell, a research analyst with the Employee Benefit Research Institute in Washington, D.C. "The more important that employee is to them, the more likely they are to do it."

Employers also assist workers through the parenthood transition by picking up much of the tab for the baby's birth. Health insurance routinely covers prenatal care and delivery costs, and the BLS finds that 83 percent of those working full-time in organizations of 100 or more employees participated in a health insurance program in which the employer paid at least some of the cost. The share for workers in smaller organizations is lower, 71 percent in 1992.

When new parents return to work, many employers help with child care. Workers in large companies are most likely to receive child-care benefits, too. Thirty percent of large employers offered resource and referral services for child care in 1993, according to Hewitt Associates, and more than three-fourths contracted with outside vendors to provide them.

The most common child-care benefit is a dependent-care spending or reimbursement account. In such an arrangement, an employee sets aside nontaxable earnings for child-care expenses. Almost three-quarters (73 percent) of large organizations offered this benefit in 1993, according to Hewitt. Also, the BLS reports that 36 percent of full-time workers in medium and large organizations could take advntage of this benefit in 1991, along with 14 percent of those employed in small establishments in 1992.

A much smaller share of employers provides or subsidizes child care, but this share is growing. The BLS found that 8 percent of full-time workers in medium and large organizations could take advan-

Bigger Benefits

Bigger companies are more likely to offer family-related benefits.

(percent of full-time employees participating in selected benefits in small private establishments, 1992, and in large private establishments, 1991)

establishments with:	fewer than 100 employees	100 or more employees
Paid vacations	88%	96%
Paid holidays	82	92
Medical care	71	83
Life insurance	64	94
Paid sick leave	53	67
Paid funeral leave	50	80
Dental care	33	60
Sickness/accident insurance	26	45
Long-term disability insurance	23	40
Unpaid maternity leave	18	37
Reimbursement accounts	14	36
Paid personal leave	12	21
Unpaid paternity leave	8	26
Child care	2	8
Paid maternity leave	2	2
Paid paternity leave	1	1

Source: Bure

tage of on-site child care, nearby child care, or a child-car
1991. This is an increase from 5 percent in 1989. Tw
those in small organizations had such benefits in 199
percent in 1990.

WELCOMING THE NEW ARRIVAL

As every new parent soon finds out, babies are exp
class couples with average incomes of $42,600 sp
$6,900 on a baby born in 1993, according to the U
Agriculture's Family Economics Research Group.

incomes averaging $79,400 spent $10,200, and those with lower incomes averaging $20,000 had a lower tab—$5,000.

To raise a middle-income child through age three, 37 percent of total estimated expenses go for housing, 16 percent for transportation, 13 percent for food, 12 percent for child care and education, 7 percent for clothing, 6 percent for health care, and 10 percent for miscellaneous items. Upper-income families pay a somewhat higher share of their baby expenses for housing (40 percent) and somewhat lower share (13 percent) for transportation. Childrearing costs in

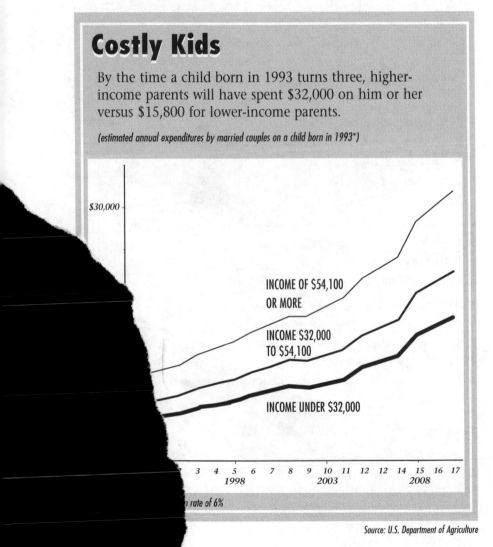

Costly Kids

By the time a child born in 1993 turns three, higher-income parents will have spent $32,000 on him or her versus $15,800 for lower-income parents.

(estimated annual expenditures by married couples on a child born in 1993*)

$30,000

INCOME OF $54,100
OR MORE

INCOME $32,000
TO $54,100

INCOME UNDER $32,000

3   4   5   6   7   8   9   10 11 12 12 14 15 16 17
        1998   2003   2008

h rate of 6%

Source: U.S. Department of Agriculture

urban areas are greatest in the West, followed by the Northeast. They are lowest in the Midwest, followed by the South.

By the time a child born in 1993 turns 18, on average, high-income parents will have spent a total of $334,600 on him or her; middle-income parents, $231,100; and lower-income parents, $170,900. (These estimates assume an annual 6 percent inflation rate.)

Keeping Baby Clean

One of the first expenses new parents encounter is keeping the baby in dry diapers. And one of the first decisions parents must make is whether or not to go with cloth or disposables.

American parents spend over $4 billion a year on diapers, according to a 1993 *Wall Street Journal* article. Ninety percent buy disposables, spending about $1,350 during the time a child is in diapers (averaging $40 to $50 a month for 30 months). About 70 percent of mothers buy disposable diapers in discount department stores, according to *American Baby*'s 1993 reader survey, followed by supermarkets (59 percent), toy stores (31 percent), price clubs (31 percent), discount drugstore chains (26 percent), and other drugstores (22 percent).

For a brief period during the late 1980s, environmental concerns prompted more parents to turn to cloth-diaper services. Between 1988 and 1991, the number of customers for cloth-diaper services increased 69 percent, reported a 1993 article in *Newsday*. But the enthusiasm was short-lived. Makers of disposables responded with ad campaigns that questioned the environmental impact of washing massive numbers of diapers, and some parents doubtless became disenchanted with the inconvenience involved. Shipments of cloth diapers began to decline in 1991, a major diaper manufacturer told the *Atlanta Constitution*.

Yet many diaper services continue to prosper because they have been able to adapt to the changing times. Lullaby Diaper Service in Atlanta was one of the first to begin offering disposable as well as cloth diapers to its customers. Currently, about one-third of Lullaby's customers receive "day-care" packages, consisting of a combination of cloth and disposables. "Some day-care providers refuse to use cloth," says manager Mary Almodovar. "But the parents still want to use cloth while they're at home." It's also more convenient for parents to use disposables when they're shopping or travelling, she says. About 15 percent of Lullaby's customers order only disposable diapers. These are often working women with other children or mothers with twins, says Almodovar. Lullaby keeps in touch with its mothers through a monthly newsletter, *Wet Set Gazette.*

Manufacturers of disposable diapers have also innovated. "Gender-specific disposable diapers were introduced in the late 1980s, followed by 'ultra-dry' and 'ultra-trim' diapers that promised more absorbency and less bulk," says Marcia Mogelonsky in *American Demographics.* "Now the companies are moving away from selling diapers only according to the weight of the child. They are offering different diapers for newborns, infants, crawlers, and walkers." And diaper manufacturer Kimberly-Clark has reached out for an entirely new market with disposable training pants for toddlers. Unlike babies, the number of children aged 18 months to four years will remain stable, at about 9.7 million between 1993 and 2000, Mogelonsky notes.

Diapers aren't the only things that keep babies fresh and clean. Parents also spend $378 million a year on baby wipes, according to *The Wall Street Journal.* More than 90 percent of parents with children in diapers buy wipes with names like Baby Fresh and Wash a-bye Baby.

"Marketers say the healthy demand is due partly to the fact that parents are putting the wipes to new uses, such as cleaning toddlers' sticky hands and faces," notes Kathleen Deveny in *The Wall Street Journal.* "But the products are also benefiting from the fact that children now wear diapers until they are 36 to 42 months old, some six months longer than when Baby Fresh was introduced 16 years ago." Parents often make purchases based on price. Lower-priced private labels have made significant inroads in this market, accounting for more than one-fourth of sales in during the year that ended February 28, 1993, according to the *Journal.*

Many parents also use a variety of other baby-grooming products. Two-thirds of households with a child under age two used baby shampoo during the previous six months, according to a 1993 survey by Mediamark Research of New York City. Over half used baby powder (54 percent), baby ointments (51 percent), and baby lotion (51 percent). Nearly half used liquid baby bath (46 percent) and baby soap (44 percent). Thirty-six percent used baby oil. Seven in ten mothers shop for these items at discount department stores, according to *American Baby*'s 1993 reader survey, followed by supermarkets (40 percent), drugstores (35 percent), and discount drugstore chains (32 percent).

Feeding Baby

There wouldn't be any need for diapers if it weren't for those other baby basics—formula and food. *American Baby* finds that just one in ten new mothers breastfeed exclusively, down from two in ten in 1984. Even so, many new mothers both breast- and bottle-feed their infants. In 1993, 82 percent reported doing at least some bottlefeeding, up from 66 percent in 1984. Two-thirds reported at least some breastfeeding, down from 73 percent in 1984. Currently, 89 percent of breastfeeding mothers use nursing pads, 89 percent use nursing bras, and 84 percent use breast pumps to express milk when they have to be away from their babies.

For those who bottle-feed, milk-based formulas are more popular than soy-based formulas, according to *American Baby*'s 1993 survey. Thirty-two percent of new mothers use a powdered milk-based formula, 23 percent use a concentrated milk-based formula, and 12 percent rely on ready-to-use milk-based formulas. Powdered formulas, usually the least costly option, have become more popular over the years, while ready-to-use mixtures have declined in popularity. Concentrated mixtures have retained a steady following.

Somewhere around the age of five months, parents start adding baby food to their infant's diet. The vast majority of American parents buy baby food in supermarkets. (This isn't the case in Canada, where parents are more likely to buy baby food and other supplies in drugstores.) Baby-food sales in the U.S. increased 13 percent between 1989 and 1990, 11 percent between 1990 and 1991, and 6 percent between 1991 and 1992, according to *Progressive Grocer*'s Supermarket Sales Manuals. Packaged Facts of New York City estimates that baby-food sales will grow 5 percent per year through 1997, when they may top $1.5 billion.

Why the slowdown in growth? Declining numbers of babies is only one reason. But Mogelonsky adds: "In 1972, American babies ate an average of 66 dozen jars of baby food a year before 'graduating' to grownup food. Then, as mothers began weaning children from baby food earlier, consumption declined to an average of 47 to 49 dozen jars per year in the mid-1980s. The current average is between 53 and 54 dozen jars." To expand their markets, Gerber and Beechnut have both introduced lines of food for toddlers.

Watching Baby

Between feeding, diapering, and other infant-care responsibilities, it is difficult to see how parents find time to work outside the home. But they often have no choice. Between 1982 and 1992, the share of new mothers in the labor force increased from 44 percent to 54 percent, according to the Census Bureau. The share is higher for first-time mothers, 59 percent compared with 50 percent for those having subsequent births. Some parents have relatives to help them out, but for others the obvious solution is professional child care.

About 17 percent of infants under age one were in group child care, according to the 1990 National Child Care Survey. Seven percent were in day-care centers, 10 percent with family day-care providers. For children with employed mothers, the share in group care was 34 percent. Children aged one and two are more likely than newborns to be in group care (26 percent), especially those with employed mothers (41 percent).

What do parents look for in child care? About six in ten parents with children of all ages in group child care said quality was the most important reason for their choice of provider. Between 10 percent and 20 percent said location was the most important reason. Less than 10 percent said cost was the overriding factor.

New parents frequently turn to their employers for help with child care. As with other benefits, workers in large companies are most likely to receive benefits related to child care. Hewitt Associates found that 30 percent of large employers offered resource and referral services for child care in 1993; more than two-thirds contracted with outside vendors to provide such services.

The most common child-care benefit is a dependent-care spending or reimbursement account in which an employee sets aside non-taxable earnings for child-care expenses. Hewitt found that 73 percent of large organizations offered this benefit in 1993. The Bureau of Labor Statistics (BLS) reports that 36 percent of full-time workers in medium and large organizations could take advantage of this benefit in 1991, as could 14 percent of those in small establishments in 1992.

A much smaller but growing share of employers provide or subsidize child care. The BLS found that 8 percent of full-time workers in medium and large organizations could take advantage of on-site or nearby child care or a child-care subsidy in 1991, up from 5 percent in 1989. Two percent of those in small organizations had such benefits in 1992, up from 1 percent in 1990.

BABY NICHES

Between 1965 and 1990, the share of preschool-aged children in day-care centers grew nearly 400 percent. This has opened up opportunities not only for day-care providers, but for those who market to day-care providers. The market is a "fast-growing segment" for makers of baby-care products, says Eric Schultz. In 1993, his Boston-based company, First Step, ltd., began marketing a catalog of baby products specifically for day-care providers.

Schultz says that many providers ordered products from the consumer catalog sent to new parents. "What we ended up doing was taking the consumer version and slowly evolving it into a professional version," he says. "We try to look for products that fulfill the need of the child-care giver. If they're going to change a dozen diapers in a row, they need a heavy-duty diaper can." This market has been underserved, he says. Other products in his professional catalog include activity nooks, sandboxes, go-carts, and videocassettes.

Schultz's response is one way to compensate for the declining numbers of babies in the next few years. Another way will be to focus directly on the consumer. Working parents of infants will probably be increasing in share if not in number in the coming years. Time-pressed parents need all kinds of labor-saving devices and services that may or may not be directly related to child care.

Another important niche for the baby industry is grandparents, who are often willing to purchase products and services young parents cannot afford. What's more, today's grandparents are in better health and stronger financial shape than their predecessors.

As Judith Waldrop of *American Demographics* observes, "Grandparents buy bibs that say 'Grandma loves me,' but they also buy high chairs. In fact, grandparents may spend even more on some products for children than parents do." Waldrop notes that households headed by 55-to-64-year-olds are nearly as likely as those headed by 25-to-34-year-olds to buy infants' furniture. The older buyers spent an average of nearly $900 on such furniture in 1991, compared with less than $800 for the younger group.

More than half of all grandparents bought their grandchildren a gift during the previous month, according to a 1992 Roper Survey. Half spent over $320 on such gifts during the year. And in real dollars, grandparents spent 11 percent more on gifts in 1992 than they did in 1988. Even nonaffluent grandparents—those with household incomes under $15,000—spent a median of $210.

About 60 million Americans are grandparents, according to the Roper survey. Fifty-nine percent are aged 60 and older, 31 percent are aged 45 to 59, and 10 percent are under age 45. *American Demographics* projects that the total number of grandparents will increase almost 15 percent between 1992 and 2000. In the 1990s, most doting grandparents are parents of baby boomers. But after the turn of the century, a changing of the guard will gradually occur. The oldest baby boomers turn 55 in 2001. At that point, boomers will constitute nearly half of grandparents.

PRODUCTS AND SERVICES FOR
The Parenthood Transition

Achieving Parenthood

Adoption services
Infertility treatment
Self-help books on infertility
Prenatal care
Maternity clothes
Childbirth classes
Books, pamphlets, and videos on childbirth and parenting
Maternity care in hospitals and birthing centers
Obstetricians and certified nurse-midwives

Preparing for Baby

Baby furniture and related items, such as car seats, playpens,
    and strollers
Security items for the home
Baby bedding and nursery decor
Toys
Baby clothes
Bigger homes
Health insurance
Nursing equipment
Diapers, especially disposable
Baby wipes and other personal-care items
Baby formula, cereal, food, and related equipment
Day care

SOURCES

American Baby/Cahners Publishing. **Baby Care Study—Baby Foods and Formula,** conducted by Bruno and Ridgway Research Associates, Inc. New York, NY: Cahners Publishing, 1993.

American Baby/Cahners Publishing. **Baby Care Study—Baby Furniture and Linens,** conducted by Bruno and Ridgway Research Associates, Inc. New York, NY: Cahners Publishing, 1993.

American Baby/Cahners Publishing. **Baby Care Study—Baby Skin Care,** conducted by Bruno and Ridgway Research Associates, Inc. New York, NY: Cahners Publishing, 1993.

American Baby/Cahners Publishing. **Baby Care Study—Baby Toys and Accessories,** conducted by Bruno and Ridgway Research Associates, Inc. New York, NY: Cahners Publishing, 1993.

American Baby/Cahners Publishing. **Baby Care Study—Children's Clothing and Expectant Mother's Maternity Clothing,** conducted by Bruno and Ridgway Research Associates, Inc. New York, NY: Cahners Publishing, 1993.

American Baby/Cahners Publishing. **Baby Care Study—Diapering and Diapering Products,** conducted by Bruno and Ridgway Research Associates, Inc. New York, NY: Cahners Publishing, 1993.

American Baby/Cahners Publishing. **Baby Care Study—Nursing Accessories,** conducted by Bruno and Ridgway Research Associates, Inc. New York, NY: Cahners Publishing, 1993.

American Hospital Association, **Survey of Obstetric Service—1992,** American Hospital Association, Section for Maternal and Child Health, Chicago, IL: 1993.

Bachrach, Christine A., Patricia F. Adams, Soledad Sambrano, and Kathryn A. London. **Adoption in the 1980s. Advance Data from Vital and Health Statistics,** No. 181, National Center for Health Statistics, Hyattsville, MD, 1990.

Bachu, Amara. *Fertility of American Women: June 1992.* Washington, DC: U.S. Bureau of the Census, 1993.

Bird, Laura. "**Lamaze Group Hopes Licensing Delivers Growth.**" *The Wall Street Journal,* June 23, 1993, p. B1.

Crispell, Diane. "**Grandparents Galore.**" *American Demographics,* October 1993, p.63.

Day, Jennifer Cheeseman. *Population Projections of the United States, by Age, Sex, Race, and Hispanic Origin: 1993 to 2050.* Washington, DC: U.S. Bureau of the Census, 1993.

Deveny, Kathlyn. "**Wipes Makers Fight to Keep Babies Fresh.**" *The Wall Street Journal,* May 4, 1993, pp. B1, B9.

Employee Benefit Research Institute. *EBRI Databook on Employee Benefits, Third Edition.* Washington, DC: Employee Benefit Research Institute, 1994.

Evans, Heidi. "**Womb with a View: Unborn Babies Star in Fetal Film Fests.**" *The Wall Street Journal,* November 30, 1993, pp. A1, A5.

Hewitt Associates. *Work and Family Benefits Provided by Major U.S. Employers in 1992.* Lincolnshire, IL: Hewitt Associates, 1992.

Hewitt Associates. *Work and Family Benefits Provided by Major U.S. Employers in 1993.* Lincolnshire, IL: Hewitt Associates, 1993.

Hofferth, Sandra L., April Brayfield, Sharon Deich, and Pamela Holcomb. *National Child Care Survey, 1990.* Washington, DC: The Urban Institute Press, 1991.

Johnston, Jo-Ann. "**Coping With the Cost of Kids.**" [Gannett News Service article published in *The Tennessean,* July 3, 1993, p. 1E.]

Klein, Paula. "**Market for Cloth Diapers Bottoms Out.**" *Newsday,* February 1, 1993, sec. 1, p. 25.

Lino, Mark. *Expenditures on a Child by Families, 1993.* Hyattsville, MD: U.S. Department of Agriculture, Agricultural Research Service, Family Economics Research Group, 1994.

Loupe, Diane. "**Time for a Change: Diaper Services Beginning to Deliver Disposables.**" *Atlanta Constitution,* June 25, 1993, pp. H1, H8.

Mediamark Research Inc. *Pet and Baby Products Report, Spring 1993*, New York, NY: Mediamark Research Inc., 1993.

Mergenhagen DeWitt, Paula. "**The Birth Business.**" *American Demographics,* Ithaca, NY, September 1993, pp. 44–49.

Mergenhagen DeWitt, Paula. "**In Pursuit of Pregnancy.**" *American Demographics,* Ithaca, NY, May 1993, pp. 48–54.

Mogelonsky, Marcia. "**Baby Food is Growing Up.**" *American Demographics,* Ithaca, NY, May 1993, pp. 20–22.

Mogelonsky, Marcia. "**Supermarket Trends North and South.**" *American Demographics,* Ithaca, NY, May 1994, pp. 22.

Mosher, William D. and William F. Pratt. *Fecundity and Infertility in the United States, 1965-88. Advance Data from Vital and Health Statistics,* No. 192, National Center for Health Statistics, Hyattsville, MD, 1990.

National Center for Health Statistics. *Advance Report of Final Natality Statistics, 1991, Monthly Vital Statistics Report,* Vol. 42, No. 3, Suppl., Public Health Service, Hyatttsville, MD, 1993.

National Center for Health Statistics. *Annual Summary of Births, Marriages, Divorces, and Deaths: United States, 1992, Monthly Vital Statistics Report,* Vol. 41, No. 13, Public Health Service, Hyattsville, MD, 1993.

National Center for Health Statistics. **Annual Summary of Births, Marriages, Divorces, and Deaths: United States, 1993, Monthly Vital Statistics Report**, Vol. 42, No. 13, Public Health Service, Hyattsville, MD, 1994.

Progressive Grocer. "**Sales Manual/Top Performers: What's Hot.**" *Progressive Grocer,* Stamford, CT, July 1993, pp. 69–80.

Progressive Grocer. "**The 1991 Supermarket Sales Manual: Building Sales-Category by Category.**" *Progressive Grocer,* Stamford, CT, July 1991, pp. 23–90.

Progressive Grocer. "**The 1992 Supermarket Sales Manual: What's Hot.**" *Progressive Grocer,* Stamford, CT, July 1992, pp. 55–60.

Reitman, Valerie. "**Diaper Firms Fight to Stay on the Bottom.**" *The Wall Street Journal,* March 23, 1993, pp. B1, B10.

Rooks, Judith P., Norman L. Weatherby, Eunice K. M. Ernst, Susan Stapleton, David Rosen, and Allan Rosenfield. **"Outcomes of Care in Birth Centers: The National Birth Center Study."** *The New England Journal of Medicine*, Vol. 321, No. 26, December 28, 1989, pp. 1804–1811.

U.S. Bureau of the Census, *Money Income of Households, Families, and Persons in the United States: 1992.* Washington, DC: U.S. Government Printing Office, 1993.

U.S. Bureau of Labor Statistics. **"BLS Reports on Employee Benefits in Small Private Industry Establishments, 1992"** (press release). U.S. Department of Labor, Washington, DC, 1994.

U.S. Bureau of Labor Statistics. *Employee Benefits in Medium and Large Establishments, 1991.* Bulletin 2422, May 1993. Washington, DC: Government Printing Office, 1993.

U.S. Congress, Office of Technology Assessment. *Infertility: Medical and Social Choices.* Washington, DC: U.S. Government Printing Office, 1988.

Waldrop, Judith. **"The Grandbaby Boom."** *American Demographics,* September 1993, p. 4.

OTHER RESOURCES

Ambry, Margaret K. **"Receipts from a Marriage."** *American Demographics,* Ithaca, NY, February 1993, pp. 30–37.

Employee Benefit Research Institute. *Public Attitudes on Child Care and Family Leave, 1993,* conducted by The Gallup Organization, Inc. Washington, DC: Employee Benefit Research Institute, 1994.

Ventura, Stephanie J., Selma M. Taffel, William D. Mosher, and Stanley Henshaw. *Trends in Pregnancies and Pregnancy Rates, United States, 1980–88. Monthly Vital Statistics Report*, Vol. 41, No. 6, Suppl., National Center for Health Statistics, Hyattsville, MD, 1992.

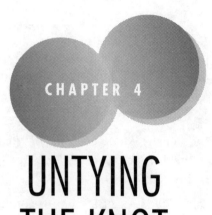

CHAPTER 4

UNTYING THE KNOT

The Divorce Transition

WHEN ELIZABETH THOMAS decided to end her marriage in 1990, she had to find a new place to live and a divorce attorney. She also needed some counseling to help her adjust to her new situation. Eventually, Thomas had to decide whether to relocate from California to her native New England. In the end, she made the move and dove into graduate school full-time.

At the time of divorce, people frequently make other transitions, like moving or returning to school. They need all the products and services that go along with these transitions, like apartments, furnishings, and career counseling. They also need help and support negotiating the legal system, coping with their divorce, and developing new social lives.

Some divorced people are in better financial shape than others to face this usually painful transition. Men's economic status may improve after a divorce, while women's usually declines precipitously. Women with careers are better off than those who have been homemakers. Those without children fare better than those with children.

The divorced population is diverse in terms of living arrangements, too. It includes people who live alone, single parents, and those who move in with other family members or roommates. Age and sex are major determinants of living arrangements. Young divorced people are likely to end up back home with their parents or with roommates. The middle-aged divorced often live alone. Women are more likely than men to live with their children as single parents.

While more single-parent families are now headed by men than in the past, men are still far more likely to be noncustodial parents. Weekend dads provide business for toy stores, movies, and amusement parks. But another group of noncustodial fathers provides work for very different types of businesses—collection agencies that seek to recover child support from "deadbeat dads."

Divorce rates increased tremendously between 1970 and the mid-1980s, but have leveled off since then. Baby boomers in their 30s and 40s are more likely to divorce than older or younger age groups. Overall, about four in ten marriages are projected to end in divorce.

The process of divorce itself provides business for a whole cadre of professionals, including lawyers, accountants, actuaries, and appraisers. The rapid growth in the ranks of these professionals is largely due to the fact that the divorce process itself has substantially changed. It has gradually moved from a fault-based system to one that does not assign fault.

No-fault divorces were first granted in California in 1970 and have now been incorporated in varying degrees in all 50 states. Instead of awards based on "fault" where the "innocent" party gets the better financial settlement, courts now attempt to make awards equitable to both parties. Hammering out what is equitable requires all types of experts.

The complexity and expense of a divorce largely depends on the age of divorcing couples because older couples tend to have more assets that must be divided. Because attorney and expert fees can be prohibitive for young people and those of modest means, a market has developed for "do-it-yourself" divorce kits. Attorneys also use books and tapes to educate clients about the divorce process.

Couples with children face child-custody issues that often involve psychologists and mediators. "Domestic relations cases"—

primarily divorce, child custody, and child support—accounted for fully one-third of all civil cases filed in general jurisdiction courts in 1991, according to the National Center for State Courts. Increasingly, courts are recommending or even requiring divorcing parents to attend classes to learn about the effects of divorce on their children.

TRENDS IN THE MARKET

In 1992, a record high 1.2 million marriages ended in divorce in the U.S., representing about 2 percent of American couples. This was a 2 percent increase over the number in 1991. In 1993, however, the number of divorces declined 2 percent, back to 1991 levels. Divorce rates have been essentially stable in recent years. "In general, the divorce rate increased dramatically during the 1960s and 1970s, declined gradually throughout most of the 1980s, and has plateaued in the early 1990s," notes a report from the National Center for Health Statistics (NCHS).

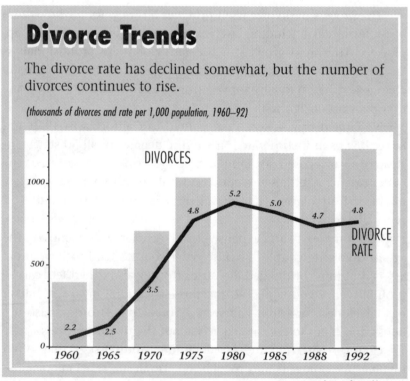

Divorce Trends

The divorce rate has declined somewhat, but the number of divorces continues to rise.

(thousands of divorces and rate per 1,000 population, 1960–92)

Source: National Center for Health Statistics

The aging of the population is one explanation for the plateau, because older people are less likely to divorce. More than half of divorces in 1988 were to people under age 35. Marriages that end are usually of short duration, too. More than one-third of couples divorced in 1988 were married less than five years, according to the NCHS.

Teens aged 15 to 19 were only a tiny portion of the married population in 1988 (less than 0.5 percent), but accounted for 1 percent of those who divorced. People aged 20 to 24 made up 5 percent of the married population in 1988, but were 12 percent of those divorced.

In absolute numbers, young baby boomers aged 25 to 34 were responsible for most divorces in 1988. They were 42 percent of those divorced, although they constituted just 24 percent of the married population. Divorce rates were lower for older boomers aged 35 to 44. Even so, this group accounted for 29 percent of those divorced, although they were just 24 percent of the married population.

Divorce rates plummet after age 45, probably because the longer marriages have lasted, the less likely they are to ever break up. People aged 45 to 54 represented 12 percent of those divorced, but constituted 17 percent of the married population. Those aged 55 or older were 5 percent of those divorced, but represented a full 29 percent of the married population.

Baby boomers may be at even greater risk than younger people of being divorced at some point in their lives. A 1992 Census Bureau report notes that "women born during the early and middle baby-boom years are likely to have higher eventual percents divorced than their predecessors or successors." The study estimates that slightly less than four in ten marriages of women who are now in their 20s will end in divorce. But for baby boomers, the share could exceed four in ten. Arthur Norton, one of the study's authors, offered the *Washington Post* this explanation of generational differences: "The vanguard of the baby boom had more direct experience with the dramatic changes of the '70s. . . . They probably paid a higher price for having been first." Among the most important changes, of course, was women's increased labor-force participation. Women who can take care of themselves economically are less likely to stay in bad marriages.

The Exploding Divorce Market

Between 1970 and 1992, the number of divorced Americans nearly quadrupled.

(number of currently divorced men and women in thousands, by age, 1970, 1980, and 1992, and percent change 1970–92)

| | 1992 | | 1980 | | 1970 | | percent change 1970–92 | |
	men	women	men	women	men	women	men	women
total	6,752	9,569	3,930	5,966	1,567	2,717	330.9%	252.2%
under 25	119	226	166	418	78	208	52.6%	8.7%
25 to 34	1,322	2,011	1,171	1,813	313	575	322.4	249.7
35 to 44	2,205	2,793	1,012	1,412	316	632	597.8	341.9
45 to 54	1,606	2,285	725	1,085	405	585	296.5	290.6
55 and older	1,501	2,253	856	1,239	455	716	229.9	214.7

The share of divorced people doubled for all age groups in the 1970s, but grew more slowly in the 1980s.

(percent of population currently divorced, by age, 1970, 1980, and 1992)

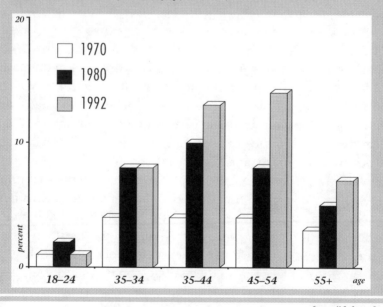

Source: U.S. Census Bureau

Call 1-800-HOTELS 1

The Seven-Year Itch

More than one-third of marriages that end in divorce lasted less than five years.

(thousands of divorces and rate per 1,000 population, 1960–92)
Median duration = seven years

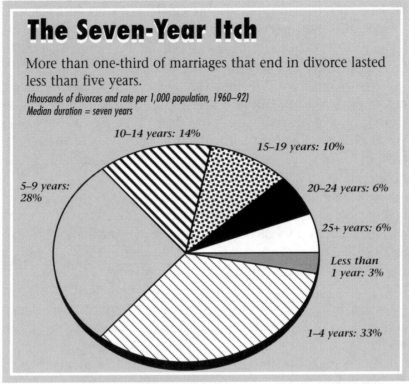

10–14 years: 14%

15–19 years: 10%

5–9 years: 28%

20–24 years: 6%

25+ years: 6%

Less than 1 year: 3%

1–4 years: 33%

Source: National Center for Health Statistics

Although economically self-sufficient women may be more inclined to divorce, some research finds that people in poverty are also more likely to split up. Not only do people with low incomes tend to marry younger, but money problems create stressful living situations detrimental to marriages.

Religion plays a role in the likelihood of divorce, too. A 1988 Gallup survey found that highly religious people are less likely to experience marital difficulty or divorce, 45 percent versus 58 percent for the less religious. The relationship persists even when age is held constant.

But people don't get divorced because they are baby boomers, because of their economic status, or even because they are not religious. When Gallup asked people what led to their split, the answers were much more personal. According to divorced people, the leading cause of breakups is incompatibility. Almost half of those who have ever been divorced (47 percent) cited this reason. Other reasons include infidelity, mentioned by 17 percent; drug or alcohol problems, cited by 16 percent; disputes about money, family, or children (10 percent); and physical abuse (5 percent).

Women are more likely than men to initiate marital separations, according to Gallup. Fifty-five percent of divorced women and 44 percent of divorced men said it was their idea to separate. Women are also more likely to file for divorce. According to the NCHS, women file in 61 percent of cases, men in 32 percent of cases, and both partners in 7 percent of cases.

How long do people remain divorced before they remarry? According to demographers Robert Schoen and Robin M. Weinick, the average duration of a divorced spell is about eight years for a man and 13 years for a woman. This includes both those who do and do not remarry. Individuals who divorce at younger ages spend less time in that state, and they are considerably more likely to remarry, according to the Census Bureau. Overall, 78 percent of divorced men and 72 percent of divorced women remarry, according to Schoen and Weinick.

Love is not always lovelier the second time around. Research by demographers Teresa Castro Martin and Larry L. Bumpass finds that divorce rates for second marriages are 25 percent higher than for first marriages.

THE DIVORCE PROCESS

Divorces range from simple to complex, depending on the couple's financial status, as well as whether or not they have children. This means that divorces also range from inexpensive to costly, and may involve any number of products and services.

"Do-It-Yourself" Divorce

Young people in marriages of short duration need the least help from divorce professionals. Because they have few assets and are least likely to have children, they may not even need a lawyer. In fact, one in five people are not represented by a lawyer at all, according to a study by the State Justice Institute (SJI) of divorce cases filed in 1989 in 16 urban courts. "It's probably just an issue of who's going to pay off the credit cards," says John Goerdt of the National Center for State Courts, who analyzed the study results.

In some courts, the philosophy is to encourage people seeking an uncomplicated divorce to file it themselves. Goerdt writes: "In Washington and Tucson, clerk's office staff provide litigants with 'divorce packets,' which include all the necessary forms and instructions on how to file for and obtain a divorce decree . . . the Legal Aid office in Tucson offers a biweekly workshop on how to obtain a

A Divorce Lawyer's Town

Just over half of divorces in Oakland, California involve a lawyer. But in Hartford, Connecticut, both husband and wife are usually represented.

(percent of divorces by attorney representation in 16 urban courts)

	no attorney	wife with attorney	husband with attorney
	18%	65%	47%
Atlanta, GA	3	72	41
Boston, MA	10	68	42
Cleveland, OH	4	80	55
Colorado Springs, CO	36	52	36
Dayton, OH	<1	79	52
Des Moines, IA	3	85	59
Detroit, MI	6	73	47
Hartford, CT	5	86	74
Houston, TX	6	65	51
Oakland, CA	47	41	28
Providence, RI	1	80	63
San Diego, CA	43	45	41
Seattle, WA	37	48	39
St. Paul, MN	3	79	61
Tucson, AZ	45	43	29
Washington, DC	40	40	33

Source: National Center for State Courts, Williamsburg VA

divorce without an attorney. In Seattle, clerk's office staff also inform litigants of the availability of divorce packets that can be obtained at stationery and bookstores in the county."

Indeed, "do-it-yourself" divorce kits can easily be obtained in bookstores anywhere in the country. "They're for people with no kids, no assets, and no debts," says Jan Warner, an attorney and businessman in Columbia, South Carolina.

Some people need more help than a kit can provide, but don't need to spend hundreds of dollars in attorneys' fees, either. According to *The Wall Street Journal*, new services in Phoenix's Maricopa Superior Court "include a do-it-yourself divorce video, which plays almost continuously in a courthouse waiting room, and an on-the-spot attorney who charges $20 for a half-hour preparation session."

Many entrepreneurial lawyers are starting to tap into this market, adding "court coaching" to their repertoire. Instead of full-service legal work, they offer advice and review court papers for a smaller fee, leaving routine matters such as filing and photocopying to the client. "More and more lawyers are doing it for self-interested reasons," Beverly Hills family-law specialist Forrest S. Mosten told *The Wall Street Journal*. "It's not the difference between a $12,000 fee and a $1,000 fee. It's the difference between a $1,000 fee and no fee."

In 53 percent of divorce cases, at least one party—husband or wife—has no attorney. This frequently happens with uncontested divorces, which constitute almost three-fourths of all cases. When only one lawyer is involved in the case, he or she more often represents the wife. This is probably because women feel at a power disadvantage, according to the SJI study.

"Soup to Nuts" Representation

For older couples who have been married a long time and have substantial assets, divorce is a complicated process requiring the assistance of lawyers and other experts. According to the SJI study, about one-fourth of divorces are contested because of disagreements over child custody, visitation, and support, or the division of property.

Most men and women with substantial assets hire attorneys. Two-thirds find one through friends and relatives, according to a survey reported in *The Arbitration Journal*. Just 41 percent say that cost is a factor in their choice, and most interview only one lawyer. Clients say they look for an attorney who specializes in divorce, is empathetic, and is a good negotiator.

Attorneys are expensive, frequently charging $200 and up per hour. They also don't typically take the time to thoroughly educate clients about the divorce process. But Jan Warner, the attorney-turned-businessman, does. His company, Life Management, produces and markets a series of audiotapes on the divorce process, some in conjunction with the American Bar Association. Attorneys buy the tapes for clients, and some clients buy the tapes on their own. "Lawyers really assume that these folks know what's going on, and they don't," says Warner. The tapes cover topics such as custody and visitation, giving depositions, and preparing for court. Warner expects to sell 1.5 million audiotapes in 1994.

Besides their own legal services, attorneys perform another important role in divorce cases. They act as gatekeepers for a variety of experts such as accountants, appraisers, and actuaries who value property of various kinds. "Generally you're not going to be called into a case unless there's some real money," says Katherine Bourgeois, a CPA in Houston. "You couldn't justify it otherwise." In most of her cases, the marriage has been lengthy and the children are grown. "A lot of times the woman has not participated in the finances. So we have to help her figure it out," says Bourgeois.

Marital property includes items that are relatively straightforward to assess, such as household furnishings. Houses may appear uncomplicated as well, but they can be difficult to appraise in an uncertain real-estate market. Nearly half (45 percent) of divorcing couples own homes, according to the SJI study.

Attorneys and accountants are often called upon to evaluate property that is even more complex, like businesses. Bourgeois researches the average income and expenses of typical businesses in an industry. But such information is not always readily available. She once had to value a tanning salon. "You don't find a lot in the library about how to do that," she says.

Property with future value also has to be divided. That's where actuaries like Marvin Snyder come in. He is the president of Pension Analysis Consultants, Inc. in Merion Station, Pennsylvania. It's his role to help attorneys place a present value on pension benefits that in most states are considered marital property. Snyder started the business in 1982 and has done over 5,000 valuations. His cases typically involve couples aged 40 to 60. The husband is usually the one with the pension, "but lately we've been getting more wives with pensions," he says, a trend that will surely continue.

Women who have been homemakers for many years of marriage need to make new lives for themselves that often include paid employment. But job training costs money, something else that divorce settlements must consider. Karen Bullard works with attorneys and their clients to develop marital "severance packages" for divorcing homemakers that usually include education or training. "Over and above their settlement, we try to get a fund that will allow them to become self-supporting," says Bullard, president of Changes/Results Plus in Wichita, Kansas. Since starting the company in 1990, her business has tripled.

Entrepreneur Jan Warner has put a new twist on hiring experts for divorce cases. He arranges teleconferences whereby they can interact long-distance with clients. Warner works in conjunction with local bar associations on such projects.

CHILD CUSTODY

Divorces involving custody disputes can be some of the most expensive, time-consuming, and emotionally wrenching. Fifty-three percent of divorces involve children, according to the NCHS. About 2 percent of American children go through a divorce in a given year, up from 1 percent in the 1950s and 1960s. As the baby boom ages, the share of divorces involving children may increase. But family size has been decreasing, so divorces may affect fewer children. The average divorce now involves less than one child, compared with 1.3 during the 1960s.

Divorces that involve children take longer to complete than those that don't, five-and-a-half months versus four months, according to the SJI study. One-fourth of divorces involving children include a legal dispute over child custody. One-third involve disputes concerning child support, and 20 percent involve debates over visitation rights and schedules.

These protracted legal fights often involve psychologists, as well as medical and education experts who can testify on behalf of one parent or the other. Increasingly, however, courts are recommending or requiring feuding parents to resolve their differences through mediation. The goal is to get parents to arrive at an agreeable settlement with the help of a neutral party without resorting to the courts. Mediation can help settle property disputes, too, but is most often used to settle issues involving child custody and visitation. Thirteen of the 16 courts analyzed in the SJI study had a mediation program; 11 required mediation.

Mediators are usually attorneys or mental health practitioners, but many other types of professionals are now seeking training. There are over 25 major training organizations for mediators, says Mary Brummer at the Academy of Family Mediators in Minneapolis. The academy had 2,400 members in 1994, up from 1,800 in 1992.

Many courts now also suggest or require that parents attend classes to learn about the effects of divorce on their children. *The Wall Street Journal* points to this trend as a national movement: "This year alone, scattered counties in Illinois, Georgia, Indiana, Missouri, New York and Ohio added divorce education, which varies from 25-minute videotapes to 18-hour seminars." Some programs are free,

Kids and Divorce

The number of children involved in divorces has grown, but the average number of children per divorce has declined.

(children involved in divorces in thousands, and average number per divorce, 1960–88)

	number	average
1988	1,044	0.89
1985	1,091	0.92
1980	1,174	0.98
1975	1,123	1.08
1970	870	1.22
1965	630	1.32
1960	463	1.18

Source: National Center for Health Statistics

but others cost more than $50 per person. Many are developed in association with a local university or social service agency. Some even include special classes for children.

DEALING WITH SEPARATION AND DIVORCE

Although just over one million couples get divorced each year in the U.S., at any point in time the country has millions of currently divorced people. Their numbers have been growing. In 1992, the U.S. had 6.8 million divorced men and 9.6 million divorced women, according to the Census Bureau, up 65 percent from 1980, compared with an 8 percent increase in the number of married people. Divorced people are also older than they used to be. The number aged 45 and older grew 96 percent between 1980 and 1992, compared with 45 percent for those under age 45.

What types of services do divorced people need? Both during and after divorce, many need counseling to deal with the emotional impact. In *Our Turn: Women Who Triumph in the Face of Divorce*, Christopher L. Hayes and colleagues found that 40 percent of the recently divorced middle-aged women they surveyed sought counseling during the divorce process. Sixty percent felt formal support groups were crucial in helping them cope. Nashville psychologist Ruth Arbitman Smith says that mothers with small children and displaced homemakers are the people who most often seek her counsel after divorces.

While most divorced women are in the labor force at the time of their divorce, many are homemakers. In 1989, 5.1 million divorced women were classified as displaced homemakers because they had lost their primary source of income through divorce. Thirty-one percent were under age 35, 52 percent were aged 35 to 64, and 17 percent were aged 65 and older, according to Jean Cilik at Women Work! in Washington, D.C.

Young and middle-aged displaced homemakers are good candidates for community colleges, vocational programs, and other types of training programs because they need marketable skills. In *Our Turn*, Hayes and colleagues found that 41 percent of recently divorced middle-aged respondents went back to school during the first year after their divorce. "One of my clients started nursing school at age 47," says Karen Bullard of Changes/Results Plus in Wichita, Kansas. "She had not been in a classroom in 30 years."

One-third of the 17.8 million ever-divorced women in 1990 received some type of property settlement, according to the Census Bureau. Fifteen percent of the 20.6 million ever-divorced or currently separated women were awarded alimony. The share receiving alimony is twice as high for women aged 40 and older as for those under age 40, 20 percent versus 9 percent.

Yet many women have little experience in dealing with finances. Hayes and colleagues found that nearly two in three respondents never discussed finances with their husbands during their marriages. Such women are good candidates for the services of financial counselors. "Women want to be educated about the process," says Barry Clark, a financial consultant with Merrill Lynch in Wichita, Kansas. Although women constitute about 80 percent of the new business he gets because of divorce, Clark also works with divorced men who are often existing clients. "They may have to restructure their portfolios in making divorce settlements," he says.

Eventually, many divorced people want to get back into the social swing and begin dating, creating a market for singles groups and dating services. In fact, at many dating services, a greater percentage of clients are divorced than never-married. Most are in their 30s and 40s. "When you were 20, you went out to clubs and met people. But when you're 35, your peers aren't at the local disco," says Trish McDermott, director of communications for the International Society of Introduction Services in San Francisco. Currently, there are about 2,500 dating services across the country, she says. McDermott fields calls not only from people who are divorced, but from those who are still going through the process. "It's not uncommon for someone to want to come into a service before their divorce is final," she says.

DIFFERENT DIVORCE MARKETS

When a couple gets divorced, one household becomes two. The former spouses each need products and services. But what they need and their ability to buy it depends on post-divorce living arrangements.

People Who Live Alone

According to the Census Bureau, 42 percent of currently divorced men and 31 percent of divorced women were living alone in 1992. The majority of divorced people who live alone are middle-aged. Just 10 percent of divorced women and 13 percent of divorced men who live alone are under age 35. Fifty-seven percent of men and 43 percent of women are aged 35 to 54. Thirty percent of men and 47 percent of women are aged 55 and older.

Traditionally, women of all marital statuses who live alone don't have as much money to spend as men who live alone, partly because they tend to be older and are either retired or have never worked, but also because those who work don't earn as much as men. But women are starting to gain parity, especially the middle-aged. Women of all marital statuses who live alone spent 77 percent as much as their male counterparts in 1990–91, compared with 72 percent in 1984–85, according to the government's Consumer Expenditure Survey. But those aged 35 to 44 spent just as much as men—an average of $24,500.

Women who live alone allocate a greater share of their expenditures to housing than men do, 38 percent versus 31 percent. While young single men spend more than young single women on housing, women aged 35 and older who live alone outspend their male counterparts.

Women are willing to spend more in housing costs to ensure safety, according to Forrest Pafenberg of the National Association of Realtors, interviewed in *American Demographics*. "Single women look for a two- or three-story building," notes real-estate analyst Kenneth Danter of the Columbus, Ohio–based Danter Company. "They don't want to live on the first floor for security reasons. That has maintained the value and premium of upper-floor units."

Men of all ages who live alone spend twice as much as women on eating out, a 1990–91 average of $1,600 compared with women's $800. Some of this is probably due to the fact that some men pick up the tab for dates, but it's mostly because women who live alone are an older group. Men who live alone also spend a lot more than women on entertainment, an average of $1,100 vs. $600 in 1990–91.

Living with Roommates and Relatives

Almost two-thirds of all divorced people don't live alone, and they tend to be younger than those who do. Because of their relative youth, they may have lower incomes than those who live alone. But since they share household expenses (or don't chip in at all), many have a considerable amount available for discretionary spending.

On Their Own—Sort Of

The most common living situation for divorced men is living alone; for divorced women, it is living with family members.

(currently divorced men and women in thousands by age, and percent distribution by living arrangement, 1992)

WOMEN	number	living alone	with nonrelatives	with family
total	9,569	31.4%	14.1%	54.5%
under 25	225	5.8%	25.3%	68.9%
25 to 34	2,011	13.5	23.0	63.5
35 to 44	2,793	16.8	14.6	68.6
45 to 54	2,285	36.4	12.1	51.5
55 and older	2,254	62.9	6.3	30.8

MEN	number	living alone	with nonrelatives	with family
total	6,753	42.1%	27.2%	30.7%
under 25	119	18.5%	37.8%	43.7%
25 to 34	1,323	26.7	37.7	35.6
35 to 44	2,204	39.7	27.5	32.8
45 to 54	1,606	46.5	23.2	30.3
55 and older	1,500	56.3	21.1	22.6

Source: U.S. Census Bureau

Twenty-seven percent of divorced men and 14 percent of divorced women live with roommmates who are unrelated to them. Thirty-three percent are under age 35. Just 14 percent are aged 55 and older. One-third of divorced men and 55 percent of divorced women live with family members, such as children and parents. They are slightly older than those who live with roommates. Twenty-seven percent are under age 35; 14 percent are aged 55 and older.

About 7 percent of divorced people live in their parents' homes. Almost half (46 percent) are under age 35. But most divorced people living with family members are single parents. Thirty-five percent of all divorced women and 10 percent of all divorced men are single parents whose children live with them. Almost nine in ten are household heads.

Single Parents

Thirty-seven percent of single mothers and 45 percent of single fathers are divorced. (The rest are never married, widowed, separated, or have an absent spouse.) In 1992, this amounted to 3.3 million divorced single mothers and 700,000 single fathers. That year, 5.5 million children under age 18 were living with divorced mothers and 900,000 with divorced fathers. Children of divorce comprise 10 percent of all children living with at least one parent and 37 percent of those living with single parents.

Women are more likely than men to be single parents; they are also poorer. Children residing with divorced fathers lived in households with a median income of $27,300 in 1992, compared with $17,500 for those living with divorced mothers. Twenty-nine percent of children living with divorced fathers were in households with incomes of $40,000 or more, compared with 13 percent of those with divorced mothers. And just 15 percent of children residing with fathers were living below the poverty level, compared with 37 percent of those with mothers.

Thirty-one percent of children who live with a divorced mother live with a parent who is unemployed or not in the labor force, and another 12 percent with a mother who works only part-time. This is true for just 17 percent and 6 percent, respectively, of those who live with their fathers.

In spite of their lower economic standing, divorced women and their children have many consumer needs. One is rental housing. Divorce is a frequently cited reason for moving, according to the Census Bureau's 1991 American Housing Survey. Children who live with mothers after divorce are more likely to live in rented dwellings than those who end up with fathers after divorce, 59 percent versus 42 percent.

The food habits of divorced mothers also provide marketing opportunities. According to Ruth L. Wynn and Jean Bowering, families headed by separated or divorced mothers eat out more often than do two-parent families. Women heading divorced/separated families report eating out an average of 2.9 times per month, compared with 1.4 times for intact families. Nine in 10 times, separated/divorced families go to fast-food or cafeteria-style restaurants, while two-thirds of the time intact families go to restaurants with table service.

Single Parents

Men are more likely than women to become single parents through divorce.

(number in thousands and percent distribution of single-parent families headed by men and women, by marital status, 1992)

	number	percent
families maintained by father who is:	1,472	100.0%
divorced	664	45.1
never married	400	27.2
separated/spouse absent	308	20.9
widowed	100	6.8
families maintained by mother who is:	9,028	100.0%
divorced	3,349	37.1
never married	3,284	36.4
separated/spouse absent	1,947	21.6
widowed	448	5.0

Source: U.S. Census Bureau

Single fathers are a very small market, but they offer opportunities for particular services, particularly those related to running a household. Single parents of both sexes are frequently overburdened with housekeeping and child-care responsibilities, and could use help. But because of their higher income, single fathers can better afford household help. Furthermore, many men are not accustomed to doing household chores on a regular basis. According to researcher Geoffrey L. Greif, single fathers are three times more likely than single mothers to use outside help for chores such as cooking, cleaning, and shopping. Men are also more likely than women to spend money on entertainment. Three-fourths of the single fathers Greif studied said they dated at least every other week, compared with just over half of the single mothers.

Noncustodial Parents

Almost nine in ten divorced noncustodial parents are men. In 1990, 6.9 million divorced, separated, or remarried women were living with children under age 21 whose father was not present. Although different studies have produced somewhat different results, all show that some noncustodial fathers maintain contact with their children on a regular basis. According to these studies, between one-third and two-thirds of noncustodial fathers see their children more than once a month.

Some noncustodial fathers also provide economic assistance for their children above and beyond child-support payments. Researcher Jay D. Teachman reports that 60 percent of noncustodial fathers sometimes purchase gifts for their children. Of those who do, one in three does so on a regular basis. Thirty-five percent pay for their children's clothes at least some of the time; of these, one in five does so regularly. Thirty-five percent take their children on vacation. Of those, one-third do so regularly. Twenty-five percent pay for routine dental care, two-thirds on a consistent basis. Similarly, 24 percent pay for uninsured medical expenses, with two-thirds doing so regularly.

But another group of fathers isn't even willing to pay for the basics. About three-fourths of divorced women with children are awarded child support, according to the Census Bureau. Of those awarded child support, half receive full payment, one-fourth receive partial payment, and one-fourth receive nothing at all. In 1989, the average child-support payment received by divorced women was $3,300, constituting 17 percent of their total income. Forty-four percent of divorced mothers were awarded health-care benefits for their children as part of their support. But just two-thirds of fathers required to provide health insurance actually did so. One in four noncustodial fathers lives in a different state than his children. This group is especially likely to be "deadbeat dads."

Three in ten women with children by noncustodial fathers have at some time contacted a government agency for assistance in obtaining or collecting child support. Government agencies have been unable to keep pace with the demand, which has created a new niche for private businesses. In 1991, David Allen Moffitt expanded his San Diego law firm, Moffitt and Associates, to include a child-support collection service. The average amount of back child support due to his clients is about $15,000, says Moffitt.

Sometimes both parents want the children to live with them, and occasionally both get their wish. Joint physical custody of children is still quite rare, however. According to sociologist Judith A. Seltzer, it happens in less than 3 percent of cases. But when it does occur, this arrangement can be beneficial not only for children, but for business as well. Children with two homes need two sets of bedroom furniture, toys, and many other items.

Regardless of custody arrangements, the majority of children do not remain in single-parent households forever. Most become members of stepfamilies when one or both parents remarries. In spite of the costs of divorce, many people are ready, willing, and able to try again.

PRODUCTS AND SERVICES FOR
The Divorce Transition

The Divorce Process

Attorneys' services
Accounting services
Actuarial services
Appraisals
Psychological assessments
Medical and educational assessments
"Do-it-yourself" divorce kits
Paralegal clinics
Books and tapes on the divorce process
Divorce education classes

After the Divorce

Apartments
Home furnishings
Real-estate services
Occupational assessments
Community colleges and training programs
Career and other counseling
Support groups
Financial planning
Dating services

Single and Noncustodial Parents

Child-care services
Cooking, cleaning, and laundry services
Takeout and fast-food
Children's toys, clothes, and furnishings
Child-support collection services

SOURCES

Arditti, Joyce A. "**Factors Related to Custody, Visitation, and Child Support for Divorced Fathers: An Exploratory Analysis.**" *Journal of Divorce and Remarriage,* Vol. 17, Nos. 3/4, 1992, pp. 23–42.

Braus, Patricia. "**Sex and the Single Spender.**" *American Demographics*, Ithaca, NY, November 1993, pp. 28–34.

Castro Martin, Teresa and Larry L. Bumpass. "**Recent Trends in Marital Disruption.**" *Demography* 26, 1989, pp. 37–51.

Colasanto, Diane and James Shriver. "**Middle-Aged Face Marital Crisis.**" *The Gallup Report*, Princeton, NJ, May 1989, pp. 34–38.

Goerdt, John A. *Divorce Courts: Case Management, Case Characteristics, and the Pace of Litigation in 16 Urban Jurisdictions.* Williamsburg, VA: National Center for State Courts, 1992.

Greif, Geoffrey L. *Single Fathers*. Lexington, MA: Lexington Books, 1985.

Greif, Geoffrey L. and Mary S. Pabst. *Mothers Without Custody.* Lexington, MA: Lexington Books, 1988.

Hauser-Dann, Joyce. "**Divorce Mediation: A Growing Field?**" *The Arbitration Journal*, Vol. 43, No. 2, June 1988, pp. 15–21.

Hayes, Christopher L., Deborah Anderson, and Melinda Blau, *Our Turn: Women Who Triumph in the Face of Divorce*. New York, NY: Pocket Books, 1993.

Lester, Gordon H. *Child Support and Alimony: 1989*. Washington, DC: U.S. Bureau of the Census, 1991.

Mergenhagen DeWitt, Paula. **"All the Lonely People."** *American Demographics*, Ithaca, NY, April 1992, pp. 44–48.

Mergenhagen DeWitt, Paula. **"Breaking Up Is Hard To Do."** *American Demographics*, Ithaca, NY, October 1992, pp. 52–58.

National Center for Health Statistics. *Advance Report of Final Divorce Statistics, 1988, Monthly Vital Statistics Report*, Vol. 39, No. 2, Suppl. 2, Public Health Service, Hyattsville, MD, 1991.

National Center for Health Statistics. *Annual Summary of Births, Marriages, Divorces, and Deaths: United States, 1992, Monthly Vital Statistics Report*, Vol. 41, No. 13, Public Health Service, Hyattsville, MD, 1993.

National Center for Health Statistics. *Annual Summary of Births, Marriages, Divorces, and Deaths: United States, 1993, Monthly Vital Statistics Report*, Vol. 42, No. 13, Public Health Service, Hyattsville, MD, 1994.

Norton, Arthur J. and Louisa F. Miller. *Marriage, Divorce, and Remarriage in the 1990s*. Washington, DC: U.S. Bureau of the Census, 1992.

Ostrom, Brian J., Karen Gillions Way, Steven E. Hairston, and Carol R. Flango. *The Pulse of Justice: The Business of State Trial and Appellate Courts*. Williamsburg, VA: National Center for State Courts, 1993.

Rawlings, Steve W. *Household and Family Characteristics: March 1992*. Washington, DC: U.S. Bureau of the Census, 1993.

Saluter, Arlene F. **Marital Status and Living Arrangements: March 1992**. Washington, DC: U.S. Bureau of the Census, 1992.

Schoen, Robert and Robin M. Weinick. **"The Slowing Metabolism of Marriage: Figures from 1988 U.S. Marital Status Life Tables."** *Demography*, Vol. 30, No. 4, November 1993, pp. 737–746.

Seltzer, Judith A. **"Legal and Physical Custody Arrangements in Recent Divorces."** *Social Science Quarterly*, Vol. 71, No. 2, June 1990, pp. 250–266.

Teachman, Jay D. "**Contributions to Children by Divorced Parents.**" *Social Problems*, Vol. 38, No. 3, August 1991, pp. 358–371.

Vobejda, Barbara. "**Baby-Boom Women Setting Divorce Record.**" *The Washington Post*, December 9, 1992, pp. A1, A8.

Wynn, Ruth L. and Jean Bowering. "**Homemaking Practices and Evening Meals in Married and Separated Families with Young Children.**" *Journal of Divorce and Remarriage*, Vol. 14, No. 2, 1990, pp. 107–123.

White, Lynn K. "**Determinants of Divorce: A Review of Research in the Eighties.**" *Journal of Marriage and the Family*, Vol. 52 No. 4, November 1990, pp. 904–912.

Women Work! *The More Things Change: A Status Report on Displaced Homemakers and Single Parents in the 1980s*. Washington, DC: Women Work! 1990.

Woo, Junda. "**Entrepreneurial Lawyers Coach Clients to Represent Themselves.**" *The Wall Street Journal*, October 15, 1993, pp. B1, B5.

Woo, Junda. "**More People Represent Themselves in Court, But Is Justice Served?**" *The Wall Street Journal*, August 17, 1993, pp. A1, A7.

Woo, Junda. "**More Courts Are Forcing Couples to Take Divorce-Education Class.**" *The Wall Street Journal*, October 1, 1993, p. B8.

OTHER RESOURCES

Kitson, Gay C. *Portrait of Divorce: Adjustment to Marital Breakdown*. New York, NY: Guilford Press, 1992.

Women Work! *Women Work, Poverty Persists: A Status Report on Displaced Homemakers and Single Mothers in the United States*. Washington, DC: Women Work! 1994.

CHAPTER 5

AIDING OUR ELDERS
The Caregiving Transition and Death

"I HAD ALMOST NO personal time. I was physically and emotionally exhausted," says Nancy Promersberger, a Nashville marketing professional who was looking after two small sons at the same time her widowed father in Chicago became seriously ill. For two years, she cared for him long-distance, spending much of her free time—scarce though it was—checking into services for him.

Just before her father died in February 1993, Promersberger switched from a full- to part-time work schedule in anticipation of moving him to Nashville. She and her husband even bought a home with an in-law suite. "My father's situation totally drove the decision-making process in the type of house we purchased," she says.

Like Promersberger, many people face this transition—becoming caregivers for aging and ill parents at the same time they are responsible for their own children. They are what has come to be known as the "sandwich generation." Three-fourths of caregivers are women. Some are in their 30s with young children, but most are in their 40s and 50s, many of whom face children's college costs. A smaller group of caregivers—those aged 60 and older—experience the declining health of a parent or spouse at the same time they must prepare for their own retirement.

The caregiving transition opens up new business opportunities because many caregivers need help. Sometimes they cannot provide the specialized medical care necessary or do not have the physical strength required to assist an elderly relative. But even caregivers who don't need these kinds of services need other ones. More than half work outside the home and don't have time to provide care. Those who do provide full-time care can get burned out. Caregivers may also need help with routine chores and transportation, as well as financial and legal matters.

A new and growing type of business called care management assesses the needs of elderly relatives and arranges for their care, often at the request of long-distance relatives. Employers, too, are realizing that many of their employees are or will become caregivers. Many have set up programs to help with this transition. This helps stem the loss of productivity that often occurs when workers become caregivers. It also promotes good will both within an organization and in the public eye. Businesses have cropped up to provide employees with services such as information and referral lines, seminars, support groups, and newsletters. Eventually, caregivers will experience the death of their loved one and require the services of various professionals, including funeral directors, counselors, and lawyers.

TRENDS IN THE MARKET

In a sense, caregiving is a "new" transition because never before have so many people lived so long. The population aged 65 and older grew 171 percent between 1950 and 1994, compared with 73 percent for the total population. The population aged 85 and older increased 509 percent. Between 1994 and 2050, the number of people aged 65 and older is projected to increase 138 percent; the number aged 85 and older could grow 402 percent.

The U.S. had more than five million chronically disabled people aged 65 and older living in private households in 1989, according to

Boomers Cause Boom in Elderly Market

In the year 2050, the youngest baby boomers will be 86 years old, and one in 20 Americans will fall into the oldest-old age group.

(millions of elderly people by age, 1970–2050)

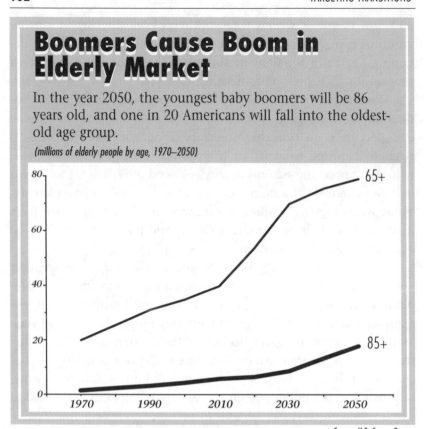

Source: U.S. Census Bureau

an analysis of National Long-Term Care Survey data by Kenneth G. Manton and his colleagues at Duke University. One-fourth had difficulties with tasks like shopping and household chores. The rest had more severe problems and needed help with personal-care activities like eating, bathing, and dressing.

Most elderly people are women, because women live, on average, seven years longer than men. Today, there are just 68 men for every 100 women aged 65 and older. The likelihood of disability increases with age, and at any given age, women experience more severe disabilities than do men. These three factors combine to make women the majority of the disabled older population.

Ninety-five percent of the noninstitutionalized disabled elderly receive care from family, friends, or other unpaid sources. A 1988 study by the American Association of Retired Persons (AARP) and the Travelers Foundation found that as many as seven million households may be involved in caring for a person aged 50 or older. Many receive outside help. Twenty-four percent of caregivers have used home-health aides while 22 percent have used homemakers and chore services. Some of these services are provided by the government but others must be purchased from private businesses.

Who are America's unpaid caregivers? The typical caregiver is an employed professional woman in her mid-40s, according to the AARP/Travelers survey. Seventy-five percent of caregivers are women. Forty-two percent are employed full-time, and 13 percent work part-time. Two-thirds are married, and 39 percent have children at home. Twenty-nine percent are aged 35 to 49; 26 percent are aged 50 to 64; 28 percent are under age 35; and 15 percent are aged 65 and older.

Women and men have different ways of caring for aging parents. "Daughters will cook, clean, shop, and do the laundry, while sons are more likely to pay for things," says Monika White, director of the Senior Care Network at Huntington Memorial Hospital in Pasadena, California. But women may become more like men in the future, because they will be more likely to work outside the home through the middle-aged primary caregiving years.

In 1992, 73 percent of women aged 45 to 54 were in the labor

Disabled at Home

The U.S. has three times as many disabled elders living in private homes as in institutions.

(millions of people aged 65 and older, by disability status and living arrangements, 1982–89)

	1982	1984	1989
not disabled	20.5	21.4	23.9
disabled	6.3	6.6	7.0
living in community	4.8	5.1	5.3
institutionalized	1.5	1.5	1.7

Source: adapted from data reported in Journal of Gerontology (Vol. 43, No. 4), 1993

force, compared with 38 percent in 1950. Their use of purchased elder-care services is bound to increase. As researcher Rhonda J. V. Montgomery observes: "The impact of employment will not alter the number of elders for whom daughters are serving as primary caregivers, but this employment will likely alter the way in which these daughters provide care." She suggests that employed women will replace their time with money—that is, they will increasingly buy caregiving services.

HELPING CAREGIVERS PROVIDE CARE

There is an almost universal belief on the part of adult children that caring for parents is a moral obligation. In a 1991 survey sponsored by the Massachusetts Life Insurance Company, 36 percent of people said "taking care of one's parents in their old age" is one of the most important values they hold. Fifty-four percent said it was a very important value; 8 percent said it was somewhat important.

The greatest share of caregivers are rendering aid to a mother (28 percent), according to the 1988 AARP/Travelers survey. This is followed by a father (12 percent), grandmother (12 percent), and spouse (10 percent). Altogether, 85 percent are providing care for some type of relative. In six out of ten cases, the elder is aged 75 or older. Many elders get help from more than one source, and the kind of help they get varies from specialized medical services to routine household help. Their caregivers also get help, ranging from needed breaks to financial advice, emotional support, and assistance with managing care itself.

Home Health Care

Home health care is an exploding industry. In 1963, about 1,100 agencies in the U.S. provided these services, according to the Washington, D.C.–based National Association for Home Care. Today, almost 14,000 do so.

About half of agencies are Medicare-certified, which means they are eligible to provide federally subsidized services. In 1978, Medicare spent $435 million for 17 million home-health care visits to 770,000 clients. In 1993, it paid $11.7 billion for 184 million visits to 3.5 million clients.

The entire home-care industry employed 401,600 people in 1992 and is projected to employ more than twice that many in 2005, according to the Bureau of Labor Statistics. In 1992, over half of the jobs were in service occupations, including 184,000 homemakers and home-health aides and 22,300 nursing and psychiatric aides. These workers perform services ranging from cooking and cleaning to bathing, dressing, and feeding. Almost one-fourth of home health employees were in professional specialty positions, including 71,300 registered nurses, 11,100 therapists, and 4,300 social workers. Among other things, these specialists administer medication, devise exercise routines, and help home-bound people access community services.

Medicare doesn't cover all home-care services because the young and middle-aged use them, too. But the elderly use a disproportionately large share. In 1987, those aged 65 and older accounted for 11 percent of the population but accounted for half of those receiving home-care services, according to the National Medical Expenditure Survey.

Growth in home care has resulted partly from the aging of the population, but also because of shorter hospital stays. People can

Home Care Use

People aged 65 and older account for half of home-care patients, but nearly three-fourths of total visits.

(millions and percent of population receiving home care, and average visits per user, by age, 1987)

	number receiving home care	percent receiving home care	average visits per user
all ages	5.9	3%	44
under 40	1.7	1	15
40 to 64	1.2	2	38
65 to 74	1.2	7	56
75 to 84	1.2	15	67
85 and older	0.6	30	71

Source: National Association for Home Care, Washington, DC

now receive services at home that used to be available only in the hospital, such as intravenous medication (also known as infusion therapy), respiratory therapy, and dialysis.

Expenditures on infusion therapy are projected to increase from $2 billion in 1990 to $5.9 billion in 1996, according to FIND/SVP of New York City. Respiratory therapy, which brought in almost $1.3 billion in 1990, is expected to increase to $2.2 billion in 1996, and expenditures for dialysis services are projected to increase from $345 million to $589 million over the same time period.

Most elders don't need such high-tech medical help, but they rely heavily on medication. In fact, 85 percent of those aged 65 and older fill at least one prescription per year, according to the American Association of Retired Persons. Medicare enrollees average $500 per year on prescription drugs, but the 11 percent who spend the most average $100 a month in prescription costs.

Elders also rely on a variety of health and safety devices that make home care possible. Kenneth G. Manton and colleagues at Duke University found that between 1982 and 1989, the use of special equipment by disabled elders aged 65 and older living in the community increased. In 1989, almost three million elders had an impairment that affected their ability to bathe. Thirty-six percent used grab bars in the bathtub area, 35 percent used a shower seat or tub stool, 14 percent a rubber mat, 6 percent a handheld shower, and 5 percent a walker or cane. Almost 2.8 million elders had an impairment that affected their ability to get around inside their home. Fifty percent used a cane, 38 percent a walker, 19 percent a wheelchair, 4 percent a railing, 4 percent crutches, 1 percent orthopedic shoes, and 1 percent an elevator. About 1.6 million had an impairment that affected their ability to use the toilet. Thirty-five percent used a raised toilet to deal with their difficulties, 31 percent a portable toilet, 26 percent a bathroom railing, 21 percent a bed pan, 9 percent adult diapers, and 4 percent a catheter.

In addition to special devices, elders frequently need personal-care assistance from workers supplied by home-care agencies. But many of the services that home-care agencies provide have nothing to do with health per se, says Linda Schoenborn, owner of Interim Healthcare of Western Massachusetts, a franchised home-health-care agency. "The biggest request from family members is to get the elderly individual up and functioning in the morning," she explains. "Maybe they've gotten the elder enrolled in a day-care program, but they can't always go to the person's home and get them dressed." Schoenborn's company even provides companions for the elderly.

Providing Relief

Adult children who care for elderly relatives often need breaks. That's where respite care comes in. Respite care can occur daily or periodically, as when the family goes on vacation. "If the family member is working, then day care is crucial," says Karen Casciato of Providence ElderPlace in Portland, Oregon, an organization offering respite care and comprehensive medical services for the frail elderly.

Day care is provided at the center, along with meals and transportation. In-home care is also available.

Respite care tends to be underutilized, says Andrew Scharlach, a professor of aging at the University of California–Berkeley. Part of the problem is that people don't really understand what it is. "It's not part of the common parlance," he says. "If you picked 1,000 caregivers out of the population and asked them if they were interested in respite care, they'd say, 'What's that?'" Scharlach feels the issue will receive more attention in the future with changes in the nation's health-care system, including long-term-care policies.

Caregivers also need a hand with the endless, mundane tasks of everyday life—taking Mom to the grocery store, helping Dad with his laundry. Silver Service, a small business in Annapolis, Maryland, saw the need and responded. "We rent ourselves out as 'daughters for a day'," says vice president Diane Kramer. She and her partner, Sally Branning, do anything and everything—chauffeuring, errand-running, visiting, housekeeping, even gardening.

Sometimes elderly people contact the service directly themselves, and sometimes it's a son or daughter. "Children are concerned about the parent driving or making sure there is enough food," says Kramer. "They may be feeling that they're not visiting as often as they should." Silver Service began operating in June 1992. A year later, it served 30 clients on a regular basis and 20 more on a one-time or occasional basis. The local enterprise gets most of its business through word of mouth.

Maria Hodges, of Sheboygan, Wisconsin, has been running another small local operation since 1987. Gifts and Groceries 2 Go is a part-time pick-up and delivery service with about 35 regular customers ranging in age from 62 to 95. Most are women in their 80s living alone. "Some of these women have never driven," says Hodges. Adult children want to know that their parents are eating right. But food is not their only concern. Hodges is successful because she provides a friendly face and a listening ear for the elders. "It's more then just grocery shopping. It's being a friend."

Some elders need more than groceries; they need fully cooked meals. Meals on Wheels are delivered by a host of volunteers through countless community-based organizations around the country. Jackie Bayless coordinates the Meals on Wheels program for Senior Citizens, Inc. in Nashville, Tennessee. The average client is in her mid-70s and usually lives alone. "The meal may be the only thing keeping them out of a nursing home or a child's home," says Bayless. Most of the elders do have relatives, sometimes out of town, "but a small percentage do not have anyone." Some elders can afford to pay the full cost of the meals; others pay on a sliding scale.

Such programs also afford opportunities for private businesses. Ziker and Company Catering prepares 1,000 meals a day for Meals on Wheels and other senior nutrition programs in the South Bend, Indiana area. Preparing meals for the elderly is about 25 percent of his catering business, says owner Robert Ziker. But such work can be complicated. Ziker must alter the meals for elders with various health conditions, including diabetes and renal problems. "We have eight different diets for Meals on Wheels," he notes.

In 1990, about 1.5 million impaired elders used a community service such as Meals on Wheels at least once, according to the American Association of Homes and Services for the Aging in Washington, D.C. That number is expected to grow to 2.4 million by 2020.

Managing Money Matters

Caregiving also involves complex financial and legal issues. A growing number of professionals are concentrating on serving these special needs of the elderly and their caregivers.

"We focus our practice on the sandwich generation," says Barry Freedman, a financial planner in Peabody, Massachusetts. "The biggest concern in that age group—45 to 55—is that they married late, had their children later in life, and now have to care for elderly parents, raise their children, and plan for their own retirement all at the same time."

Freedman's clients are usually upper-middle-class, dual-earner couples. A professional couple with combined income of $150,000 is typical, he says. They want to know how much money they need to set aside for both family obligations and their own future needs. Such couples are also interested in protecting their inheritance. "They ask, 'What happens to Mother's house if she dies or goes into a nursing home?'" Although caregivers may arrange for their parents' legal and financial services, the recipient of the services frequently pays for them.

Questions about money often become legal questions, and that's when elder-care specialists like Tucson attorney Allan Bogutz become involved. About one-fourth of his practice involves clients from out of state who have elderly parents living in the Tucson area. To help with care-management issues, Bogutz even employs a nurse.

Elder law is a rapidly growing specialization. In 1987, the National Academy of Elder Law Attorneys was incorporated with 30 members. By 1993, the academy had 2,100 members, with the largest concentrations in New York and California, followed by Florida and Arizona. While the overall elderly population is predominantly female, Bogutz deals with more elderly men. This is because elderly women generally have fewer financial resources and more difficulty paying for legal services, he says.

In dealing with the financial and legal issues that caregivers face, professionals should keep in mind that emotions run high. Understanding the social and psychological needs of the sandwich generation is as important as understanding their portfolios. "This is a wide-open area for financial planners," says Freedman. "But if I had it to do over again, I would probably have gotten my degree in sociology with a focus on geriatrics."

Managing Care

Many adult children have so many commitments that they become overwhelmed by the needs of their parents and find it difficult, if not impossible, to coordinate services themselves. "Most of them are working. They usually have children that they're still involved with—either at home, in college, or who are beginning to have their own families," says Rona Bartelstone, a care manager in Fort Lauderdale, Florida. "We are usually called when there has been a crisis."

B.J. Curry Spitler of San Diego says that when she first began offering care-management services to the families of elderly individuals, "nobody knew what I was doing." That was in the mid-1980s, and the U.S. had only about 25 care managers. But Spitler, president of Age Concerns, soon gained colleagues. By 1993, the National Association of Professional Geriatric Care Managers boasted 450 members.

Care managers assess the well-being of elderly people and coordinate home-care services for time-strapped caregivers. They are not usually hired by recipients themselves, but by family members typically in their 40s, 50s, and 60s. Many of Bartelstone's clients are adult children who live far from their parents, not surprising for a business based in Florida. But 74 percent of care recipients who live on their own reside within a 20-minute drive of their caregivers, according to the AARP/Travelers survey. Children who live close to elderly parents are better able to coordinate care themselves.

Many care managers are primarily brokers of services. Some, like Bartelstone and Spitler, not only broker services, but provide them as well, by dispatching their own personnel such as nurses, homemakers, and home-health aides. Bartelstone works with clients for an average of ten months, but her services have ranged from one-time assessments to ten years of ongoing management. The average age of the elderly people she serves is 86; her oldest is over 100. Her business served ten families in 1989; by 1993, it was serving 160.

SENIOR HOUSING

Home-care, financial, and other services can go a long way toward keeping elderly people in their own homes. But when a parent

becomes too disabled, he or she may no longer be able to live inde-
pendently. According to the AARP/Travelers survey, 37 percent of
disabled elders live with their caregivers. Some caregivers, like Nancy
Promersberger whose story opened the chapter, purchase homes
with additional rooms or a suite to accommodate an elderly parent.
Some build additions to their present homes.

But others may not be capable of caring for an elder at home.
They may not have the time, resources, skills, or desire. And some
elderly people have no children or other relatives to care for them
once they are unable to live on their own. Fortunately, senior housing has become a major industry in the U.S., offering a variety of
facilities for a range of needs.

Independent-care residences are for elders with no serious health
problems. Individuals may own or rent units, often in a building
that provides meals, housekeeping, transportation, and activities,
but usually no personal-care services.

Assisted-care housing is designed for an older and more impaired group, though not so impaired that they need the acute care
provided in a nursing home. They receive more hands-on care than

Dependent Living

People usually enter Continuing Care Retirement
Communities (CCRCs) in their late 70s, then move to
assisted-living or nursing-home level care several years later.

(selected characteristics of senior housing residents, 1990)

	average age at entry	average age at death	percent male	percent married
independent-living units	78.8	84.9	25%	30%
assisted-living personal care	83.7	87.6	17	11
nursing-home care	84.2	88.4	17	15

Source: American Association of Homes and Services for the Aging, Washington, DC

is usually available in independent-care residences, including assistance with medication monitoring, bathing, dressing, and eating. Adult children become very involved in the selection of assisted-care facilities for their parents.

"They [the children] are what is called the 'influencer'," says Chris Ourand at the National Association for Senior Living Industries in Annapolis, Maryland. "They go on tours of the facilities with their parents, who tend to be in their early 80s." The U.S. has approximately 50,000 assisted-care facilities, says Ourand, and their rate of growth has been higher than that of retirement facilities in general.

Nursing homes are often seen as a last resort by adult children and their elderly parents. According to a 1992 survey sponsored by the Alliance for Aging Research, 70 percent of people agree with the statement: "Losing my independence and having to spend the last years of my life in a nursing home is what I fear most about old age."

According to research by Lois Grau and colleagues at the Robert Wood Johnson Medical School, caregivers feel guilty and depressed when they place their relatives in nursing homes. These feelings do not dissipate with time, the research found. Grau studied 422 caregivers with relatives at two New York City–area nursing homes— 45 percent were daughters, 20 percent were sons, 13 percent were spouses, and 22 percent were other relatives. Spouses felt the worst about their decision, followed by daughters and other relatives, with sons the least affected.

Nevertheless, nursing home placement is a necessary option. Twenty-four percent of disabled elderly people reside in nursing homes; many have no living relatives. Nearly half are aged 85 and older, according to the 1985 National Nursing Home Survey. Nursing-home care accounts for a considerable portion of total U.S. personal health-care expenditures—9 percent, or $53 billion, in 1990, when 1.8 million Americans lived in these facilities. On average, nursing-home care costs $35,000 a year, Richard Coorsh of the Health Insurance Association of America recently told *American Demographics*. About 40 percent of these costs are covered by Medicaid.

During the 1980s, the nursing-home population grew 24 percent, more than double the growth rate of the U.S. population, notes

Patricia Braus in *American Demographics*. Researchers offer different projections of the size of the nursing-home population in years to come, ranging from two million to four million by 2020. The actual number will depend on changes in death rates as well as payment policies for long-term home-based versus institutional care. But all researchers seem to agree that after the oldest baby boomers turn 75 in 2021, the nursing-home population will expand rapidly.

Some residential communities offer different levels of care, ranging from independent living to nursing-home service. These types of residences are known as continuing-care retirement communities (CCRCs). Individuals typically pay an entrance fee and then make monthly payments. According to a 1990 survey by the American Association of Homes and Services for the Aging, average entrance fees for a one-bedroom unit ranged from a low of $34,352 to a high of $95,152, depending on the level of service desired. The most expensive arrangements include lifetime medical care. Average monthly fees in 1990 ranged from $694 to $1,299. The typical CCRC resident is an unmarried (usually widowed) woman in her early 80s.

The U.S. currently has 1,000 CCRCs; 85 percent are run by non-profit organizations. But private companies are also entering the market. Bentley Village, a Classic Residence by Hyatt, is a CCRC located in Naples, Florida. Its 374 independent apartments stay 99 percent occupied, says Mary Leary, vice president of sales and marketing. The community has 18 assisted-living units and 93 nursing-home beds available if needed. Those who move to such communities "are looking toward the future," says Leary. "They are planners." One-third of residents move in as married couples, higher than the share that move to residences that are exclusively independent- or assisted-living, says Leary. If one spouse requires nursing-home care, the other will be conveniently located nearby. "They know that one may pass away before the other, and they want to be settled."

Even if nursing homes aren't always as horrible as people imagine, keeping disabled elderly out of them as long as possible is still a priority for concerned relatives. It is also a challenge, especially for relatives who have to work. Employers are trying to help adult children maintain their parents' independence, creating business opportunities in the process.

EMPLOYERS INVOLVED IN CAREGIVING

Elder-care services are often marketed to employers rather than to caregivers. This makes sense, because more than half of caregivers are employed outside the home. Employed caregivers spend a median of ten hours per week on care-related tasks, according to the AARP/Travelers study.

Like Nancy Promersberger, the Nashville resident who cared for her father long-distance, some employees change their work hours or employment situations in response to caregiving duties. Nine percent of working caregivers took a leave of absence, and 6 percent reduced their hours from full- to part-time, according to AARP/Travelers. More than one-third lost time from work because of caregiving duties.

Employers like Tenneco, Inc., of Houston, are responding to the needs created by the caregiving transition. "The demands of working and trying to care for both children and parents puts the squeeze on people," says Diana Freeland, the company's corporate manager of employee assistance programs. A 1993 survey of 1,034 major U.S. employers by Hewitt Associates of Lincolnshire, Illinois, found that 20 percent of large organizations offered some type of elder-care benefit to employees. Of companies that provide such benefits, 22 percent offer counseling, 22 percent offer long-term care insurance, and 76 percent offer resource and referral services. Most employers contract with outside firms for many of these services.

Helping Employees Find Services

Boston-based Work/Family Directions is one of the nation's largest providers of resource and referral services. In 1988, it had just one client for elder-care services—IBM, with 200,000 covered employees. By 1993, it had 60 elder-care clients, including General Electric and AT&T, covering two million employees.

Fourteen counselors at Work/Family headquarters serve as initial contacts for employees with elder-care concerns. But the company itself contracts with 200 additional organizations around the country to help families locate and select services in their communities.

"Our philosophy is that people really need to talk with a local expert who understands that community very intimately," says Diane Piktialis, Work/Family's vice president for elder-care services. "We've contracted with experts in locations where we have employees or retirees, as well as in communities where you would find a heavy retirement population, like Florida and California," she explains.

Work/Family Directions is primarily used by the children of elders rather than spouses or other relatives. Ninety percent of employees who use the company's resource and referral service are calling about their parents or parents-in-law. Another 6 percent are calling about a grandparent. Sixty percent of callers are women. More than half live 50 or more miles from their elderly relative.

The largest share of users are aged 45 to 54 (36 percent), followed by those aged 35 to 44 (28 percent). Twenty-two percent of people using the service are aged 55 and older. "Many retirees actually call for parents in their 90s," says Piktialis. Nearly one-fourth of the elders for whom services are sought are aged 85 and older. Forty-five percent are aged 75 to 84.

While Work/Family serves Fortune 500 companies that are national in scope, other resource and referral providers target smaller and more localized markets. About one-fourth of companies with 100 to 500 employees either offer elder-care services or are considering them, according to a 1992 survey by the Society for Human Resource Management in Alexandria, Virginia.

Working Families, Inc., of New York City provides elder-care resource and referral services to 20 medium-sized employers in the New York metropolitan area. "We try to target companies with between 200 and 3,000 employees," says president Patricia Schiff Estess. "The larger companies have really taken the lead [in work-family programs]. But coming along right behind them are smaller companies, especially in the public utilities and securities industries."

Some mid-size employers are banding together to provide more affordable resource and referral services. Several New York City advertising agencies designed an elder-care program for their employees with the help of the New York Business Group on Health, a nonprofit business coalition that focuses on issues regarding health care. Having companies in the same industry work together on such a plan is advantageous, says Judith Barr, who spearheaded the initiative. "The demographics of the work force and the nature of the work activity are similar," she says.

Not all employees in need of elder-care services take advantage of them. Only 2 percent to 10 percent of employees eligible for Work/Family's resource and referral services use them, says vice president Piktialis. Yet research suggests that between 12 percent and 15 percent of all employees have some caregiving responsibility for elders, according to Andrew Scharlach at the University of California-Berkeley.

For company-sponsored programs to be effective, employers must constantly promote them. "When we do outreach and advertising, we get an influx of calls for our resource and referral services," says Penny Breiman, director of health services at Equitable Life Assurance Society in New York City.

One Canadian company has successfully launched a convenient phone-in resource and referral service. Microchip Human Services in suburban Toronto maintains a computerized database with information on elder-care services throughout Canada. Employees from client companies call an 800-number and immediately receive a report containing detailed information on elder-care services anywhere in the country. The service is available 24 hours a day.

"What we're concentrating on is making information as accessible and convenient as possible," says founder Mark Frankel, a clinical psychologist. "We're allowing people to pick up the phone in the middle of the night," he says. Some people prefer talking to a computer about their elder-care needs to dealing with a real person, Frankel adds, although the service also offers the option of talking to a live human being.

Frankel started Microchip in 1988 to provide child-care resource and referral services. A year-and-a-half later, he added elder-care services, after focus-group research showed strong interest among employees of client firms. Child-care requests still outnumber elder-care requests, but the margin has been declining, says Frankel. "All of our clients now ask for both services," he notes. His services cover 100,000 employees in more than 30 Canadian companies, including the Bank of Montreal, Imperial Oil, General Electric–Canada, and Xerox-Canada.

Providing Education and Support

In addition to its company-sponsored resource and referral services, Equitable Life Assurance Society offers employee seminars on a variety of elder-care topics, like choosing a nursing home and financial and legal issues. Independent consultants—attorneys, psychiatrists, and social workers—make the presentations. A New York theatrical group has even performed plays on elder-care topics.

As part of its program, the Senior Care Network at Huntington Memorial Hospital facilitates on-site support groups for employees of client companies at the companies' offices. "We've found that lunch hour is the best time for the groups because people don't have to leave their workplace," says Monika White, director of the Pasadena, California organization. However, support groups for caregivers are more popular with some employees than others. Attendance is greater among older caregivers and those dealing with Alzheimer's patients, according to a 1992 study by Deborah J. Monahan and colleagues at Syracuse University.

At least one newsletter for employed caregivers is growing in popularity as well. Working Families, Inc. publishes a bimonthly newsletter called *WorkingFamilies* that covers elder- and child-care issues. It debuted in March 1993; within five months, 12 companies had signed on to receive it. "We also have individual subscribers," says Patricia Schiff Estess of Working Families. "Professionals like therapists and lawyers want to leave this in the waiting room in their offices."

But many caregivers don't work outside the home or don't have employers who provide elder-care information. Fortunately, there are other sources of help. Life Management of Columbia, South Carolina, markets informational audiotapes to caregivers through hospitals, insurance companies, rehabilitation centers, and associations that deal with caregiving issues. Owner Jan Warner began marketing the tapes in 1993 and says he sold about 10,000 during an eight-month period. Two of the tapes deal with general issues such as locating resources and managing care; another is designed for individuals who face the prospect of caring for someone with Alzheimer's disease. "There are two million Alzheimer's patients [in the U.S.], and that number is increasing significantly," says Warner.

The publisher John Wiley and Sons also finds that the care of Alzheimer's patients is a topic of growing interest. Sales of *Alzheimer's: A Caregiver's Guide and Sourcebook* have increased significantly over the past few years, says Kit Allan, associate publisher with New York City–based Wiley. The book is sold to hospital libraries and associations as well as bookstores. Mid-life women are the target audience. The increasing emphasis on home-based care rather than institutional care means more people in need of self-help books, says Allan. "There are a lot of things a caregiver has to know that aren't that simple if they're not medically trained."

LOSING A LOVED ONE

Eventually, caregivers will be faced with the inevitable: the loss of their loved ones. They will have to make funeral plans and adjust to life without the people to whom they have been devoted. Funeral homes, counselors, and lawyers all provide services during this transition.

Although not all Americans who die are elderly, three in four are. Of the 2.2 million people who died in the U.S. in 1991, 72 percent were aged 65 and older, according to the National Center for Health Statistics. Seventeen percent were aged 45 to 64, and 11 percent were under age 45. Because women live an average of seven years longer than men, 79 percent of female deaths occur to women aged 65 and older, versus 65 percent of deaths for males.

So far, baby boomers have been more conscious about diet and exercise and less likely to smoke than their elders, which should decrease their risk of both heart disease and cancer, the nation's two leading killers. But they can't forestall the grim reaper indefinitely. The number of deaths, which has been holding steady for several years, will begin to grow at the turn of the century as boomers begin to enter their late 50s. According to the Census Bureau's middle series of population projections, the U.S. will have 2.3 million deaths in 1995, 2.5 million in 2005, and 2.9 million in 2020.

Most Americans today die in hospitals, 60 percent. Sixteen percent die in nursing homes, and 22 percent die elsewhere, including at home.

Although the funeral industry may seem ghoulish to some, it's one of the most reliable businesses, with a guaranteed steady stream of customers. "The funeral service industry probably has one of the lowest failure rates of any business," says Susan Little, an industry analyst with Raymond James and Associates in St. Petersburg, Florida. But even this estimated $10 billion industry is seeing changes. Specifically, it is becoming franchised.

Traditionally, funeral homes have existed as local family-owned businesses. More than nine in ten of the nation's 22,500 funeral homes still operate that way. But more and more are being bought out by chains.

One such chain is two-year-old Prime Succession, headquartered in Batesville, Indiana. Between April 1992 and April 1994, it acquired 124 funeral homes, 12 cemeteries, three monument companies, and an insurance agency, according to vice president Steven Tidwell. To retain the hometown flavor, chains typically keep the personnel and names of the homes they buy. Name recognition and reputation is extremely important to customers, says Tidwell. People typically do business with funeral homes that have served other members of their family. "People don't shop around," says analyst Little.

Most families still send off their loved ones in a traditional manner. In 1991, more than two-thirds of funerals involved a service and ground burial, according to a survey by the National Funeral Directors Association. But some facilities have offered nontraditional twists. One of the most unusual is that offered by Verrette's Pointe Coupee Funeral Home near Baton Rouge, Louisiana. It has a drive-through window so busy people who can't make visiting hours can stop by to pay their respects to the deceased.

An increasing number of people are foregoing traditional caskets and burial and instructing their loved ones that they prefer cremation. Cremations have increased from 5 percent of deaths in 1972 to 19 percent in 1992, according to Jack Springer, executive director of the Cremation Association of North America. The association predicts that this share will rise to 27 percent in 2000 and 36 percent in

2010, because people are dying at ever-older ages. The older people are, the more likely they are to prefer cremation, says Springer.

Better-educated people and those with higher incomes are also more likely to prefer cremation, he adds. One in four respondents to a 1990 Gallup poll said they would choose to be cremated. The share for college graduates was 38 percent. "These people are less bound by tradition and usually have less close religious ties," Springer says. Geographic differences show up, too. Western states like California have cremation rates of more than 40 percent, while those in the Southeast (except for Florida) have rates averaging just 4 percent.

The average cost for a no-frills cremation, a process in which the remains are returned in a cardboard box, is $600 to $1,000. But cremations can also rival the cost of a traditional funeral when they include ceremonies, urns, and niches (resting places for the ashes). While many people opt for fancy urns, some want to keep their loved ones closer to their hearts—literally. Madelyn Co. of Janesville, Wisconsin, sells gold and sterling-silver pendants to fill with ashes. "Either people love the idea or they hate it. There doesn't seem to be any in-between," co-owner Joni Cullen told the *Business Journal-Phoenix*.

People often make their preference for a simple cremation known ahead of time, perhaps to spare their relatives the expense and bother of a funeral service. But they can also send themselves off in style without putting anyone out. "There is a trend for people to buy their funerals ahead of time so loved ones don't have to," says analyst Susan Little. Virtually all funeral homes in the U.S. offer some type of pre-funded funeral arrangements, according to a 1991 survey by the National Funeral Directors Association. About one-third of funerals that year had been arranged beforehand.

The primary market for "pre-need" funerals, as they are called, are mature consumers, says Steven Tidwell of Prime Succession. Fifty-seven percent of people aged 50 and older told Gallup in 1990 that they had made at least some arrangements for their own funerals, including buying burial plots, prepaying expenses, or detailing funeral plans in their wills. Few people under age 50 have gone to these lengths to give themselves the send-off they want, just 24 percent of those aged 30 to 49 and 12 percent of those aged 18 to 29.

Funeral Costs

Nearly half the cost of a funeral goes to purchase a casket.

(average total and selected funeral costs, 1992)

total cost	**$4,208**
casket	$2,039
professional service charges	761
transfer of remains to funeral home	100
embalming	270
other preparation	101
use of viewing facilities	206
use of facilities for ceremony	202
other use of facilities	195
hearse (local)	132
limousine (local)	107
other automotive	75
acknowledgement cards	20

Source: National Funeral Directors Association, Milwaukee, WI

Funeral homes can sell pre-need services by appealing to people's sense of thrift as well as their desire to spare bereaved ones' feelings. Buying a funeral ahead of time saves money. In 1992, the average funeral cost $4,200, according to the National Funeral Directors Association. This doesn't include burial costs such as cemetery plots, vaults, or monuments.

In the past, the funeral director's job may have ended with the funeral, but he or she is becoming more involved with "after-care" services, says Andrea Waas, public relations specialist with the National Funeral Directors Association. In 1992, 45 percent of funeral homes sent a follow-up letter to the family; 44 percent provided bereavement brochures; 38 percent provided referrals to community support groups; 31 percent offered a bereavement library; 24 percent sponsored community seminars; 15 percent sponsored their own support groups; and 11 percent conducted holiday memorial services for survivors. "Holidays are a particularly difficult time for people who have lost a loved one," says Waas, "especially the first year."

Survivors may need even more support than a funeral home can provide, however. Clinical psychologist Therese Rando sees many such people in her Warwick, Rhode Island, bereavement counseling practice. While most people seeking her help have experienced the unexpected or untimely death of a loved one, she also sees clients who have experienced the "on-time" death of an elderly relative.

"The loss of a parent when one is an adult tends to be a loss that gets devalued quite a bit," says Rando. "The expectation is that our parents will die before we do. The problem is that people do not get enough support and validation for their mourning." For caregivers whose lives have been consumed with a relative's care, "there is a relief, but some people feel, 'What do I do now?'"

When a relative dies, people also need legal help to settle estates, especially large ones. Many baby boomers expecting inheritances may be in this situation in coming years. Fortunately or not, depending on the circumstances, many of those decisions are out of survivors' hands. More than two-thirds of people aged 50 and older have a will, according to a 1990 Gallup poll. The share is higher among those with high incomes.

PRODUCTS AND SERVICES FOR
The Caregiving Transition and Death

Home Care

Nursing services
Personal-care services—bathing, feeding, etc.
Medical equipment and supplies
Day care, respite care, and companion services
Household services—shopping, cleaning, etc.
Transportation services

Business Matters

Financial planning and counseling
Legal services
Self-help market—books/tapes

Senior Housing

Retirement communities
Independent-care facilities
Assisted-care facilities
Nursing homes

Employer-Provided Services

Dependent-care accounts
Resource and referral services
Seminars
Newsletters

Death-Related

Funeral homes
Cremation services
Counseling
Legal services—wills, trusts, and estates

SOURCES

American Association of Homes and Services for the Aging. *Background: Community Services* (fact sheet). Washington, DC: American Association of Homes and Services for the Aging, 1994.

American Association of Homes and Services for the Aging/Ernst and Young. *Continuing Care Retirement Communities: An Industry in Action.* Vol. 1 and 2. Washington, DC: American Association of Homes and Services for the Aging, 1993.

American Association of Retired Persons/The Travelers Foundation. *A National Survey of Caregivers: Final Report.* Washington, DC: American Association of Retired Persons, 1988.

American Association of Retired Persons/The Travelers Foundation. *A National Survey of Caregivers: Working Caregivers Report.* Washington, DC: American Association of Retired Persons, 1989.

Braus, Patricia. "**When Mom Needs Help.**" *American Demographics,* March 1994, pp. 38–47.

Buglass, Karen. "**The Business of Eldercare.**" *American Demographics,* September 1989, pp. 32–38.

Burns, Barbara J., H. Ryan Wagner, John E. Taube, Jay Magaziner, Thomas Permutt, and L. Richard Landerman. "**Mental Health Service Use by the Elderly in Nursing Homes.**" *American Journal of Public Health,* Vol. 83, No. 3, March 1993, pp. 331–334.

Coward, Raymond T., Claydell Horne, and Jeffrey W. Dwyer. "**Demographic Perspectives on Gender and Family Caregiving.**" Pp. 18–33 in *Gender, Families, and Elder Care* (Jeffrey W. Dwyer and Raymond T. Coward, eds.), Newbury Park, CA: Sage Publications, 1992.

Crispell, Diane. "**People Patterns: Nursing-Home Decisions Pain Spouses the Most.**" *The Wall Street Journal*, September 13, 1993, p. B1.

Day, Jennifer Cheeseman. *Population Projections of the United States, by Age, Sex, Race, and Hispanic Origin: 1992 to 2050*. Washington, DC: U.S. Bureau of the Census, 1992.

Gallup Poll Monthly. "**Fear of Dying.**" Princeton, NJ, January 1991, pp. 51–59.

Giblin, Paul. "**The Last Good Buy: Reaping the Profits.**" *Business Journal-Phoenix and the Valley of the Sun*, February 25, 1994, sec. 1, p. 1.

Hewitt Associates. *Work and Family Benefits Provided by Major U.S. Employers in 1993*. Lincolnshire, IL: Hewitt Associates, 1993.

Manton, Kenneth G., Larry S. Corder, and Eric Stallard. "**Estimates of Change in Chronic Disability and Institutional Incidence and Prevalence Rates in the U.S. Elderly Population From the 1982, 1984, and 1989 National Long Term Care Survey.**" *Journal of Gerontology: Social Sciences*, Vol. 48, No. 4, July 1993, pp. S153–S166.

Manton, Kenneth G., Larry Corder, and Eric Stallard. "**Changes in the Use of Personal Assistance and Special Equipment from 1982 to 1989: results from the 1982 and 1989 NLTCS.**" *The Gerontologist*, Vol. 33, No. 2, April 1993, pp. 168–176.

Monahan, Deborah J., Vernon L. Greene, and Patricia D. Coleman. "**Caregiver Support Groups: Factors Affecting Use of Services.**" *Social Work*, Vol. 37, No. 3, May 1992, pp. 254–260.

Montgomery, Rhonda J.V. "**Gender Differences in Patterns of Child-Parent Caregiving Relationships.**" Pp. 65–83 in *Gender, Families, and Elder Care* (Jeffrey W. Dwyer and Raymond T. Coward, eds.), Newbury Park, CA: Sage Publications, 1992.

National Association for Home Care. *Basic Statistics About Home Care 1992*. Washington, DC: National Association for Home Care, 1992.

National Association for Home Care. *Basic Statistics About Home Care 1993*. Washington, DC: National Association for Home Care, 1993.

National Center for Health Statistics. *Advance Report of Final Mortality Statistics, 1991, Monthly Vital Statistics Report*, Vol. 42, No. 2, suppl., Hyattsville, MD, 1993.

National Center for Health Statistic. *Annual Summary of Births, Marriages, Divorces, and Deaths: United States, 1992, Monthly Vital Statistics Report*, Vol. 41, No. 13, Hyattsville, MD, 1993.

National Funeral Directors Association. *1992 Survey of Funeral Home Operations*. Milwaukee, WI: 1992.

National Funeral Directors Association. *1993 Survey of Funeral Home Operations*. Milwaukee, WI: 1993.

Spanberg, Erik. **"Funeral Home Offers Mourners an Alternative."** *Greater Baton Rouge Business Report*, January 11, 1994, sec. 1, p. 50.

Waldrop, Judith. **"People Patterns: Odds and Ends."** *The Wall Street Journal*, May 23, 1994, p. B1.

Waldrop, Judith. **"Who Are the Caregivers?"** *American Demographics*, September 1989, p. 39.

OTHER RESOURCES

Boaz, Rachel F. and Charlotte F. Muller. **"Paid Work and Unpaid Help by Caregivers of the Disabled and Frail Elders."** *Medical Care*, Vol. 30, No. 2, February 1992, pp. 149–158.

Greene, Vernon L., Mary E. Lovely, and Jan I. Ondrich. **"The Cost-Effectiveness of Community Services in a Frail Elderly Population."** *The Gerontologist*, Vol. 33, No. 2, April 1993, pp. 177–189.

Lee, Gary R., Jeffrey W. Swyer, and Raymond T. Coward. **"Gender Differences in Parent Care: Demographic Factors and Same-Gender Preferences."** *Journal of Gerontology: Social Sciences*, Vol. 48, No. 1, January 1993, pp. S9–S16.

PART II

JOBS AND SUCH

CHAPTER 6

FINDING A PLACE IN THE WORLD

The School and Graduation Transition

WHEN SEDRIK NEWBERN graduated from Western Kentucky University in 1993, he didn't plan to move home for an extended period. "My plan before I graduated was to move home, save money for the summer, and be in my own place by fall," he says.

But between May and August, Newbern changed his mind. He was paying off a new home stereo, and the tape player in his car began malfunctioning, necessitating another purchase. He got a great price on a cellular phone for his new car, and he enjoyed buying gifts for his girlfriend. There was also the credit-card debt he had accumulated in college. Newbern revised his plan and gave himself an extra year at home before venturing out on his own to face the added costs of housing, utilities, and food.

Transitions into and out of school are big opportunities for businesses. High school graduation involves rituals like the senior prom, which are becoming more elaborate all the time. Many high school graduates also need help preparing for college and choosing a school.

Most young people make a variety of purchasing decisions for the first time in college; it is a time when they form brand loyalties.

The transition from college into the "real world" provides additional opportunities as graduates seek new cars, apartments, jobs, and things for their homes. High school graduates who don't go on to college need the same things, but usually sooner.

While the majority of college students are aged 18 to 24, a growing percent are aged 25 or older. Older students have different needs because they often have families, jobs, and other responsibilities that vie for their time. The same is true for graduate students.

TRENDS IN THE MARKET

Graduation transitions out of high school and into and out of college traditionally happen to people between the ages of 18 and 24, an age group that has been declining. In 1980, the U.S. had 29 million 18-to-24-year-olds born during some of the peak baby-boom years. In 1994, there were 26 million—all members of the baby-bust generation. The 18-to-24-group will grow again around the turn of the century, as the children of boomers reach these ages.

The share of minorities in this group will grow, too. The share of 18-to-24-year-olds who are white fell from 85 percent in 1980 to 80 percent in 1994. By 2010, the share should fall further, to 77 percent, according to Census Bureau projections.

Since an increasing number of "older students" are going back to school, it is important to monitor trends in the 25-plus population, too. While the number of 18-to-24-year-olds declined during the 1980s, the number of 25-to-34-year-olds expanded with an infusion of baby boomers. However, the youngest boomers will exit this age group after 1998. At that point, the 35-to-44 age group will be growing rapidly—from 37 million in 1990 to to 45 million in 2000. This group will provide a large pool of potential students. Nevertheless, competition for the "older" student will intensify.

High School Graduation

Chronologically, high school graduation occurs first. In 1992, nearly 2.4 million young people graduated from high school, according to the Bureau of Labor Statistics (BLS). Teenagers are about as likely to finish high school today as they were 20 years ago.

Teenagers have much of their own money to purchase many of

the goods and services they need around the time of high school graduation—from prom clothes to yearbooks. Teens spent a total of $58 billion on themselves in 1993, according to Teenage Research Unlimited in Northbrook, Illinois. A 1992 study by marketing professors Dennis H. Tootelian and Ralph M. Gaedeke found that 51 percent of high schoolers receive an allowance. One-third receive $25 or more a week. One-third of high schoolers work part-time. Nearly half work at least 15 hours a week, and almost two-thirds make more than $50 a week.

Teen Buying Power

Older teens spend more than younger teens, but most of the money is their own.

(average weekly spending of teenagers, by sex and age, by source of money, 1993)

	total spending	own money	family money
boys	$62	$43	$19
girls	59	35	24
12 to 15	$43	$19	$14
13 to 17	66	43	23
18 to 19	92	77	15

Source: © Teenage Research Unlimited, Northbrook, IL

College Enrollment

High school graduates are now more likely to go to college than in the past. Sixty-two percent of the 1992 graduating class went on to college, according to the BLS, compared with 49 percent in 1972.

In 1992, the college enrollment rate for women was higher than for men, 64 percent versus 60 percent. This is a turnaround from 1972, when the rate for men was higher than for women, 53 percent versus 46 percent. The share of black high school graduates attending college fell in the 1970s before rising again. It has barely returned to the 1972 level, while the share of white high school graduates attending college has grown from 49 percent to 63 percent.

Going to College

Since the late 1980s, women have been more likely than men to enroll in college directly after graduating from high school, whites more likely than blacks.

(percent of high school graduates enrolled in college that October, by sex and race, 1977–92)

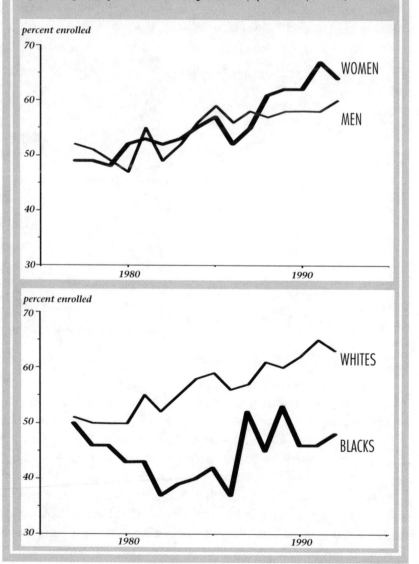

percent enrolled

WOMEN

MEN

percent enrolled

WHITES

BLACKS

Source: Bureau of Labor Statistics

Because the share of high school graduates who go to college has increased over the years even as the number of teens has dropped, the number of new college students has remained fairly stable. According to the BLS, nearly 1.6 million 1977 high school graduates were enrolled in college that fall. The number peaked at nearly 1.7 million for the 1984 high school graduating class, and declined to 1.5 million for 1992's graduating class.

Total enrollment for all institutions of higher education has increased considerably, up 67 percent between 1970 and 1991—from less than nine million to more than 14 million. The National Center for Education Statistics predicts that the number will reach 15 million in 1998. Two important trends in higher education are the aging of the student body and the increasing percentage of part-timers. In 1970, 32 percent of all students enrolled in higher education were part-time. By 1991, this had increased to 43 percent. In 1970, 28 per–cent were aged 25 or older. By 1991, this had climbed to 45 percent.

Another trend of considerable importance is the greater presence of foreign students on U.S. campuses. In 1991, 416,000 students from foreign countries were enrolled in U.S. institutions of higher education, according to the National Center for Education Statistics.

College students are in school longer than they used to be, according to the National Center for Education Statistics. Just 31 percent of those receiving a bachelor's degree in 1990 did so within four years, compared with 45 percent of those who graduated in 1977.

The college student population has great buying potential. In 1993, full-time undergraduates at four-year colleges accounted for $27 billion in buying power, including $7 billion for discretionary spending, according to Roper CollegeTrack, a division of New York City–based Roper Starch Worldwide. Many students arrive at college with a history of work experience. Once in college, 60 percent work during the school year and 82 percent during summer break, according to Roper CollegeTrack. Their average annual earnings in 1993 were $4,100.

Nontraditional and Postgraduate Students

Of course, not all 18-year-olds head off to college. Thirty-eight percent of the high school class of 1992 did not—at least not immediately. The potential of this market should not be written off. Although their unemployment rate is relatively high, most of these young people are earning a paycheck. In addition, many will begin a college program sometime in the future and become a part of the fastest-growing segment in the educational world today—the "older student."

Aging Student Bodies

College students have become older over the years.

(fall enrollment in institutions of higher education in thousands and percent distribution*, by age, 1970–98)

	1970	1980	1990	1998†
number:	8,581	12,097	13,820	15,111
under 25	6,196	7,560	7,752	8,187
25 to 34	1,561	3,114	3,423	3,550
35 and older	823	1,422	2,644	3,376
percent:	100%	100%	100%	100%
under 25	72	62	56	54
25 to 34	18	26	25	23
35 and older	10	12	19	22

*Numbers do not add exactly to totals due to rounding

† projected

Source: National Center for Education Statistics

Some people going back to school these days never even made a traditional transition from high school. Nearly one in six high school diplomas awarded in the U.S. is based on passage of the General Educational Development (GED) exam, according to the American Council on Education in Washington, D.C. Almost 800,000 people took the GED in 1992. Fifty-six percent were under the age of 25. Sixty-one percent of 1992 test-takers indicated that they planned to go on to postsecondary education. "Many go to community colleges to attain job skills," says Janet Baldwin of the council.

College students aged 25 and older have more than made up for the declining ranks of 18-to-24-year-olds. According to the National Center for Education Statistics, one-third of 1991 undergraduates were aged 25 and older.

Older students make up an even larger share of the graduate student population. Half of graduate students in 1991 were aged 30 and older. Many of these people hold down jobs while attending school. They may be short on time, but they usually have money, and they will probably have even more once they get their degrees. An additional 280,500 students enrolled in professional schools to attain degrees in fields such as law and medicine can look forward to some of the most affluent lifestyles after they graduate.

Taking Attendance

Women undergraduate and graduate students are more likely than men to attend college part-time.

(fall enrollment in institutions of higher education in thousands and percent attending part-time, by sex, 1991)

	number	all	attending part-time men	women
total	14,359	43%	40%	47%
undergraduate	12,439	42	38	45
graduate	1,639	61	55	66
professional	281	10	10	10

Source: National Center for Education Statistics

Commencement Exercises

The number of bachelor's degrees conferred has risen from 839,730 in 1970–71 to 1,165,000 in 1993–94, an increase of 39 percent. The number of associate degrees awarded doubled over the same time period, from 252,610 to 504,000. By the turn of the century (2000–01), the number of bachelor's degrees awarded should increase to 1,203,000 and the number of associate degrees to 538,000.

In 1970–71, 57 percent of both bachelor's and associate degrees went to men. But by 1993–94, women dominated. Fifty-four percent of bachelor's and 58 percent of associate degrees went to women that year.

In short, since more than 14 million individuals make transitions into and out of academia each year, this market is certainly worth paying attention to. But it isn't the same as it was 20 years ago.

PROMS AND PICTURES

The senior prom is an important rite of passage marking the transition out of high school. Although proms are an old tradition, they have taken on a new flavor—a more profitable one.

"When we [baby boomers] were kids, we used to sit down after school and make flowers to decorate the school gym. They don't do that anymore. They buy everything," says Christine Maloy of East Greenbush, New York, editor of *The Perfect Prom Guide*. The guide, a how-to book for proms, is distributed free to 15,000 high school students through schools in the Albany, New York area. Local vendors of prom-related services—limousines, formal wear, photographers—as well as substance-abuse prevention groups advertise in the booklet. Maloy had 15 sponsors for her first two booklets, published in 1992 and 1993.

A 1993 survey of the readers of *Your Prom*, a national magazine from Cahners Publishing, found that, on average, girls spend $546 on prom-related products and services, including $181 for a dress, $210 for other clothing and accessories, and $52 for jewelry. Girls begin shopping for these items an average of nine weeks before the prom. Their dates spend an average of $352, including $78 for a rented tux, $30 for accessories, $18 for a corsage, $41 for dinner, $37 for prom tickets, and $98 for a limousine.

The expenses may seem like a one-shot deal, but this is not necessarily the case. Says Maloy: "When I go to my advertisers, I say, 'Do you realize that six or seven years down the road, these are the same people who are going to come back to you for the same services for a wedding?'"

The cost of a prom dress is a hefty sum for any teen. In 1993, Maloy started Gowns Again, a consignment shop for second-hand prom dresses. Many teens are also interested in renting prom dresses, she says, to cut down on the cost.

But the price for proms remains steep. How do kids afford it? "A lot of them have part-time jobs, and they start putting money aside for it," says Maloy. "I hear kids say, 'Mom, you pay half, and I'll pay half.'" When shopping for clothes and accessories, 58 percent of teens go to four or more stores, according to a 1992 study by marketing professors Dennis H. Tootelian and Ralph M. Gaedeke. Girls shop in more stores than do boys. One in four teens say that friends are the most important source of information for purchasing clothes and accessories, followed by magazines (15 percent), television (13 percent), and newspapers (10 percent).

Proms provide good opportunities for photographers, but senior portraits are even more important. Most seniors want to be in their school yearbook, and many buy picture packages on top of that. Senior portraits accounted for 36 percent of all school portrait sales in 1991, according to the Professional School Photographers of America in Jackson, Michigan. Senior picture packages are larger than other school photography packages, consisting of 25 prints at an average cost of $112. Seniors in the South and West, and those in places with populations of less than 50,000 are most likely to buy senior portraits.

High school graduations, like weddings, are gift-giving occasions. Although many businesses have bridal registries, few have graduation registries. Service Merchandise, a Brentwood, Tennessee-based catalog showroom with over 400 stores in 37 states, is an exception. It offers a registry for both high school and college graduates, although most customers are high school students, according to registry director Laura Walther. The most commonly purchased items include microwave ovens and small refrigerators, she says. "High school graduates are leaving the nest and will be living in a dorm room or apartment for the first time." Other popular items include telephones, answering machines, calculators, computers, and jewelry.

PREPARING FOR COLLEGE

Well before the prom and commencement, however, most high school students are already involved with a variety of tasks in preparation for their next transition—going to college. The first obstacle is the dreaded SAT. Despite their high school success, many graduates are not confident of their ability to take the standardized tests colleges require. In a 1992 survey of high school students commissioned by Kaplan Educational Center, a major test-preparation company, 49 percent of those who planned to attend college said that taking the SAT/ACT had them "very worried"; 34 percent were "somewhat worried." To get ready for the exams, 54 percent said they had used or planned to use test-preparation books, 36 percent a test-preparation course, and 15 percent a computer. The number of students who use Kaplan programs to prepare for standardized tests has doubled in ten years, to 150,000, says public relations director Melissa Mack.

Finding the Money

Getting into college is only one worry. There is also the matter of paying for it. The price of a college education has increased astronomically. In the 1976–77 academic year, students paid an average of $2,300 for tuition, room, and board, according to the National Center for Education Statistics. The fees at private institutions averaged $3,900; at public schools, they averaged $1,800. These costs pale in comparison with those for 1992–93—an average of $7,500 for all students—$14,700 for those at private schools and $5,400 for those at public schools.

Eighty-six percent of college-bound high school students surveyed by Kaplan said that finances would be an important factor affecting their choice of college. "More and more students are deciding on college based on cost, which was not happening in the 1980s," says Diane Saunders, vice president of the New England Education Loan Marketing Corporation (Nellie Mae), the nation's largest nonprofit provider of educational loans.

To finance their educations, about 55 to 60 percent of students take out some type of loan, according to Saunders. The average student taking a loan leaves school with a debt of $8,000 to $10,000, she says. "Students are having to borrow more as tuitions increase. There are fewer federal grant dollars available." In 1992–93, student aid, consisting primarily of loans, amounted to $35 billion, according to a report from the College Board, an increase of 41 percent in inflation-adjusted dollars in ten years. Three-fourths is federally guaranteed aid.

Fifteen to 20 percent of students have problems repaying their loans, but not all are equal risks for lenders. "Over 70 percent of all defaults are people who went to trade and technical schools. Half of these students default," says Saunders. Four-year college students are excellent risks, she adds, with women being slightly better than men. "Most have the ability to repay what they borrow."

While the student loan market has increased considerably over the years, and will continue to increase, the nature of the industry will be changing quite soon. The federal government recently authorized a new program whereby it will directly fund an increasing proportion of student loans. Banks and other financial institutions will provide a declining share as the program is phased in over the next few years.

Picking a School

According to a 1992–93 survey by Kaplan, many college-bound students start to look at colleges early in their high school careers. Twenty-six percent started looking or planned to start in their sophomore year and 45 percent in their junior year.

Colleges have been busy trying to keep up enrollment. Although a record-high share of high school graduates go on to college, the base numbers began to decline in the 1980s as baby busters replaced baby boomers. The number will slowly start to grow again in the mid-1990s as the numerous children of baby boomers reach college age.

Even so, in a 1993 report commissioned by the National Institute of Independent Colleges and Universities, researcher Harold L. Hodgkinson warns that certain schools may continue to see declines in potential student populations. Private schools are heavily represented in states where the youth population will decrease between

1990 and 2010, including Indiana, Massachusetts, Michigan, Ohio, and Pennsylvania. In states where the youth population will be increasing—California, Texas, and Florida—independent colleges are not well represented, which will place an added burden on state-supported colleges and universities.

Competition for students will continue to be intense at many institutions, requiring schools to add new strategies to their marketing arsenals. With fear of crime on campus at an all-time high, some schools are selling their safety records. After *USA Today* published a school safety ranking, Adelphi University placed promotions in several publications touting itself as "the safest campus in America." Others, like the University of Pennsylvania and Temple University, use their ratings in promotional literature.

Most universities today produce promotional videos to entice students to visit their campuses. This fact has put Shelly Spiegel in business. Her company, Philadelphia-based Search by Video, mails out complimentary college videos to targeted high school students. Students can also contact her directly for a customized tape of one or more schools.

"Videos are an excellent way for schools that are recruiting nationally to make sure that students see their campus, because all students can't travel," says Spiegel. Her 300 client colleges and universities are her best sources of student referral. Seventy-five percent are private institutions that recruit nationally, but she also represents some large state universities.

The business has grown considerably since its inception in 1987, when Spiegel had 23 college clients and sent out 6,000 videos. In 1993, she sent out 300,000 videos (including some for boarding schools), totaling sales of $1.2 million. She's recently added a new travel service, Campus Connections, for students who want to visit a campus in person. "We guarantee them the lowest fares to and from college campuses on any of the airlines."

THE COLLEGE CONSUMER

When Mom and Dad finally deposit Junior on campus, they are doing more than starting his career in higher education. His life as an independent consumer has also begun. "When students go to college, for the first time in their lives, they're going to be purchasing products their parents have been buying for them. For marketers, it's a primary time to reach those people," says Michael Hogan, president of Hogan Communications, a Burbank, California, marketing company specializing in the college market.

College students, while not always rich, are likely to have spare cash on hand because more than half of them work part-time while in school. The "care package" from home containing snacks and personal-care items doesn't last long. "Eventually they run out and have to go buy the products themselves," says Hogan.

Before they do, they will be barraged by free samples from businesses hoping to build brand loyalty among the young consumers. MarketSource, a Cranbury, New Jersey, college marketing company, supplies a Campus Trial Pack to 1,000 college bookstores around the country, distributing 2.4 million boxes of free samples of food and personal-care products to students.

Teens aged 18 and 19—those of college age—are much more likely to buy personal-care products for themselves than those aged 16 and 17. In a 1993 study, Teenage Research Unlimited found that

Health, Beauty, and Youth

Older teens are much more likely than younger teens to buy a variety of health-and-beauty aids.

(percent of teens who purchased selected health-and-beauty aids for themselves in past three months, by age, 1993)

	16- and 17-year-olds	18- and 19-year-olds
regular bar soap	7.0%	22.1%
vitamins	4.3	11.2
toothpaste	12.5	30.4
headache remedy	7.9	18.9
allergy or cold remedy	5.0	11.9
regular shampoo	12.5	27.6
menstrual-pain medication	5.0	10.4

Source: ©Teenage Research Unlimited, Northbrook, IL

83 percent of 18- and 19-year-olds purchased health and beauty aids in the past three months, compared with 69 percent of 16- and 17-year-olds. Eighteen- and 19-year-olds are three times as likely as 16- and 17-year-olds to buy regular bar soap and more than twice as likely to buy headache, allergy, or cold remedies, menstrual pain medication, vitamins, toothpaste, and regular shampoo.

The same is true for food. According to a 1992 Roper High School Report survey, 43 percent of tenth-, eleventh-, and twelfth-graders shopped in supermarkets during the past week. This share was 62 percent for full-time undergraduates at four-year colleges, according to a Roper CollegeTrack survey conducted the same year. Students living off campus are naturally more likely than those living on campus to shop for food in a given week, 72 percent versus 54 percent.

Michael Hogan says that in the absence of marketing and advertising, students are inclined to continue using the brands with which they grew up. But on a college campus, an absence of marketing and advertising is highly unlikely.

In 1988, MarketSource Corporation began holding Campus Fests so sponsors could offer a variety of activities and product samples to students. "The category of event marketing has been the fastest-growing of all marketing to college students," says Chip Underhill of MarketSource. From two schools in 1988, Campus Fest had increased to 50 by 1992. Underhill says that between 25 and 55 percent of students attend the events. It has been so successful, several competing companies now offer their versions of Campus Fest to colleges.

In 1993, MarketSource joined forces with *Sports Illustrated* and began touring the Sports Illustrated Sports Festival at Campus Fest. Additional sponsors range from food and personal-products companies like Hershey, Häagen Dazs, and Nuprin to vendors of big-ticket items like Toyota and IBM, as well as Pier I, which sells home furnishings. "Students may need a futon mattress if they live off-campus," explains Underhill.

Advertising to college students is smart strategy, and it gets results. MarketSource conducted a survey that asked students "Are you using a different brand of _____ in college than you did in high school?" "We tracked it across class," says Underhill. "When you looked at it from freshman to senior year, in every case the share who switched increased over time." Overall, 47 percent of students used a different deodorant in college than they did in high school; 45 percent a different cough/cold remedy; 30 percent a different sun-care product.

College students have past experience with most personal-care products, but in other categories they are first-time consumers. For example, most high school students do not have experience with credit cards, but that changes in college. In 1993, 56 percent of full-time undergraduates at four-year colleges had a major credit card, according to Roper CollegeTrack. Nine in ten cards were in students' names rather than their parents'.

Sedrik Newbern, the 1993 graduate of Western Kentucky University introduced earlier, says he was deluged with credit-card applications the moment he stepped on campus as a freshman. "I was at the limit [of my card] for three of the years I was in college," he says.

One reason why credit-card companies are so eager to sign up college students is because they are comparatively good risks. Their rate of default is less than that of the general population. "Students understand this is the first step in getting credit history, so they are conscientious about their payments," says Betty Riess, a spokeswoman for Bank of America in San Francisco.

The desire to obtain loyal customers early on is equally important. "Marketing studies show that it costs three times as much to switch a person to your product as it does to get them to try your product in the beginning stages," says Michael Hogan of Hogan Communications. "That's why financial services and credit-card companies are going after students younger and younger. They're looking for that long-term loyalty."

Banks want to build loyalty for other services as well. In 1992, 70 percent of full-time undergraduates at four-year colleges had a savings account and 75 percent had a checking account, according to Roper CollegeTrack. A full 90 percent had one and/or the other.

AmSouth Bancorporation, headquartered in Birmingham, Alabama, markets a "no-monthly-fee" combined checking and savings account called Passage designed for students. The account includes a "no annual fee" credit card and ATM card. "The credit feature and the 'one-price' fee is very important in the college market," says AmSouth assistant vice president Steve Reider. "They don't have a lot of cash to be paying service fees with."

AmSouth has marketed the account through special promotions on college campuses since fall 1992. Within one year, Passage accounts comprised over 5 percent of AmSouth's checking accounts, says Reider. Banks don't make much money on accounts like Passage, he notes, but "we hope to grow with the person. Most people buy houses and cars at some time in their lives. Mortgages and installment loans are wonderfully profitable products." The majority of Alabama college graduates remain in the state after graduation, says Reider, and AmSouth has branches all over the state.

The ATM is a very important part of the Passage account, says Reider. "Each succeeding graduating class is more inclined to want to use technologically oriented banking products." According to Roper CollegeTrack, 68 percent of full-time undergraduates at four-year colleges had ATM cards in 1992.

Some technologies are familiar to students before they get to college. Even so, their needs change once they get there. For instance, most high school students use the telephone a great deal. They don't stop using the phone when they get to college; on the contrary, they spend even more on long-distance calls. In 1993, 53 percent of full-time undergraduates at four-year colleges had a long-distance calling card, according to Roper CollegeTrack. "Students are looking for a convenient way to make calls," says Roper vice president Stuart Himmelfarb. "They are living away from home, and their friends are scattered."

INTO THE "REAL WORLD"

Eventually, nights spent studying for exams and weekends spent in the library pay off. The actual graduation ceremony presents the same kind of opportunities for businesses as high school graduations—photographs, celebration dinners, graduation registries. But those entering the working world for the first time also need things unlikely to be found on most gift registries—namely a job, a car, and a place to live.

The Job Hunt

In a 1991 survey of college students by Philadelphia-based Right Associates, nearly half said they began their job search six months prior to graduation. In the search, 45 percent used personal contacts and 44 percent their college career center. Twenty-six percent checked newspapers, and 15 percent looked at professional journals.

Although most young people do not avail themselves of formal search services other than their college career center, employers are more likely than in the past to use formal services when recruiting graduates. This has created business opportunities for Information Kinetics, Inc. The Chicago-based firm maintains a database of 175,000 job candidates from 1,900 colleges and universities across the country. It furnishes résumés to its client organizations—Fortune 500 companies, branches of government, and major regional employers—on CD-ROM. Sixty percent of the database consists of recent or pending graduates; the rest are experienced candidates, says Al Copland, director of marketing communications.

New graduates who obtain jobs do best if they majored in engineering. The 1993–94 starting salary for a chemical engineering major was $40,300, followed by mechanical engineering at $35,400, and electrical engineering at $35,000, according to a survey by L. Patrick Scheetz at the Collegiate Employment Research Institute at Michigan State University. Starting salaries for most academic majors, however, range between $20,000 and $30,000, with telecommunications and journalism majors lowest at averages of $20,700 and $20,600, respectively.

Cars and Homes

Graduates need a set of wheels to get to their jobs. According to a 1993 Roper CollegeTrack survey, 62 percent of full-time undergraduates at four-year colleges own or have access to a vehicle, but 70 percent of these were purchased used. When commencement rolls around, many graduates are ready for a new car or truck. In 1992, 47 percent of seniors told Roper CollegeTrack they planned to buy one in the next two years.

General Motors offers a special program for new college graduates, with low downpayment requirements and the opportunity to defer the first payment for up to 90 days. It is valid for six months prior to graduation and one year afterward. There's one important catch, of course: the graduate must have a job-commitment letter.

Since the program started in 1985, about 250,000 college graduates have taken advantage of it, says Linda Kosinski, spokeswoman for GMAC, the financing arm of General Motors. In 1993, those eligible for the program were offered a special test drive and free gift. "The idea was to get the students into the dealerships and looking at the cars," says Kosinksi. "Hopefully, we're building future customers who will return down the line."

Other car companies have similar programs. Keith Magee, general marketing manager for Ford Division, told *Automotive News* that 18-to-29-year-olds buy 23 percent of all new cars and 17 percent of all new trucks. "It's our future because these buyers are going to be in the market for 50 years."

Another critical need of the college graduate is a place to live. For most, this means an apartment. According to the government's 1991 American Housing Survey, five million households had heads under the age of 25; 86 percent were renters.

"Young people coming out of college who used to stay in the apartment market until they were in their late 20s tend to be staying longer now," says Kenneth Danter, president of the Danter Company, a Columbus, Ohio research firm specializing in the real-estate market. Danter says that today's younger people have greater expectations for a house, so they can't afford what they want as soon as they want it. In the meantime, however, they can afford a very nice apartment. "College graduates, a year or two after college, are going to be paying in the upper quartile of rents in the marketplace," says Danter. This amounts to between $600 and $800 a month, depending upon the area of the country. Apartment complexes with clubhouses, swimming pools, and saunas target this youthful group, he says.

Student loans do not seem to deter most college graduates from striking out on their own. According to a 1991 study by student-loan financier, Nellie Mae, 78 percent of New England graduates paying off student loans said their debt did not prevent them from moving out of their parents' homes. Of course, those who can't find decent jobs, have hefty credit-card bills, or want to use their money for things other than rent may end up back at home—at least for a time. Twelve percent of 25-to-34-year-olds were living in their parents' households in 1992, according to the Census Bureau's Current Population Survey.

The Noncollege Market

Not everyone goes to college immediately after high school. Thirty-eight percent of the class of 1992 didn't. Many went directly into the working world. Because this group is not "upscale" like college students and has lower income potential, marketers show less interest in it. But eight in ten noncollege young adults are in the labor force and making money.

Like college students, these young people are also starting to develop brand loyalties. But they don't constitute a "captive audience" like those on college campuses, so they aren't as easy to find. They must be reached through the same advertising avenues as the general population—TV, radio, print, billboard. Nevertheless, they do pay more attention to particular stations and publications.

After its Passage account was such a hit with the college crowd, AmSouth Bancorporation decided to market it to the young noncollege group, too. To reach them, the bank advertises on Fox TV stations and top-40 radio stations, says assistant vice president Steve Reider.

Service Merchandise, a Brentwood, Tennessee–based catalog showroom company, visits high schools each fall to display items from its graduate gift registry. It targets both college- and noncollege-bound students. Whether they are moving away from their parents' home for college or a job, "they will need all the basics of setting up a home," says Laura Walther of Service Merchandise. The registry includes products such as dishes, TV sets, and answering machines.

Many in the noncollege group will buy houses sooner than their college-graduate peers, partly because they marry earlier, but also because their expectations are lower, says Kenneth Danter of the Danter Company. They are a good market for entry-level housing. "People who don't go to college are going to move into a single-family home before the college graduate does," says Danter. "They are going to buy a $60,000 house, whereas the college graduate wants a $120,000 house."

CONTINUING EDUCATION

It's likely that many members of the noncollege group will go back to school some day, probably because they want to get ahead in their jobs. These people form the backbone of a current trend—increasing numbers of people aged 25 and older returning to school.

A number of universities are gearing programs around the non-traditional student. New York University's School of Continuing Education caters to the older working student. The school offers both credit and noncredit courses. Of those taking credit courses in fall 1992, 57 percent were aged 25 to 35, and 25 percent were over age 35. Those taking noncredit courses were even older; 51 percent were aged 25 to 35, and 43 percent were over age 35. Night and weekend schedules make it possible for full-time workers to attend.

Older students have to get used to being in school again. "If you're going back to school, you're going to have to do a lot of reading that you're not accustomed to doing," notes Letitia Chamberlain, director of NYU's Center for Career and Life Planning. "When you're away from school, you don't have to take timed tests or do research papers."

The center offers a variety of courses for this group, such as "improving reading skills" and "overcoming math anxiety." "If people are phobic about numbers, they won't go on and get a degree because they think they can't take the SAT math test," says Chamberlain. A class on time management helps those who must juggle the responsibilities of families, jobs, and school.

Some students take noncredit courses to help them in their present careers or to help them change careers. Others work toward the bachelor's degree they never earned. Yet others go back to pursue a graduate degree.

Graduate School

The number of master's degrees conferred has risen from 230,500 in 1970–71 to an estimated 370,000 in 1993–94, according to the National Center for Education Statistics. It is projected to increase to 389,000 by 1996–97 and then decline to 363,000 by 2002–03, as baby busters replace baby boomers in the ranks of graduate students. In 1970–71, 32,100 doctoral degrees were conferred. This number is projected to increase to 41,400 in 1996–97 and stay at that level through the beginning of the next century. There were 37,946 professional degrees conferred in fields such as law and medicine in 1970–71. There will be about 74,700 conferred in 1996–97, then a decline for several years.

The composition of the U.S. graduate student population has changed significantly in recent years. Notably, fewer students are Americans. Eleven percent of graduate students enrolled in fall 1991 were from other countries. During the 1990–91 academic year, 28 percent of the 37,500 doctorates awarded went to foreign students, according to the National Academy of Sciences. In the field of engineering, the share was 55 percent, up from 46 percent in 1979–80. The presence of foreign students is less pronounced in humanities disciplines, but the shares of doctorates awarded to them still doubled between 1979–80 and 1990–91, from 9 percent to 18 percent.

Some companies are taking advantage of this trend. Kaplan Educational Center recently expanded its international locations to include France, Hong Kong, Italy, and the United Kingdom. "There is a great demand among international students to study at American universities," says public relations director Melissa Mack. "In order to do so, they need to pass these [standardized] tests."

In some fields, foreign graduate students will be especially helpful in bolstering sagging application rates. Even top-ranked management schools like Northwestern's Kellogg School, which received 4,328 applications for 582 slots in the 1993–94 term, is doing more recruiting in foreign countries. Twenty-five percent of Kellogg's 1993–94 entering class was foreign, up from 13 percent six years earlier, says admissions director Stephen Christakos.

As a whole, graduate students today take longer to complete their programs, are more likely to do so on a part-time basis while working, and are older when they complete their degrees. According to the National Academy of Sciences, the median age of those receiving education doctorates in 1990–91 was 42 years. On average, 18 years passed between receipt of a bachelor's and doctorate in this field. In 1979–80, the median age was 37 years, with an average of 13 years between bachelor's and doctorate. The increase has been less dramatic, but still discernible, in other fields. Overall, the average doctoral recipient in 1990–91 was 34 years old and had spent ten years between receiving his/her bachelor's and doctorate degrees.

This trend is partly caused by the aging of the baby boom. Another reason is a growing acceptance of career change and schools' desire for students with "real world" experience. "Ten years ago at Kellogg, about 10 to 12 percent of students came right from college. Now it's well under 1 percent," says admissions director Christakos. "Ten years ago, the average age was 24 or 25. Now it's 27."

The percent of female graduate students has also increased in all disciplines. In 1970–71, 40 percent of master's degrees went to women, according to the National Center for Education Statistics. By 1993–94, this share had increased to 52 percent. The share of doctorates going to women grew from 14 percent in 1970–71 to 39 percent in 1993–94. Professional degrees in fields such as law and medicine have seen the largest gains. In 1970–71, women received just 6 percent of such degrees. By 1993–94, the share had leaped to 41 percent.

Older students are more likely to have family responsibilities as well as school work on their minds. Growing shares of women students contribute to this likelihood because family responsibilities still fall more heavily on women. Students today need a wide range of services, like day care, that were relatively unimportant in the past.

Says Kellogg's Christakos: "The dual-career and family issues come up [with students]. 'Can you tell me about housing? What about the schools in the area?' The concerns are far different than they were ten years ago." In 1988, just 18 percent of entering Kellogg students were married. In 1993, 33 percent had "partners," primarily spouses, says Christakos. Good job prospects for spouses in the Chicago metropolitan area have been a real drawing point for the school, he adds.

Businesses located in the vicinity of graduate and professional schools can take advantage of the changing composition of this population by providing services for time-pressed students with families. These might include diaper and laundry services, chore services, and take-out food.

Schools themselves can help prospective students who are short on time. Kellogg now offers its application form on computer disk. "Our prospects are in the workforce and have access to personal computers. It's pretty hard to find typewriters," says Christakos. Twenty-three percent of U.S. applicants used this option the first year it was offered. Candidates with modems can now go online to retrieve the application form, too.

PRODUCTS AND SERVICES FOR
The School/Graduation Transition

For High School Graduation

Prom clothes and accessories
Yearbooks and school rings*
Caps and gowns*
Party items*
Senior portraits*
Gifts*

Preparation for College

Test-preparation services
College selection services—
videos, catalogs
Student loans
Items for dorm rooms and
apartments— microwaves,
small refrigerators,
telephones, computers,
calculators

For College Students and Graduates

Health/beauty/personal-care
items
Credit cards
Telephone calling cards
Banking services
Cars
Stereo systems
Apartments
Home furnishings
Career clothing

For Nontraditional and Graduate Students

Relocation and orientation
services for foreign students
Test-preparation services,
especially for foreign
students
Seminars on time manage-
ment and school
adjustment for returning
students
Time-saving ways to apply to
schools
Time-saving family-related
services

* Also pertains to college graduation.

SOURCES

Cahners Publishing Company. *Your Prom: Lifestyle and Purchasing Study.* New York, NY: Cahners Publishing, 1993.

The College Board. *Trends in Student Aid: 1983 to 1993.* New York, NY: The College Board, 1993.

Day, Jennifer Cheeseman. *Population Projections of the United States by Age, Sex, Race, and Hispanic Origin: 1993 to 2050.* Washington, DC: U.S. Bureau of the Census, 1993.

GED Testing Service/The Center for Adult Learning and Educational Credentials. *1992 GED Statistical Report.* Washington, DC: American Council on Education, 1993.

Graham, Ellen. "**Fortress Academia Sells Security.**" *The Wall Street Journal*, October 25, 1993, p. B1.

Hodgkinson, Harold L. *Independent Higher Education in a Nation of Nations.* Washington, DC: National Institute of Independent Colleges and Universities, 1993.

Kaplan Educational Center. *1992/93 High School Survey.* New York, NY: Kaplan Educational Center, 1993.

Pedalino, Marilyn, et al., *The New England Student Loan Survey II.* Braintree, MA: Massachusetts Higher Education Assistance Corporation/The New England Education Loan Marketing Corporation (Nellie Mae), 1991.

Professional School Photographers of America/Photo Marketing Association International. *1991–92 PMA Industry Trends Report.* Jackson, MI: Photo Marketing Association International, 1992.

Right Research Report No. 7. *College Students, Career Expectations, and Attitudes: A Three-Year Comparison.* Philadelphia, PA: Right Associates, 1992.

Roper Starch Worldwide. *Roper CollegeTrack and Roper High School Report.* New York, NY: Roper Starch Worldwide, 1992, 1993.

Scheetz, L. Patrick. **Recruiting Trends 1993–94.** East Lansing, MI: Collegiate Employment Research Institute, Michigan State University, 1993.

Serafin, Raymond. **"'X' Marks Target Group in Ford Ad Campaign."** *Automotive News*, March 15, 1993, p. 6.

Teenage Research Unlimited. **Teenage Marketing and Lifestyle Study.** Northbrook, IL: Teenage Research Unlimited, 1993.

Tootelian, Dennis H. and Ralph M. Gaedeke. **"The Teen Market: An Exploratory Analysis of Income, Spending, and Shopping Patterns."** *The Journal of Consumer Marketing*, Vol. 9, No. 4, Fall 1992, pp. 35–44.

U.S. Bureau of the Census/U.S. Department of Housing and Urban Development. **American Housing Survey for the United States in 1991.** Washington, DC: U.S. Government Printing Office, 1993.

U.S. Bureau of the Census. Current Population Survey, March 1980, 1990, 1992, published and unpublished reports.

U.S. Bureau of Labor Statistics. Current Population Survey, October School Enrollment Supplement, various years.

U.S. National Center for Education Statistics. **Digest of Education Statistics, 1993.** Washington, DC: Government Printing Office, 1993.

OTHER RESOURCES

Dunn, William. **The Baby Bust: A Generation Comes of Age.** Ithaca, NY: American Demographics Books, 1993.

Riche, Martha Farnsworth. **"The Boomerang Age."** *American Demographics*, May 1990, pp. 24–30, 52–53.

Waldrop, Judith. **The Seasons of Business**, Ithaca, NY: American Demographics Books, 1992.

CHAPTER 7

DISCOVERING A NEW PATH
The Career-Change Transition

In 1991, Julia Triplett was working as a nurse in Los Angeles, managing the practice of a group of doctors who treated cancer patients. Although Triplett had a lot of responsibility and cared deeply for her patients, she knew she needed a change. "It became depressing," she says. "We got the patients who had been told, 'There's nothing more we can do.'"

Triplett wanted to remain in the medical field in a different capacity and hoped to parlay her knowledge into a new career in health administration, but she lacked the business background. The average nursing student is not exposed to courses in finance and operations management.

In 1992, at age 28, Triplett decided to re-tool and entered an M.B.A. program. There she discovered that she had a knack for business. "I found that I really liked cost accounting," she says.

Like Julia Triplett, many people change the type of work they do. Ten percent of the work force make a change each year, according to the Bureau of Labor Statistics. In a 1993 Gallup poll, 24 percent of American workers said it was very likely that they would switch careers sometime during their working lives; another 24 percent said it was somewhat likely.

Most people do in fact make at least one change at some point, according to the Census Bureau. Some return to school for advanced degrees. Many more leverage on-the-job training or off-the-job coursework into new positions. According to research by Lakewood Publications, U.S. organizations budgeted $48 billion for training in 1993. Colleges, training organizations, and consultants will continue to benefit from employers' increased willingness to train and retrain their workers.

Many employees turn to career counselors and self-help materials for guidance in finding more satisfying work. A large outplacement industry deals with the unique needs of laid-off workers, a group that is increasingly likely to include white-collar professionals and managers.

A growing number of people are deciding that the most satisfying thing they can do is go to work for themselves, often out of their own homes. Currently, about 41 million individuals work out of their homes in some capacity, according to LINK Resources of New York City. This is an excellent market for all types of office products, from computers and fax machines to furniture and workstations.

TRENDS IN THE MARKET

In 1991, 10 percent of American workers aged 16 and older—about ten million people—were doing a different type of work than they were doing a year earlier. The Bureau of Labor Statistics (BLS) calls this the "occupational mobility rate." It may involve changing employers, but this is not essential. A research scientist promoted to a managerial position in the same company qualifies as occupationally mobile.

The occupational mobility rate has remained fairly stable over a 25-year period, fluctuating between 9 percent and 12 percent, according to the BLS. But the number of people making changes has increased considerably because the U.S. labor force nearly doubled in size during that time period, from 74 million to 125 million. The number of people changing occupations also grew rapidly—from 6.6 million to 10.3 million.

Age is the strongest predictor of occupational mobility. Young people are, by far, the most likely to make changes. One-third of 16-to-19-year-olds changed occupations in 1990, mostly the result of going from one part-time job to another. The rate among 20-to-24-year-olds, although lower, was still substantial, at 24 percent. "People in their 20s are exploring," says New York City career counselor Elinor Wilder.

By their mid-20s, young adults begin to settle down. The occupational mobility rate for 25-to-34-year olds is 12 percent. The rate

Occupational Mobility

Men were less likely to make occupational changes in 1990 than in 1965, but women were more likely to do so.

(percent of employed men and women who changed the type of work they did between January of one year and January of the next year, by age, 1965–66 and 1990–91)

	1965–66*	1990–91
men aged 16 and older	9.9%	9.2%
16 to 19	—	32.6
20 to 24	28.5	22.9
25 to 34	13.8	11.6
35 to 44	7.4	6.3
45 to 54	5.2	4.5
55 to 64	3.8	3.1
65 and older	2.7	2.0
women aged 16 and older	6.9%	10.7%
16 to 19	—	33.2
20 to 24	14.9	25.0
25 to 34	8.5	12.3
35 to 44	5.3	8.1
45 to 54	4.7	5.5
55 to 64	2.4	3.4
65 and older	1.8	2.5

* Data for 1965–66 are for persons 18 years and older.

Source: Bureau of Labor Statistics

falls steadily with age, to 2 percent for people aged 65 or older still in the workforce. Older workers are less likely to make changes, not necessarily because they resist change, but because they have so much more to lose in terms of seniority and accumulated benefits.

Men today are no more likely to career hop than their counterparts in the preceding generation. In fact, in 1990, the occupational mobility rate for men was actually slightly lower than in 1965, 9 percent compared with 10 percent. But for women, it's a different story. Their occupational mobility rate increased from 7 percent to almost 11 percent. The number of women in the labor force has doubled, from 26 million in 1965 to 57 million in 1990, and they have many more options. No longer confined to the traditional female occupations of nurse, teacher, and secretary, they are more likely to change careers. Twenty-five or 30 years ago, few women like Julia Triplett would have left nursing careers to enter management school. Today, it's a common occurrence.

Women have slightly higher rates of occupational mobility than men in most age groups. "Women look for opportunities, and men look for stability," because men are expected to be stable breadwinners, says Mary Ann Kipp, a Nashville career counselor. Among those aged 35 to 44, women's occupational mobility rate is 8 percent, compared with 6 percent for men. "At that age, many women are just getting started," says Kipp. "They're getting freed up from child care."

Men and women in certain occupations are more likely than others to switch to a different line of work. Those in managerial and professional jobs have lower annual occupational mobility rates (8 percent and 7 percent, respectively) than those in sales and service positions (12 percent and 13 percent, respectively).

Individuals get help with career transitions through both formal and informal sources. According to a 1989 Gallup survey commissioned by the National Career Development Association, 7 percent of American workers said they needed help with their job search. Many turned to informal sources: 24 percent went to friends, 18 percent to relatives, 7 percent to community leaders, and 5 percent to teachers. One-third visited government job-service workers, and 22 percent turned to professional counselors.

Mobility by Occupation

Laborers, sales people, and service workers are most likely to change occupations, while professionals, farmers, managers, and craftspeople are least likely.

(thousands of people employed, both in 1990 and 1991, and percent who changed occupations during that time, by 1991 occupation)

	number employed	percent changed to occupation
total aged 16 and older	104,889	9.9%
executive/administrative/managerial	14,283	7.8
professional specialty	15,091	6.5
technicians	3,597	8.1
sales occupations	12,349	12.4
administrative support	16,695	11.4
private household service	548	11.5
protective service	1,877	10.2
other service	10,549	12.5
precision production, craft, repair	12,586	7.8
machine operators, assemblers, inspectors	7,003	10.0
transportation workers	4,275	10.2
helpers and laborers	3,496	18.5
farming, forestry, fishing	2,541	7.3

Source: Bureau of Labor Statistics

CAREER COUNSELING AND SELF-HELP

According to the Bureau of Labor Statistics's Consumer Expenditure Survey, about 6 percent of American households cited unreimbursed job-related expenses in 1992, including career counseling. The average expenditure for unreimbursed job-related expenses for these households was about $1,600. In 1992, 234,000 educational and vocational counselors were in business to help with career transitions, up from 216,000 in 1989.

The Center for Career and Life Planning at New York University's

School of Continuing Education has grown considerably since it opened in 1979. That first year, it served about 300 clients, says director Letitia Chamberlain. Over the years it has broadened its services; in 1993, it served several thousand individuals.

Although people in their teens and early 20s are most likely to make occupational changes, the majority of people who come to the center for counseling and workshops are in their late 20s and 30s. "When people begin work in their 20s, they don't necessarily do a lot of planning," says Chamberlain. "By the time they are in their late 20s or early 30s, they might reach a point where they say, 'I want something that's more satisfying.'"

"It's very complicated for most of the people coming here," adds Chamberlain. "They are working. This is a transition on top of conducting a normal life. It takes juggling of time and responsibilities." To help clients in this juggling act, the center offers individual counseling and workshops during the day and at night, on weekends and weekdays.

When the center first opened, Chamberlain says only one-fourth of the clients were men. The share has risen to one-third. Elinor Wilder, a counselor at the center, says men mainly come for individual counseling. "It's predominantly women in the group workshops," says Wilder. "Men may be a little more reticent to admit [in front of a group] that they're floundering."

Those who feel uncomfortable talking to a counselor about their career difficulties may seek assistance on their own. Ronald Krannich is there to help. His Manassas Park, Virginia–based Impact Publications specializes in the career area. "Career books within business sections of book stores sell very well," he says. "A few years ago, we were only publishing four career titles a year. Now it's 16 to 18." General how-to books on résumés, cover letters, and job interview techniques sell best, says Krannich, although several specialty niches do well, too, such as career help for those leaving the military.

As with career counseling, those in their late 20s and 30s are most likely to buy such books for themselves. Although college students themselves are not an especially good market for career books, says Krannich, their parents are. Just before the holidays, he receives requests from parents saying, "Send this résumé book to my son or daughter with a note saying, 'Merry Christmas and good luck with your career.'"

Impact also distributes a catalog of books, videos, audiocassettes, CD-ROMs, and software programs to 300,000 individuals, schools, libraries, and other institutions. The 80-page catalog lists over 2,700 career resources from 60 publishers. For all but the books, the biggest buyers are "institutions with renewable budgets," says Krannich. "Individuals still tend to be very book-oriented. Seventy percent of the [book] buyers are female."

Men are more interested in job banks which, for a fee, electronically transmit résumés to employers, Krannich adds. "When it comes to electronic jobs banks, 80 percent of the people who participate are men. They think: 'For $30, I can put my résumé in there and wait for employers to call me.' Women take it a little more seriously. They will seek out the assistance [that books offer]." To appeal to the men's market, Impact is publishing a new book on how to write an electronic résumé.

CORPORATE RESTRUCTURING TAKES ITS TOLL

Although most people who make occupational changes do so voluntarily, many are forced to make changes when they lose their jobs. Corporate restructuring has taken a heavy toll, and many of these people need a considerable amount of help.

Between January 1987 and January 1992, 5.6 million workers who had been with their employer for three years or more lost their jobs because of job cuts, company closings, and the like. Half had been in white-collar positions: 22 percent held professional and managerial positions; 28 percent were in technical, sales, and administrative-support roles. Seasoned workers were hardest hit. Those aged 35 to 54 accounted for 47 percent of the labor force aged 20 and older in 1992, but 53 percent of those who lost jobs. Those aged 55 and older accounted for 13 percent of the labor force, but 17 percent of those who lost jobs.

According to a survey by the American Management Association (which had a disproportionately high representation of large employers and manufacturing firms), 19 percent of job cuts between July 1992 and June 1993 were in middle management, up from 17

Job Losses

The average employee laid off from a job between 1987 and 1992 was a white-collar man aged 35 to 44.

(thousands of workers aged 20 and older with employer tenure of three or more years who lost jobs due to restructuring, slack work, or company closings between January 1987 and January 1992, and percent distribution by age, sex, and occupation)

	workers who lost jobs	percent of job losses
total aged 20 and older:	5,584	100%
20 to 24	203	4%
25 to 34	1,447	26
35 to 44	1,742	31
45 to 54	1,227	22
55 to 64	750	13
65 and older	214	4
sex:		
men	3,447	62%
women	2,137	38
occupation:		
managerial/professional	1,210	22%
technical/sales/support	1,559	28
service	354	6
production/craft/repair	1,021	18
operator/fabricator/laborer	1,301	24
farming/forestry/fishing	76	1

Source: Bureau of Labor Statistics

percent four years earlier. Twenty percent of lay-offs were professional/technical jobs in 1992–93, up from 16 percent in 1988–89. Supervisory job cuts comprised 15 percent of the total in both time periods. "For the first time in the survey's seven-year history, a majority of the jobs eliminated belonged not to hourly workers but to exempt non-hourly employees . . . ," says an AMA report.

Although middle-aged workers have lower occupational mobility rates than younger workers, more of their changes are involuntary. In a 1986–87 survey on occupational mobility (unfortunately not repeated in 1990–91), the Bureau of Labor Statistics asked whether occupational changes were voluntary (for better pay, better working conditions, etc.) or involuntary (due to layoff, plant closing, etc.). Only about one-third of moves among workers aged 55 and older were voluntary, compared with about four in ten for those aged 45 to 54 and half for those under age 45.

Outplacement Services

Corporations that lay off employees hire outplacement firms, a relatively new and growing branch of the career-planning industry. Seventy-eight percent of U.S. businesses that reduced their workforces between July 1992 and June 1993 used outplacement services, according to the American Management Association, up from 64 percent four years earlier.

In 1991, 800,000 Americans received outplacement services, and revenues for outplacement firms stood at $500 million, according to the Association of Outplacement Consulting Firms International (AOCFI) and Kennedy Publications. In 1993, 1.4 million individuals received services, and revenues climbed to $700 million. According to a 1993 AOCFI member survey, one-third of people served are women. The average person going through outplacement is in his or her mid-40s, says executive director Steven Worth.

As with other types of career counseling, outplacement services can be delivered in group settings or through one-on-one counseling. Most of those who receive individual counseling are management-level employees, says Paul Wesman of Right Associates, a major outplacement firm headquartered in Philadelphia. Of over 4,000 individuals who received Right's full one-on-one program and landed new positions between January 1992 and September 1993, 23 percent were under age 40, 48 percent were aged 40 to 49, 26 percent were aged 50 to 59, and 3 percent were aged 60 and older.

In general, older and higher-salaried individuals must wait longer to find new jobs. It took 24 weeks for those under age 40 to find a new position, on average, while those aged 50 to 59 had to wait an average of 36 weeks. It took 26 weeks for those who had been making less than $40,000 a year, but 34 weeks for those who had been in positions paying $100,000 or more.

Older and higher-salaried individuals are more likely to become entrepreneurs or consultants. Right Associates data reveal that 21 percent of those making $100,000 or more before they were displaced went into business for themselves, versus 10 percent of those making less than $40,000. Just 11 percent of those under age 40 try it on their own the next time around, compared with 20 percent of those in their 40s, 27 percent of those in their 50s, and 45 percent of those aged 60 and older.

Working from Home

Many displaced workers are joining the growing ranks of those who work out of their homes. Most home-based workers own their own full- or part-time businesses. But a growing number have employers who allow them to work from home (i.e., telecommute). Both groups need home-office products.

LINK Resources, a New York City–based research and consulting firm, reports that 41 million Americans worked from home in some capacity in 1993. For 12 million, self-employment was their primary

Working at Home

Between 1989 and 1993, the number of people doing some or all of their work at home increased 53 percent.

(numbers in millions and percent of homeworkers, 1989–93)

	number	percent of work force
1989	26.8	22.3%
1990	34.3	28.0
1991	38.4	31.2
1992	39.0	31.4
1993	41.1	33.0

Source: LINK Resources Corporation, New York, NY

source of income; for another 12 million, self-employment was a part-time venture. Eight million were company employees doing their regular work at home on a part- or full-time basis (telecommuting), and nine million did extra work at home after business hours.

Home-based workers are an excellent market for high-tech office products. In 1993, 58 percent of homeworker households owned personal computers, according to LINK. The average price paid for PC hardware was $1,800, and the average price tag for an entire PC system was $2,500. Seventy-two percent of homeworker households own answering machines, 50 percent have cordless phones, and 19 percent have cellular phones. One-fourth own pocket electronic devices, 11 percent have fax devices, and 11 percent have photo-copiers. Home-based business owners are also good customers for standard office equipment: desks, workstations, and multiline tele-phones. *The Wall Street Journal* reports that it costs about $3,000 to $5,000 to equip a home office with computer, printer, fax machine and furniture. The estimate was made by Ithaca, New York–based consultant Thomas Miller.

Office Depot, a chain of office supply stores, recently told *The Wall Street Journal* that 15 percent of the merchandise it sells is des-

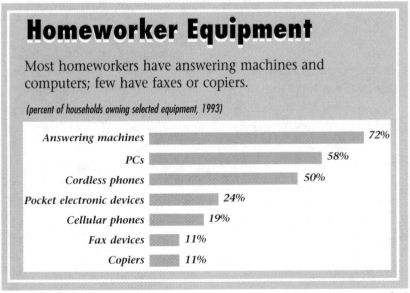

Homeworker Equipment

Most homeworkers have answering machines and computers; few have faxes or copiers.

(percent of households owning selected equipment, 1993)

Equipment	Percent
Answering machines	72%
PCs	58%
Cordless phones	50%
Pocket electronic devices	24%
Cellular phones	19%
Fax devices	11%
Copiers	11%

Source: LINK Resources Corporation, New York, NY

tined for home offices, double the share of a few years ago. In 1990, Hewlett Packard's home-office market "barely existed." By 1994, the home market accounted for 40 percent of its ink-jet printer sales.

People who work at home are well able to afford such equipment and technology. The average income of home-based workers, including those in business for themselves and those working for others, is between $48,000 and $55,000, according to Abhijeet Rane of LINK Resources.

Many people who work from home are professionals, says Rudy Lewis, president of the National Association of Home Based Businesses in Owings Mills, Maryland. Lewis says that the average age of home-based business owners is about 40. More than one-third are women, and the majority are married and have attended college. Many are sales and marketing consultants, although one of the hottest home-based businesses for the 1990s will be importing and exporting, says Lewis.

UPGRADING SKILLS

Many fortunate individuals are able to learn new skills on the job and use them to enhance and upgrade their careers without necessarily changing employers. Employer-sponsored training has become widespread in recent years.

In 1991, one in five people aged 17 and older took part in some type of educational program with which their employer was involved, according to the National Center for Education Statistics. Those aged 35 to 44 and 25 to 34 are most likely to receive training with employer involvement, 31 percent and 25 percent, respectively.

In 1993, U.S. organizations budgeted $48 billion for formal training, according to Lakewood Research, a division of Lakewood Publications, which publishes *Training* magazine. Seventy-two percent pays for salaries of training staff, and 8 percent goes for facilities and overhead. The remaining 20 percent covers outside expenditures, including seminars and conferences, equipment, and materials. A variety of independent management consultants, seminar producers, and training companies, as well as community colleges that have developed specialized business-training divisions, make up this $9 billion industry.

Building computer skills is one of the surest ways for employees to make themselves promotable or attractive to other employers. According to *Training* magazine: "It's no longer enough that Nola can file or input data; now she has to use a desktop-publishing system and understand spreadsheets and be conversant with three new software programs a year." Nine in ten employers currently offer employees some type of basic computer training.

Oakland County Community College near Detroit has a Business and Professional Institute that provided training for 60 employers and almost 7,000 employees in 1993. The school offers not only basic computer training, but sophisticated instruction in areas such as computer-aided design of automobiles and airplanes. "We hold most of the classes directly at the company site, so people don't have to travel," says dean Carol F. Stencel.

The need for training will surely grow in the future, fueled by several trends. One of the most important will be the continuing shift away from the use of mainframes and stand-alone PCs toward networked personal-computer systems. *The Wall Street Journal* reports that almost half of the nation's PCs—22 million of them—will be networked by the end of 1994. The forecast, by Forrester Research of Cambridge, Massachusetts, is a 54 percent increase over 1992.

This trend is explored in *Paradigm Shift: The New Promise of Information Technology,* by Don Tapscott and Art Caston. The authors detail major shifts involving the integration of data systems and work units. Ultimately, this will involve refocusing and retraining employees, not only in terms of computer usage, but in the whole area of workplace dynamics.

What types of employees currently receive training? According to Lakewood Research, mostly middle managers and executives. Three-quarters of all U.S. organizations with 100 or more employees offered training to middle managers and executives in 1993, compared with 41 percent that offered training to salespeople, 52 percent to customer-service employees, and 37 percent to production workers. Training for managers and executives is also more likely to involve outside consultants, according to Lakewood.

The training that higher-level employees receive tends to be less focused on concrete technical skills like computer usage and more focused on global skills like interpersonal relations. It might include the type of one-on-one "career coaching" that BeamPines, a New York City–based consulting firm, provides. "A corporation will engage us to work with executives or managers who might be experiencing blocks in their career or individuals they may be grooming for broader roles in the future," says chairman Jerome C. Beam.

The firm often works with those who are long on technical skills but short on people skills. "People can advance just so far on the basis of technical competence alone," says Beam. "It's the interpersonal skills that become of increasing importance as the individual moves up the ladder." Over a six- to 12-month period, executives learn techniques to aid their interpersonal relationships at work, such as negotiation and listening skills.

Victoria Tashjian, president of Tashjian and Company in Wilmington, Delaware, has developed a special niche in the area of career coaching. She works with major companies, such as General Electric, Prudential, Dupont, and Kodak, to develop high-potential executive women. "Companies recognize that some factors make [career development] different for women than for men," says Tashjian.

Using both one-on-one and group sessions, she helps executive women identify and deal with gender-related barriers to advancement. Women are still disproportionately found in staff areas, rather than having direct responsibility for running businesses, says Tashjian. This can hurt their prospects for advancement. "We really try to help women strategize about how they might get the kinds of experiences they need to advance."

Even MTV has had its effect on the world of training. Videos are the most common method of corporate training. Fully 95 percent of companies used videotapes in their training in 1993, according to Lakewood Research. This trend keeps Tom Heisler in business. A victim of management downsizing himself, Heisler was laid off from his corporate job in merchandising. With a marketing background and entrepreneurial spirit, in 1991 he teamed up with a friend with technical expertise in video and started Heisler and Associates, Inc., a St. Louis video production and communications company.

Within two-and-a-half years, Heisler's company produced about

150 training videos for corporate clients such as Ralston Purina. Thirty percent of the company's video business is now in training tapes. "That's been going up," says Heisler. "Two years ago, the training video business was marginal."

The company produces tapes on motivational management, total quality management, selling strategies, and telephone etiquette, among others. "Anything you can imagine in the training arena that you would do in a classroom environment, we do on video," says Heisler. "There was a time when large companies had in-house capability. But the trend now is for it to be outsourced." Smaller and medium-sized companies are an up-and-coming market, says Heisler.

Aside from videotapes, companies deliver training in a variety of ways. According to the Lakewood survey, 93 percent use lectures; 76 percent use one-on-one instruction; 58 percent use computer-based training; 54 percent use audiotapes; 53 percent use self-assessment/self-testing instruments; 21 percent use interactive video; and 16 percent use video teleconferencing.

"User-Friendly" Education

Many people are willing to better themselves in their careers through education even if their employer does not pay for it. One-third of the 57 million people aged 17 and older who received adult education/training in 1991 did so on their own, according to the National Center for Education Statistics. Men and women are equally likely to participate in educational programs, but women are less likely than men to have employer involvement. Forty-three percent of women who participated did so on their own, compared with 27 percent of men.

Employers that don't pay for training probably don't provide time off for it, either. This can make a dedicated program of study difficult for working people. In response, some schools are trying to break down barriers and be as "user-friendly" as possible.

Thomas Edison State College is located in Trenton, New Jersey, but almost half of its students do not even live in the state. Courses are not delivered in the traditional fashion because the school has no classrooms. Students receive course materials through the mail

Adult Education

Women and men are equally likely to participate in adult education, but men are more likely to get assistance from employers.

(number of adults aged 17 and older in thousands, and percent who participated in adult education in past year by age, sex, race, and education, 1991)

	number	percent participating in adult education*	percent with employer involvement
total aged 17 and older	57,391	32%	64%
age:			
17 to 24	7,125	33%	54%
25 to 34	17,530	37	68
35 to 44	17,083	44	70
45 to 54	8,107	32	71
55 to 64	4,516	23	64
65 and older	3,031	10	18
sex:			
men	25,923	32%	73%
women	31,469	32	57
race:			
white non-Hispanic	47,401	33%	65%
black non-Hispanic	4,586	23	59
Hispanic	4,032	29	58
other races non-Hispanic	1,371	29	56
education:			
less than high school	3,437	12%	35%
high school graduate**	31,602	29	62
associate degree	2,461	49	76
bachelor's or higher	19,891	52	71

*Adult education is defined as all non-full-time education such as part-time college attendance, classes, or seminars given by employers, and classes taken for adult literacy purposes or for recreation.

** Includes those with some college but no degree.

Source: National Center for Education Statistics

and are assigned a "faculty mentor." "The student could be in Idaho, and the mentor could be in Texas," says director of communications and college relations Linda Holt, "Some of the courses are offered on a computer network as well." Students can transfer credits toward degrees at Thomas Edison from schools they currently attend or have attended in the past. They can also receive credit for courses they've taken at work or in the military, or what they have learned from life experience.

Many people who wish to change or advance their careers don't go as far as earning new degrees, however. "A lot of people can't

Jobs vs. Bosses

People stay longer in occupations than they do with employers.

(thousands of employed people and median years with current employer and occupation, by age, sex, and education, January 1991)

	number employed	median years with current employer	median years with current occupation
total aged 16 and older:	114,979	4.5	6.5
16 to 24	17,357	1.2	2.0
25 to 34	32,808	3.5	5.1
35 to 44	30,718	6.0	9.9
45 to 54	19,721	10.0	13.2
55 to 64	11,193	12.4	17.4
65 and older	3,183	11.1	18.1
sex:			
men	62,396	5.1	7.7
women	54,651	3.8	5.5
education:			
less than high school	16,065	3.2	5.2
high school graduate	45,348	4.6	6.4
some college	25,358	4.0	5.9
college graduate	28,208	5.4	7.9

Source: Bureau of Labor Statistics

afford to retrain, or they don't want to take the time for a long retraining," says Dallas career counselor David Connerty. More and more are attending classes to qualify for certificates in specialized fields, such as financial planning, health administration, direct marketing, and human resources. "These are fields that are projected to have a future," says Connerty, and a number of schools now offer these short-term programs. "People who already have a degree don't necessarily need more formalized education," he says. "They can go through a much shorter process."

Sometimes people don't want a different job, but need a change of scene nonetheless. Many people change employers without changing occupations. In 1991, American workers had spent a median of 6.5 years in their current occupation, but just 4.5 years with their current employer. According to the BLS's *Occupational Outlook Quarterly*: "The greater occupational tenure compared with employer tenure implies that the labor force is more willing, and perhaps more able, to switch employers than occupations."

Changing employers may be just as much—or more—of a transition than changing occupations. It not only involves adapting to a new work environment and new colleagues, but frequently involves relocation as well. But whether they find new jobs or new bosses, people are generally willing to spend some time and money to find more meaningful employment. A work life can last 40 or more years, and most people are not willing to stay put for that length of time.

PRODUCTS AND SERVICES FOR
The Career-Change Transition

Finding New Work

Career counseling and "coaching"
Career development centers
Electronic job banks
Résumé preparation
Self-help books, video/audiotapes, CD-ROMs, and
    software programs
Outplacement services

For the Home Office

Personal computers
Software
Telephones
Fax machines
Photocopiers
Office furnishings
Office supplies

Upgrading Skills

Consultant/seminar training
Training videos, software, and multimedia
Self-testing materials
Schools that provide advanced degrees and
    certificate programs

SOURCES

American Demographics, **"Career Hopping."** December 1993, p. 6.

American Management Association. *1993 AMA Survey on Downsizing and Assistance to Displaced Workers*. New York, NY: American Management Association, 1993.

Bleakley, Fred R. **"Huge and Diverse Home-Office Market is hard to Crack."** *The Wall Street Journal,* May 9, 1994, pp. B1, B8.

Braus, Patricia. **"Homework for Grownups."** *American Demographics,* August 1993, pp. 38–42.

Kotite, Erika, **"Home Improvements."** *Entrepreneur,* March 1993, pp. 97–100.

Kotite, Erika, **"Home Tech."** *Entrepreneur,* September 1993, pp. 82–84.

Huber, Janean, **"Homing Instinct."** *Entrepreneur,* March 1993, pp. 82–87.

Huber, Janean, **"The Quiet Revolution."** *Entrepreneur,* September 1993, pp. 76–81.

The Gallup Poll Monthly. "Workers Concerned They Can't Afford to Retire." May 1993, pp. 16–25. Princeton, NJ: The Gallup Poll, 1993.

LINK Resources Corporation. *1993 Home Office Trend Fact Sheet, 1993 Home Office Electronics Product Usage Trends*. Press Releases. New York, NY: LINK Resources, 1993.

Maguire, Steven R., "Worker Tenure in 1991." *Occupational Outlook Quarterly*, Spring 1993, pp. 25–37. Washington, DC: U.S. Bureau of Labor Statistics, 1993.

Markey, James P. and William Parks II, **"Occupational Change: Pursuing a Different Type of Work."** *Monthly Labor Review*, September 1989. Washington, DC: U.S. Bureau of Labor Statistics, 1989.

Mergenhagen, Paula. **"Doing the Career Shuffle."** *American Demographics*, November 1991, pp. 42–44, 53–54.

Tapscott, Don and Art Caston. *Paradigm Shift: The New Promise of Information Technology*. New York, NY: McGraw Hill, Inc., 1993.

Training magazine. Special section. October 1993, pp. 29–65. Minneapolis, MN: Lakewood Publications, 1993.

U.S. Bureau of Labor Statistics. 1991 Consumer Expenditure Survey, unpublished data, 1992.

U.S. Bureau of Labor Statistics. *Displaced Workers, 1987–91*. Bulletin 2427, July 1993. Washington, DC: Government Printing Office, 1993.

U.S. Bureau of Labor Statistics. *Employment and Earnings*. January 1993. Washington, DC: Government Printing Office, 1993.

U.S. Bureau of Labor Statistics. 1990–91 Occupational Mobility, unpublished data, 1992.

U.S. Bureau of Labor Statistics. Workers Who Lost Jobs Between January 1987 and 1992, By Occupation of Job Lost, and Employment Status in January 1992, unpublished data, 1993.

U.S. National Center for Education Statistics. *Digest of Education Statistics, 1993*. Washington, DC: Government Printing Office, 1993.

Wilke, John R. *"Computer Links Erode Hierarchical Nature of Workplace Culture."* *The Wall Street Journal*, December 9, 1993, pp. A1, A7.

OTHER RESOURCES

Amirault, Thomas. **"Job Training: Who Needs It and Where They Get It."** *Occupational Outlook Quarterly,* Winter 1992–93, pp. 18–31. Washington, DC: U.S. Bureau of Labor Statistics.

Carey, Max. **"Occupational Advancement from Within."** *Occupational Outlook Quarterly.* Winter 1991/92, pp. 19–25. Washington, DC: Bureau of Labor Statistics, 1991.

Silvestri, George. **"Who Are the Self-Employed? Employment Profiles and Recent Trends."** *Occupational Outlook Quarterly,* Spring 1991, pp. 26–36. Washington, DC: U.S. Bureau of Labor Statistics.

U.S. Bureau of Labor Statistics. ***How Workers Get Their Training. A 1991 Update.*** Bulletin 2407, August 1992. Washington, DC: Government Printing Office, 1992.

CHAPTER 8

SAYING GOOD-BYE TO THE WORLD OF WORK

The Retirement Transition

AS PRESIDENT AND CEO of American General Life and Accident Insurance Co., Carroll Shanks oversaw 8,000 employees in 250 offices around the country. After a decade at the helm, Shanks retired in 1992 at age 65, and he's been busy ever since. "My transition to retirement has been absolutely great," he says.

Always involved in civic activities during his corporate days, Shanks continued with numerous volunteer activities, like serving as board chair of the local performing-arts center. He became an "ambassador" for the trust department of an area bank, keeping him in contact with community business leaders. He and his wife also began spending more time at their summer home and making other vacation trips around the country. It's no wonder he had little time to miss corporate life.

Shanks is a good example of the active lifestyle that defines the retirement transition today. Retirement is the start of a major—but relatively new—phase of life. At the turn of the century, when life expectancy was barely 50 years, most people couldn't look forward to such a period in their lives. Today, it can last for 20 years or longer.

Although their incomes may be lower than those of younger groups, retirees' net worth is greater. And unlike the income of younger age groups, which has been declining, that of retirees has been rising. Businesses can profit from this life stage by making the years of retirement as meaningful as possible. Retirees are an especially good market for products and services that deal with finances, recreation, housing, and education, to name a few.

Conventional wisdom maintains that retirees want nothing more to do with the world of work and are interested only in a life of leisure. While this may be true for some, most retirees desire continued involvement and attachment. Many return to work, in either a full- or part-time capacity. Others go back to school to increase their knowledge or obtain a degree they never got. Retirees are also concerned with keeping abreast of their finances, insuring plenty of work for financial planners, attorneys, and insurance agencies. Businesses in the travel industry needn't worry, either—retirees are very much interested in travel because it provides them with rich new experiences. And a small group of affluent retirees starts afresh by relocating.

The next generation of retirees—baby boomers—will be even more likely to desire continued involvement and growth. They are the best-educated generation in history and have always been willing to pay for a variety of personal services. This will continue into their retirement years.

TRENDS IN THE MARKET

About 14 million men and 22 million women aged 55 and older are not in the labor force, according to 1993 data from the Bureau of Labor Statistics (BLS). Among those under age 60, 22 percent of men and 43 percent of women are not in the labor force. At ages 60 to 64, the shares increase to 49 percent of men and 63 percent of women. And among those aged 65 to 69, 75 percent of men and 84 percent of women aren't part of the labor force. At age 70 and older, the shares reach 90 percent of men and 95 percent of women.

These labor force participation rates are not a perfect measure of permanent withdrawal from the labor force. Many older adults who don't work will eventually return to other full- or part-time jobs. Some find that their retirement benefits do not sustain their lifestyle; others miss the structure and social interaction that a job provides.

If retirement is defined as permanent withdrawal from the labor force, then an average 1.3 million individuals retired each year between 1985 and 1990, according to Georgetown University senior research scholar Jacob Siegel. Today, the median age of retirement is about 63 for both men and women, according to research by Siegel and colleague Murray Gendell. During the early 1950s, the retirement age was about 67 for men and 68 for women.

"A person's readiness to retire is prompted by the receipt of a private pension," says Siegel, and such pensions have become more widespread over the years. About 49 percent of men and 22 percent of women aged 65 and older who have income receive some of their income from a company, union, or government pension, according

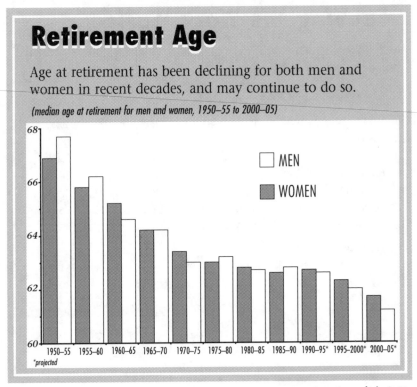

Retirement Age

Age at retirement has been declining for both men and women in recent decades, and may continue to do so.

(median age at retirement for men and women, 1950–55 to 2000–05)

☐ MEN

▨ WOMEN

1950–55 1955–60 1960–65 1965–70 1970–75 1975–80 1980–85 1985–90 1990–95* 1995–2000* 2000–05*

*projected

Source: Bureau of Labor Statistics

to the 1992 Current Population Survey. So do 13 percent of men and 5 percent of women aged 45 to 64.

But the trend toward earlier retirement is leveling off. Between the early 1980s and the mid-1990s, the median age at retirement is expected to hover around 63. Based on BLS employment projections, Gendell and Siegel say that retirement age will then resume its decline and dip below 62 between 2000 and 2005.

Not all researchers agree with them. "The retirement age is constant now. If anything, it will go up a bit because there has been a major change in government policy," says Syracuse University economist Richard Burkhauser. The age at which Social Security recipients can receive full benefits will increase to 67 in a phased-in process that will start after 2000. Some of the financial penalties that recipients face by continuing to work are being removed as well. And in many workplaces, mandatory retirement ages have been eliminated.

Leaving the Work World

In 1950, almost two-thirds of men in their late 60s were still working. That share declined to one-fourth in 1990.

(labor force participation rate of men and women aged 55 and older, by age, 1950–2000)

	1950	1960	1970	1980	1990	2000*
men:						
55 to 59	89.9%	91.6%	89.5%	81.7%	79.8%	79.2%
60 to 64	83.4	81.1	75.0	60.8	55.5	54.2
65 to 69	63.9	46.8	41.6	28.5	26.0	27.3
70 to 74	43.2	31.6	25.2	17.9	15.4	15.6
75 and older	21.3	17.5	12.0	8.8	7.1	7.3
women:						
55 to 59	29.7%	42.2%	49.0%	48.5%	55.3%	61.9%
60 to 64	23.8	31.4	36.1	33.2	35.5	39.5
65 to 69	15.5	17.6	17.3	15.1	17.0	19.7
70 to 74	7.9	9.5	9.1	7.5	8.2	8.5
75 and older	3.2	4.4	3.4	2.5	2.7	2.7

* projected

Source: Bureau of Labor Statistics

Who is most likely to retire early? According to Mark Hayward, a Pennsylvania State University sociologist, blue-collar workers are most likely. Professionals, managers, and salesworkers are least likely. "If the nature of work remains attractive and the demand for their labor continues, workers may be more likely to delay retirement," write Hayward and his colleagues. Blue-collar workers are a declining share of the work force, while professionals, managers, and salesworkers are increasing in share; these trends should work against early retirement.

Many women reaching retirement age today did not participate in the labor force, or did so only sporadically. In 1992, 39 percent of women Social Security recipients aged 62 and older were receiving benefits because of their husbands' employment, not their own. This proportion is decreasing—it was 43 percent of women in 1980, 49 percent in 1970, and 57 percent in 1960—and it will continue to decline in the future. The career histories and earnings of baby-boom women are more closely resembling those of men. In 1960, just 40 percent of women aged 25 to 44 were in the labor force, compared with 98 percent of men. In 1993, 75 percent were, compared with 94 percent of men. This will mean greater affluence for baby-boom women when they retire because more will be receiving pensions.

The Pre-Retirement Years

Judith Waldrop of *American Demographics* refers to households headed by 55-to-64-year-olds as "pre-retirement" households. According to a 1991 Current Population Survey, 64 percent have heads who are still in the labor force, and 63 percent consist of married couples. In some cases, householders are retired, but younger spouses (usually wives) are still working. In all, 78 percent of these households have at least one earner. Forty percent have two or more.

Median income for households in this age group was $34,100 in 1992, compared with $30,800 for all households. It derives from a variety of sources aside from earnings. Three in ten receive Social Security income, and one-fourth collect pensions.

The number of Americans aged 55 to 64 will grow from 21 million in 1994 to almost 23 million in 1998, according to Census Bureau projections. In 2004, the group should number 28.5 million

Retiring Households

As households age, they are less likely to contain married couples and more likely to consist of women living alone.

(thousands of households headed by people aged 55 and older, by age, 1993)

	55 to 64	65 to 74	75 and older
total households	12,438	11,834	9,062
families:	9,117	7,350	3,911
married-couple	7,674	6,223	3,084
female-headed	1,178	913	679
male-headed	265	213	148
nonfamilies:	3,321	4,484	5,151
men living alone	1,057	1,046	948
women living alone	1,976	3,284	4,077
living with nonrelatives	288	154	126

Source: U.S. Census Bureau

and comprise 10 percent of the U.S. population, up from 8 percent in 1994. By 2010, this group will leap to 35 million (12 percent), and by 2015, it will number 40 million strong, representing 13 percent of the population.

The Early Retirement Years

Judith Waldrop also discusses households headed by people aged 65 to 74—the "newly retired." This group is less likely than pre-retirees to consist of married couples (53 percent) and more likely to be headed by women with no spouse present (38 percent), mostly widows. Thirty-seven percent of householders in this age group live alone.

These households rely more heavily on Social Security and pension benefits than on wages and salaries. Just one in five has a householder who still works, and four in ten have any earners. Median income for these households was $20,400 in 1992.

Although income may be lower after retirement, net worth (assets minus debts) is higher. According to an analysis of the Census Bureau's 1988 Survey of Income and Program Participation by Charles F. Longino, Jr. and William H. Crown, median net worth is at its highest for householders aged 65 to 69, at $83,500. Furthermore, this age group saw its net worth increase 10 percent between 1984 and 1988 in constant dollars, while that of younger groups declined.

The number of Americans aged 65 to 74 will fall slightly between 1995 and 2005, from 18.8 million to 18.5 million, as the relatively small generation born during the Depression enters this group. Then it will pick up again, to 21 million by 2010 and 26.5 million by 2015, as more and more baby boomers reach typical retirement age.

PREPARING FOR RETIREMENT

Retiring from a lifetime of work is a momentous event. It can be exhilarating, but also depressing. It opens a world of opportunity, as well as economic insecurity. Employers provide a variety of services to help retiring workers make the most of their post-career life. Many retirees also strike out on their own to find a new way of filling the days.

Employers Ease the Transition

People may not plan to retire in their mid- or late 50s, but in these days of corporate downsizings and early retirement packages, they may have little choice. Many are ill-equipped to handle such a sudden and unexpected change, creating a market niche for companies involved in outplacement services.

Corporations that downsize routinely employ outplacement consulting firms to help prepare and counsel their laid-off workers. (See Chapter 7 for more information about displaced workers.) A subgroup of these workers consists of those offered, or forced to take, an early retirement. Capitalizing on this opportunity, Right Associates, an outplacement firm headquartered in Philadelphia, implemented an enhanced retirement counseling program in 1993.

"I see a big market for it," says Graham Smith, a Right consultant in Canada who developed the program. Most of those for whom he provides retirement outplacement services are in the 60-to-65 age group. "But I'm finding that age is dropping to 57 or 58. I'm even getting some people who are 55," he says. "Companies are beginning to realize that having a person retire early is cheaper than giving them a severance package."

Smith's program deals not only with financial issues surrounding retirement, but with social and emotional topics—marital adjustment during retirement, relationships with adult children and grandchildren, and areas such as relocation and volunteering. He says these issues are as important to deal with as financial matters. "Retirement is one of the top-five stress producers. It ranks up there with the death of a family member."

It's not just downsizing companies that provide pre-retirement preparation to employees. According to a 1993 Merrill Lynch survey of benefits managers around the country, seven in ten employers offer their employees some type of pre-retirement preparation. Smaller employers are just as likely as large employers to offer this kind of service.

Most employees in companies offering such benefits take advantage of them. Seventy-six percent read retirement brochures, 67 percent participate in seminars, 53 percent use multimedia resources like video- or audiotapes, and 49 percent take part in counseling.

Many companies use outside vendors to provide retirement planning programs, and this is good news for investment firms like Merrill Lynch. Kirk Brenner and Chris Brooke, financial consultants at the firm's Indianapolis office, spend the majority of their time producing seminars for a wide variety of companies, from offices to factories. The seminars either totally focus on retirement issues or offer retirement planning as a major component. Many include not only financial experts, but gerontologists, nurses, and attorneys who deal with various aspects of retirement. Estate planning tends to be one of the most popular topics, says Brenner.

Most companies open the program up to employees of all ages, but three-quarters of those who attend are aged 50 and older. Nevertheless, the word spreads to the younger generation, says Brenner. "A lot of people will go home and tell their kids—who are 30 or 35— what they found out."

Between 1988 and 1992, Brenner and Brooke worked with more than 100 companies in Indiana; 100 other Merrill Lynch consultants offer similar programs around the country. Although the consultants do not make sales pitches during presentations, the Merrill Lynch name receives favorable exposure, and many participants ultimately become clients.

Methodist Hospital of Indiana began its own in-house retirement seminars for employees in 1990, but demand soon outstripped capacity, so it turned to an outside vendor to provide additional seminars. "We had been doing them in-house about twice a year," says benefits representative Jeff McKinney. "We would announce them, and they would be full within a week. We just didn't have the time to do more ourselves."

Financial Planning

Many people who are on the verge of retirement don't wait for their employers to provide assistance. They go to financial planners on their own. Eight in ten certified financial planners have a specialty in retirement planning, according to a 1993 survey by the College for Financial Planning in Denver.

Jane King, president of Fairfield Financial Advisors in Wellesley, Massachusetts, is one of them. "People will come to me with a retirement account or a 401K plan and say, 'I'm 55 and I want to retire at 65. Tell me how I need to invest my money.'" As baby boomers edge closer to retirement age, they will be even more likely to want and need this type of help. According to the 1993 Merrill Lynch survey, 64 percent of women and 50 percent of men aged 25 to 44 agreed that they "could really use some help from a financial advisor or planner."

"They [baby boomers] are concerned about getting guidance about taking [investment] risks," says King. "They know they have to take risks because no one else is going to take care of them. The pendulum has swung from the company planning your retirement to your having to plan it."

Financial planning often goes hand in hand with insurance planning. At this point in their lives, retirees may need more insurance protection, particularly certain types of protection. The average

Retiring Households

Social Security is the most common income source for older people, but for those who have them, earnings are the largest source.

(percent of people aged 65 and older receiving income from selected sources, and average amount received, 1992)

	percent with income source	average income received
Social Security	92.7%	$6,634
Interest	66.7	2,970
Pensions	33.0	8,278
Dividends	18.6	3,308
Earnings	14.9	15,781
Rent/royalties/estates/trusts	10.0	4,399
Survivors' benefits	7.0	6,486
Supplemental Security Income	5.6	2,276
Veterans' benefits	3.9	4,264
Disability benefits	1.1	7,297
Public assistance	0.5	1,599

Source: U.S. Census Bureau

age of those who purchase long-term-care insurance is 66, says Lance Gish, vice president of Long Term Preferred Care in Brentwood, Tennessee. According to a 1990 survey by the Health Insurance Association of America, purchasers of long-term-care policies have higher incomes and education than nonpurchasers and are more likely to be female and married.

People going through the retirement transition are also good prospects for investment firms of all types. "Our typical mutual-fund shareholder is over age 55," says Steven Norwitz, vice president of T. Rowe Price, a mutual funds company in Baltimore. "These are the people who have accumulated the most assets." Norwitz noticed that many firms had developed retirement planning kits for people in their 30s and 40s—those with many years to prepare. He also discovered that older individuals on the verge of retirement wanted such information, too, but there was little in the way of planning kits available.

In 1992, T. Rowe Price introduced one. The "Retirees Financial Guide" provides not only valuable retirement information, but an introduction to the company as well. Within a year-and-a-half of its introduction, 350,000 kits had been requested. "We get many requests from our own investors," says Norwitz, "but more than half are from outsiders."

Return to Work

Regardless of whether they receive pre-retirement preparation through their employer, an investment firm, or a financial planner, many people still have a hard time adjusting to retirement. Right Associates' Graham Smith says that senior managers have the most difficult time due to the loss of power and control so prominent in their jobs. "At work, they could pick up the phone and move heaven and earth. Now they're at home, and their wife tells them they've got to take out the garbage." He usually counsels senior managers in one-on-one sessions that include the spouse.

Smith generally works with middle managers, administrators, and blue-collar workers in group sessions. "One of the big issues for them is [the absence of] the social activity and structure that work provides," he says. Many retirees want or need to continue working, particularly if the retirement is early or forced.

Sterling Dimmitt works with retired managers as an outplacement consultant with Lee Hecht Harrison in New York City. "People formerly in senior management often continue in consulting and board work," he says. "If they've been a middle manager, it will probably be something like part-time selling." If a retirement happens early or unexpectedly, most will return to some type of work, says Dimmitt.

Pennsylvania State University sociologist Mark Hayward and his colleagues tracked a group of retired men over 17 years. They found that almost one-third of the men returned to work at some point, and most returnees came back in the first year after retirement. Professionals, salesworkers, farm laborers, and self-employed individuals were most likely to return to work, as were younger retirees. Over two-thirds of all who returned took full-time jobs.

Some retirees return to work but forego pay. They join the ranks of America's volunteers. Forty-nine percent of people aged 55 to 64 and 42 percent of those aged 65 to 74 volunteered in 1991, according to a Gallup survey commissioned by Independent Sector, a national association of philanthropic and voluntary organizations. While this is actually lower than the share for younger age groups (61 percent for 35-to-44-year-olds and 56 percent for 45-to-54-year-olds), older people are important volunteers because their time is flexible. They can take on the weekday assignments that a younger person cannot.

Many retirement-age people learn about volunteer activities through organizations they belong to, especially churches and synagogues. Over one-third of volunteers aged 55 and older told Gallup they learned about their volunteer activities that way.

RETIREES ON THE MOVE

When Right Associates' Graham Smith counsels prospective retirees, the issue of relocation often comes up. Although many think about it, the majority do not go through with it.

The idea that most retired people head immediately for sunny places like Florida and Arizona is a myth. According to the Census Bureau's 1992 Current Population Survey, just 6 percent of Americans aged 60 to 64 made a move during the previous year, as did 8 percent of those aged 55 to 59. The shares are even lower for those aged 65 to 69 (6 percent) and 70 to 74 (5 percent). This compares with a much more mobile younger population—35 percent of those in their 20s and 20 percent in their 30s made a move in the year before the survey.

Even when older people move, they usually don't go far. More than half of movers aged 55 to 74 move to another home in the same county. All told, three in four don't move across state lines. The one-fourth who do are the most affluent. "It's not the poor people that are moving long distances," says Census Bureau analyst Kristin Hansen. "You have to have a reasonable amount of money."

Southern and southwestern states like Arizona, Texas, Arkansas,

Florida, and Georgia all have large numbers of retirees moving in, says Hansen. "If you're talking about the 'young' retired—people in their 60s—they're going to places where it's warm, where they don't have to shovel the walk, and where there are recreational activities."

Significant numbers of retirees are also moving to places like Maine, Vermont, and New Hampshire, says Hansen. "It's rural, the

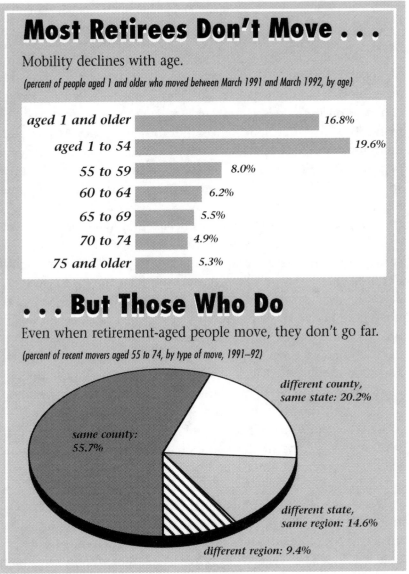

Most Retirees Don't Move . . .

Mobility declines with age.

(percent of people aged 1 and older who moved between March 1991 and March 1992, by age)

aged 1 and older	16.8%
aged 1 to 54	19.6%
55 to 59	8.0%
60 to 64	6.2%
65 to 69	5.5%
70 to 74	4.9%
75 and older	5.3%

. . . But Those Who Do

Even when retirement-aged people move, they don't go far.

(percent of recent movers aged 55 to 74, by type of move, 1991–92)

different county, same state: 20.2%

same county: 55.7%

different state, same region: 14.6%

different region: 9.4%

Source: U.S. Census Bureau

cost of living is lower, and the crime rate is lower." According to Nina Glasgow of Cornell University, about one-fifth of U.S. nonmetropolitan counties attract significant numbers of migrating retirees.

Kenneth F. Backman and Sheila J. Backman of Clemson University directed a 1991 study of people aged 55 and older who migrated to South Carolina during the previous year. "This was a fairly active group. They didn't perceive themselves as being old," says Kenneth Backman.

The group was primarily composed of married couples (81 percent); their average age was 58. Sixty-five percent had incomes of over $30,000 a year, with 28 percent over $60,000. Their top reasons for choosing South Carolina as a retirement destination were: climate, housing values, recreation/leisure opportunities, and cost of living. The most prevalent sources of information they used to plan their moves were the advice of friends or relatives, magazines, newspapers, and chambers of commerce. One-third of the sample—those with the highest incomes—ended up in special retirement communities and resorts.

Cooper Communities, based in Bella Vista, Arkansas, has developed retirement communities in rural areas of South Carolina, Arkansas, and Tennessee. Residents of its McCormick County, South Carolina village have an average household income of $71,900; 21 percent have incomes surpassing $100,000. The average age of household heads in the community is 61. Sixty-one percent are retired, and 39 percent still work.

But not all retirees want to be surrounded by people their own age. According to the Backmans' research, nearly half of retirees relocate in traditional neighborhoods. Of all retirees in their sample, including those who chose retirement communities/resorts and those who chose traditional neighborhoods, one-third moved to small towns, 30 percent picked the suburbs, 11 percent went to rural areas, and 8 percent landed in an urban environment. Another 19 percent gave no answer or said they went elsewhere.

States are eager to attract these residents, with good reason. A 1992 analysis for the Appalachian Regional Commission found that the local economic impact of the average retirement migrant household is $71,600 per year. "They bring an investment portfolio," says

Patrick Mason at the Center for Carolina Living in Columbia, South Carolina. "They also bring a series of tax payments. They buy or build a home; they end up on the school board."

Gleason and Ann Pebley retired in 1985 and relocated to Cookeville, Tennessee (population: 24,000) one year later. Gleason, aged 55 at retirement, had spent 30 years in management positions with AT&T, most of them in the Northeast. Ann had a teaching career. The energetic couple bought a home in Cookeville and soon immersed themselves in the social and civic life of the community. Gleason eventually took on the very demanding volunteer role of board chair for the local United Way. "I'm able to participate in making something better, and that's a blessing," he says.

To attract such individuals to his state, Patrick Mason has arranged with South Carolina's tourism division to distribute relocation packages at the state's roadside welcome centers. "One million of the 30 million visitors are here for the primary purpose of investigating retirement and relocation opportunities," he claims.

Indeed, the majority of retirees who relocate do a considerable amount of "shopping around" before choosing a destination. "We looked all over the Southeast," says Gleason Pebley. "We would take work and vacation trips to places my wife had already researched."

The Backmans' study of relocated retirees found that the average time between thinking about the move and making the move was more than three years. "Most of them used their vacations in their later working years as a pre-retirement search," says Kenneth Backman. "We had one gentleman in the survey who told us he looked at 20 communities in 11 states before he chose to come to South Carolina."

The "Snowbird" Phenomenon

Some people aren't ready for an all-out move upon retirement, but they still want to soak up the sun and fun at least part of the year, particularly during the winter. These individuals, dubbed "snowbirds," head for places with warm winter temperatures like Florida, Arizona, and California, and stay anywhere from several weeks to several months each year.

Snowbirds are an economic boon to the communities they enter. An estimated 300,000 snowbirds landed in Arizona during the 1992–93 winter season, spending more than $600 million, according to a study by the Center for Business Research at Arizona State University. "They start showing up in October and they pretty much leave by April," says center director Tim Hogan.

Founders Bank of Arizona, a small, one-branch institution in upscale northern Scottsdale, has developed a unique method to attract snowbirds and other retired customers. People aged 50 and older who keep a minimum level in a savings/checking or CD account are entitled to membership in the "Founders Club." The club has its own director and offers cooking and yoga classes, financial seminars, excursions to local restaurants and theaters, as well as a wide variety of trips, both domestic and abroad.

The program started in 1988 with about 100 members, says bank vice president Christine Kovach. By 1993, membership had grown to 500. Almost half of the members are snowbirds. "The busiest [club] months are December through March," says Kovach. "These people keep an active social calendar. They have unbelievable energy."

In the Phoenix area, the average male snowbird is 69 and the average woman is 68, according to Tim Hogan's study. Their median household income is $32,500, with median monthly expenditures of about $1,000 during their winter visit. The median length of stay is 4.3 months, and two-thirds come from Midwestern states. "They spend like they were permanent residents," says Hogan. "They're buying things like groceries and gasoline. But since they're retired, they do recreational kinds of things rather than go to work." One-fourth live in recreational vehicles, commonly known as RVs.

Retirees are the mainstay of the RV industry. Nearly half of the nation's approximately 8.5 million RVs are owned by people over the age of 55, according to Phil Ingrassia at the Recreation Vehicle Industry Association (RVIA). The proportion is higher for motor homes, the most costly type of RV; the average age of first-time owners is 54, and their average income is $45,300.

Twenty-five percent of RV owners claim to be snowbirds, according to a 1993 study by the RVIA. Four in ten spend eight weeks or more a year away from home. Three in ten spend at least 12 weeks away. The most popular destinations are Florida and Arizona, followed by southern California, Texas, and Nevada. Most stay in RV parks and campgrounds at multiple locations during their trips. The parks offer a wide variety of social activities that appeal to retirees, says Ingrassia.

RVers are prime customers for of all types of businesses. A lot of marketing is done through the many RV clubs around the country, including the Good Sam Club, which boasts over 800,000 members. A survey of RVers who use *Woodall's Campground Directories* found that RVers on the road spend an average of more than $100 a day on services including food, entertainment, and accommodations. Sixty percent of RVers go on foliage tours, 39 percent go to harvest festivals, 33 percent go touring and sightseeing, 31 percent go to flea markets, and 28 percent shop at outlet malls.

Not all snowbirds explore the country by RV. Tim Hogan's survey found that 26 percent of Phoenix snowbirds set up their winter quarters in mobile homes. Twenty-five percent stay in apartments, 9 percent in single-family homes, 7 percent in a condo or townhouse, 4 percent in a hotel/motel/resort, and 3 percent with friends or relatives.

Snowbirding is a way of life for many people, not necessarily the prelude to a permanent move. Over half of respondents in Hogan's Phoenix study had been snowbirds for more than five years. Deborah A. Sullivan of Arizona State University studied three year-round retirement communities outside Phoenix and found that 9 percent of households resided there half the year or less. These "seasonal in-migrants" were younger, had higher income and education, and were more likely than permanent residents to be married couples.

Sullivan concludes: "There is little evidence that seasonal migration is only a search procedure in preparation for a relocation decision.... Perennial seasonal migration to and from fixed-base retirement communities, like the seasonal migration to adult mobile home and travel-trailer parks, appears to be an alternative lifestyle for healthy, white...married, well-educated retirees who are pulled by the amenities of the retirement community but are inhibited from relocating on a permanent basis." These inhibiting factors include ties to another community and to children and grandchildren.

MAKING TRAVEL PLANS

Even if they don't relocate for part of the year, retirees often want to expand their horizons in a more limited way—through travel. Americans aged 55 to 64 made 11 percent of the 651 million round-trips of 100 or more miles made by adults during 1992, according to the U.S. Travel Data Center of Washington, D.C., proportionate to their share of the adult population. Those aged 65 to 74 made 8 percent of the trips and constituted 10 percent of the adult population.

Retired people don't travel for business, of course, but they are also less likely than younger people to take vacation trips. Forty-three percent of people aged 45 to 54, 39 percent of those 55 to 64, and 30 percent of those 65 and older took a vacation trip to a domestic location during the past 12 months, according to a 1993 survey by Mediamark Research. Another 17 percent, 16 percent, and 11 percent, respectively, took foreign vacations.

However, retirement-age travelers spend more time on trips than younger people do, says Shawn Flaherty, manager of media relations for the U.S. Travel Data Center. While travelers aged 35 to 54 spent an average of 3.8 nights away from home during 1992, those aged 55 and older spent an average of 4.9 nights. "Older people have the time and the means" to take longer trips, says Flaherty, whereas younger people "have more conditions set on their time" and may only be able to get away for weekends.

Young retirees are somewhat more likely than younger or older people to be big vacation spenders. Twenty-nine percent of domestic travelers aged 55 to 64 said they spent $1,500 or more on vacations during the previous year, according to Mediamark's 1993 survey. Just 23 percent of vacation travelers aged 45 to 54 and those aged 65 and older said they spent this much. Those under age 55 were even less likely to be big spenders.

Foreign spending is also high for mature travelers. Over one-third of those ages 45 and older told Mediamark that they spent $1,000 or more during the year on their foreign vacations. Just one-fourth of foreign travelers aged 18 to 34 spent that much.

A 1990 study conducted for the National Restaurant Association also found that people aged 50 to 64 are more likely than any other age group to visit upscale restaurants while on vacation; such visits comprise 17 percent of their meals while on trips.

Most retirees want to be on the go during their vacations. According to a 1988 survey directed by Michael A. Blazey at California State University, Long Beach, 77 percent of retired respondents went sightseeing and 71 percent shopped during vacations taken during the previous year. Fifty-six percent visited scenic areas, 48 percent historic sites, 35 percent museums, 24 percent national parks, 21 percent resorts, 20 percent theatrical events, 17 percent theme/amusement parks, and 17 percent cultural events. Seventeen percent went on package tours, 13 percent went on cruises, 13 percent attended festivals, 11 percent went to sports events, 10 percent visited zoos, and 7 percent golfed.

Rental-car companies benefit from vacationing retirees because older people are not as comfortable as younger people are with flying. They prefer to drive. Of all round-trips of 100 miles or more taken by adult Americans in 1992, automobiles were used for 70 percent and airplanes for 26 percent, according to the U.S. Travel Data Center. Among travelers aged 65 to 74, just 19 percent of trips were taken by air.

Retirees are more likely than younger people to take upscale vacations like cruises. A 1992 survey by the Cruise Lines International Association found that people aged 60 and older accounted for 36 percent of adults aged 25 and older who had taken cruises during the previous five years, higher than their 26 percent share of the population.

While some cruise lines specifically target retirees, the majority do not aim their marketing at this population, says association controller Stephen O'Connor. "Most advertising is addressed at baby boomers," he says, the reason being that younger people are worth more as long-term customers. "The research shows that once a person has taken a cruise, you've got them for life. They'll be cruising for 30, 40, or 50 years," says O'Connor.

In fact, the entire travel industry is anxiously awaiting the entrance of baby boomers into their retirement years. As noted in *The*

Mature Market, a recent publication of the Travel Industry Association (TIA): "As World War II babies and early baby boomers (who travel significantly more than older Americans today) enter the mature market, its share of travel will increase dramatically. . . . Tomorrow's mature market should be a more lucrative international and domestic market for airlines, hotels, travel agents, and tour operators."

The TIA urges its members to look toward the future by enhancing accommodations for those with limited mobility, for instance by providing additional ramps and handrails. It also points out that older travelers are more concerned than younger travelers with personal security, increasing the need for deadbolt locks and the like.

The airline industry may benefit from tomorrow's retirees, too. As the TIA points out, baby boomers' familiarity with air travel should make them more likely to opt for this transportation mode during their retirement years.

The TIA also expects that retirees of the future will favor international travel, rural destinations, and outdoor recreation, and the social interaction and learning experiences that travel can provide.

DESIRE FOR LIFELONG LEARNING

The fact that older baby boomers will be interested in vacations that provide opportunities for learning is hardly surprising. They are the best-educated generation in history. But today's retirees also have a substantial interest in educational opportunities.

Witness the phenomenal success of the Boston-based Elderhostel program, an educational residential program for people aged 60 and older. It began in 1975 as a summer program on college campuses where a group of seniors spent a week in dorms—sharing bathrooms, taking courses, and eating in the cafeteria. As the program grew, the format branched out to include hotels, conference centers, national parks, museums, and private baths.

The average age of the hostelers is 70, and two-thirds are fully retired, according to Elderhostel marketing director Karyn Franzen. They are a highly educated and well-to-do group. Over half have done post-graduate work. Twenty-seven percent have net incomes of more than $50,000. Two-thirds are married. The sex ratio is representative of the elderly population at large—60 percent female and 40 percent male.

During the program's first year, 200 hostelers participated. In 1993, more than 270,000 elders participated, and the organization's mailing list ran to 600,000 names. "We're now getting into adventure programming, which is incredibly popular," says Franzen. Seniors participate with gusto in such activities as rock climbing in the Continental Divide and white-water rafting. The typical Elderhostel program, however, is tamer and more academic in nature.

Retirees' thirst for knowledge is not limited to vacation time. In fall 1991, almost 300,000 part-time students aged 50 and older were enrolled as undergraduate, graduate, and professional students across the country. Nearly 50,000 were enrolled full-time, according to the Department of Education, a number that will surely expand after the turn of the century as the baby boom enters its retirement years.

Some educational programs are aimed specifically at the retired population. Northwestern University's Institute for Learning in Retirement operates differently than traditional academic programs because participants plan and organize their own "study groups."

"No faculty is used. They are all peer-led," says program director Beth Hart. "Topics that lend themselves most to discussion are the most popular." Study groups on international affairs are well-attended, as are those concerning politics and the press, she says.

In 1987, the program started on the Evanston campus with an enrollment of 20. By 1993, the program expanded to include the Chicago campus and had a total enrollment of 300. The Northwestern success story is not unique. Colleges and universities around the country offer 175 "learning in retirement" programs, with close to 30,000 estimated participants. Their appeal is greatest with highly educated retirees. Hart says that most of her members have college degrees, and many have advanced degrees. Baby boomers, whose education level considerably exceeds that of today's retirees, should flock to such programs when they enter retirement.

"The more education that people have, the more they will seek," says Pat Thaler, associate dean at New York University's School of Continuing Education. Currently, 7 percent of nondegree students at the school are over the age of 55. "Some people leave demanding careers and choose school as a very positive substitute," says Thaler.

Classrooms are not the only places for learning. Many retirees prefer to learn in the privacy of their own homes through newspapers, books, and magazines. Retirement is when people finally have time to devote to such pleasures as reading. In 1985, consumers aged 55 to 64 spent an average of 2.7 hours per week reading books and magazines, according to a study by John P. Robinson at the University of Maryland, College Park. Women spent more time than men (2.9 hours versus 2.5 hours). This is much higher than for other age groups (1.3 hours for those aged 35 to 44, and 1.7 hours for those aged 45 to 54).

Retirement-aged people spent an average 1.9 hours per week reading newspapers. Here men had higher averages than women (2.3 hours versus 1.5 hours). Older people devote much more time to this than younger people. Those aged 18 to 24 spent just 0.3 hours per week, those aged 25 to 34 spent 0.6 hours, those aged 35 to 44 spent 1.0 hours, and those aged 45 to 54 spent 1.4 hours.

Television is often blamed for the decline of reading in the population. This may be true for young people, but it doesn't seem to hold for the older crowd. When the Gallup Organization asked adults in 1990 about their favorite way to spend an evening, 24 percent said watching television and 15 percent said reading. Both shares were higher for people aged 50 and older—37 percent said television and 18 percent said reading. Younger people were more likely to choose group activities like going to the movies and being with friends and family.

Many newly retired people also enjoy another home-based activity—gardening. Sales of seed, soil, tools, and other items have pushed gardening to a $9 billion industry. According to a 1992 survey commissioned by *Organic Gardening* magazine, 23 percent of America's 61 million gardeners are aged 50 to 64, although this group makes up just 17 percent of the adult population. The survey divides gardeners into four basic types. The oldest are the "masters," with an average age of 53. Fifty-four percent of "masters" are women. They have been gardening for an average of 16 years, and had a median household income of $28,300 in 1991. This group spends the most on gardening supplies, an average of $271 per year.

If women like gardening, golf definitely appeals more to men. Three-fourths of golfers are male, according to a survey by the National Sporting Goods Association. Golf courses are generally thought to be populated by retirees, but, in fact, young people are most likely to play golf. Between 1988 and 1991, an average of 23 percent of those aged 25 to 34 and 18 percent of those aged 35 to 54 played golf at least once a year. But the share was still a substantial 13 percent for those aged 55 to 64 and 12 percent for those who had passed their 65th birthday. As Diane Crispell of *American Demographics* points out, with the aging of baby boomers, golf will fare better than sports where participation peaks at very young ages and then declines sharply. Whatever pastimes retirees choose, it's important to remember that they differ from younger consumers.

"Mature consumers tend to be motivated more by the capacity of a product or service to serve as a gateway to experiences than by the generic nature of a product or service," writes David B. Wolfe, author of *Marketing to Boomers and Beyond: Strategies for Reaching America's Wealthiest Market*. Retirees today are finding many fulfilling substitutes for their careers: travel, education, hobbies, part-time work, volunteering. "There are those who didn't think I could ever enjoy retirement because I enjoyed my work so much," says Carroll Shanks, the former CEO whose story opened this chapter. "But I do."

PRODUCTS AND SERVICES FOR
The Retirement Transition

Planning for Retirement

Financial planning services
Banking and investment services
Long-term care insurance
Retirement counseling
Résumé services and career counseling for second careers
Legal services—wills, trusts

Relocating and Recreation

Retirement communities and resorts
Real-estate services
Golf courses and equipment
Boats and boating supplies
Gardening products

Travel and Education

Cruises, tours, and other travel packages
RVs and related equipment
Mobile homes
RV and mobile home parks and resorts
Campgrounds
Rental cars
Upscale hotels, motels, and restaurants
Dining clubs
Souvenirs
Continuing education and "learning in retirement" programs
Educational travel programs (e.g., Elderhostel)
Book clubs

SOURCES

Arizona State University, College of Business, Center for Business Research. "**1992–1993 CBR Study Tracks State's Winter Residents**," *Arizona Business*, Vol. 40, No. 6, June 1993, pp. 1–6.

Backman, Kenneth F. and Sheila J. Backman. "**New South Carolinian Study: A Profile of New Movers**," The Strom Thurmond Institute, Clemson University, Working Paper Series, September 1992.

Blazey, Michael A. "**Travel and Retirement Status**," *Annals of Tourism Research*, Vol. 19, 1992, pp. 771–783.

Crispell, Diane. "**Putters and Steppers**." *American Demographics*, July 1993, p. 59.

Crispell, Diane and William H. Frey. "**American Maturity**," *American Demographics*, March 1993, pp. 31–42.

Cruise Lines International Association. *The Cruise Industry: An Overview*, New York, NY: Cruise Lines International Association, July 1993.

Day, Jennifer Cheeseman. **Population Projections of the United States, by Age, Sex, Race, and Hispanic Origin: 1992 to 2050**. Washington, DC: U.S. Bureau of the Census, 1992.

Gallup, George, Jr. and Frank Newport. "**Americans Have Love-Hate Relationship with Their TV Sets**." *The Gallup Poll Monthly*, October 1990, pp. 2–14.

Gendell, Murray and Jacob S. Siegel. "**Trends in Retirement Age by Sex, 1950–2005**," *Monthly Labor Review*, July 1992, pp. 22–29.

Glascow, Nina. "**A Place in the Country**," *American Demographics*, March 1991, pp. 24–31.

Hansen, Kristin A. *Geographical Mobility: March 1991 to March 1992*, Washington, DC: U.S. Bureau of the Census, 1993.

Hayward, Mark D., William R. Grady, Melissa A. Hardy, and David Sommers. "**Occupational Influences on Retirement, Disability, and Death**," *Demography*, Vol. 26, No. 3, August 1989, pp. 393–409.

Hayward, Mark D., Melissa A. Hardy, and Mei-Chun Liu. "**Work After Retirement: The Experiences of Older Men in the U.S.**" *Social Science Research*, Vol. 23, No. 1, March 1994, pp. 82–107.

Health Insurance Association of America. *Who Buys Long-Term Care Insurance?* Washington, DC: Health Insurance Association of America, December 1992.

Independent Sector. *Giving and Volunteering in the United States: Findings from a National Survey*, 1992 Edition. Washington, DC: Independent Sector, 1992.

Longino, Charles F., Jr. and William H. Crown. "**Older Americans: Rich or Poor?**" *American Demographics*, August 1991, pp. 48–52.

McCallin, Rose C., et al. *CFP Survey of Trends in Financial Planning*, Denver, CO: College for Financial Planning, July 1993.

Mediamark Research, Inc. *Automobiles, Motorcycles, Trucks, Driving Report*. New York, NY: Mediamark Research, Inc., 1993.

Mediamark Research, Inc. *Travel, Insurance, Real Estate Report*. New York, NY: Mediamark Research, Inc., 1993.

Mergenhagen, Paula. "**A New Breed of Volunteer.**" *American Demographics*, June 1991, pp. 54–55.

Merrill Lynch. *Retirement Savings in America: The Fifth Annual Merrill Lynch Retirement Planning Survey*, Princeton, NJ: Merrill Lynch, 1993.

Paulin, Geoffrey. "**Consumer Expenditures on Travel, 1980–87,**" *Monthly Labor Review*, June 1990, pp. 56–60.

Robinson, John P. "**Thanks for Reading This.**" *American Demographics*, May 1990, pp. 6–7.

Social Security Administration. *Social Security Bulletin, Annual Statistical Supplement, 1993*. Washington, DC: U.S. Government Printing Office, 1993.

Sullivan, Deborah A. "**The Ties that Bind**," *Research on Aging*, Vol. 7, No. 2, June 1985, pp. 235–250.

Travel Industry Association of America. *The Mature Market: A Report on the Impact of the Changing Mature Market on the U.S. Travel Industry*, Washington, DC: Travel Industry Association of America, 1990.

U.S. Bureau of the Census, *Money Income of Households, Families, and Persons in the United States: 1992*. Washington, DC: U.S. Government Printing Office, 1992.

U.S. Travel Data Center. *1992 National Travel Survey*, Washington, DC: U.S. Travel Data Center, 1993.

Waldrop, Judith. *"Garden Variety Customers." American Demographics*, April 1993, pp. 44–48.

Waldrop, Judith. "**Old Money**," *American Demographics*, April 1992, pp. 24–32.

Waldrop, Judith. "**Winter Wonderland**," *American Demographics*, February 1993, p. 4.

Wolfe, David B. *Marketing to Boomers and Beyond: Strategies for Reaching America's Wealthiest Market*. New York, NY: McGraw-Hill, 1993.

OTHER RESOURCES

Braus, Patricia. "**Women of a Certain Age**," *American Demographics*, December 1992, pp. 44–49.

Burkhauser, Richard V. and Dallas L. Salisbury (eds.). *Pensions in a Changing Economy.* Washington, DC: Employee Benefit Research Institute/National Academy on Aging, 1993.

Kragie, Evelyn R., et al. "**Do Americans Plan For Retirement? Some Recent Trends**," *The Career Development Quarterly*, Vol. 37, March 1989, pp. 232–239.

Schewe, Charles D. "**Strategically Positioning Your Way into the Aging Marketplace**," *Business Horizons*, May–June, 1991, pp. 59–66.

Siegel, Jacob S. *A Generation of Change: A Profile of America's Older Population.* New York, NY: Russell Sage Foundation, 1993.

Spiller, Lisa D. and Richard A. Hamilton. "**Senior Citizen Discount Programs: Which Seniors to Target and Why**," *Journal of Consumer Marketing*, Vol. 10, No. 1, 1993, pp. 42–51.

Szinovacz, Maximiliane, et al. *Families and Retirement.* Newbury Park, CA: Sage Publications, 1992.

Wiatrowski, William J. "**Factors Affecting Retirement Income.**" *Monthly Labor Review*, March 1993, pp. 25–35.

PART III

MAKING THE LINK

CHAPTER 9

PULLING UP ROOTS
The Moving Transition

ANNETTE HOOK wasted no time after she and her husband moved from Shreveport, Louisiana to Tampa, Florida. Her first project was to paint and wallpaper the house because "it was new and they had painted everything—woodwork and walls—white." At the same time, she ordered new curtains, had an entertainment center made, purchased ceiling fans, and planned for shelving in the study. The house finally began to feel like a home.

Improvements like these often occur within the first year of a move, and many businesses benefit—home-supply stores, carpet centers, furniture makers, curtain manufacturers, and interior designers. People frequently purchase new appliances when they move, too. Handymen profit from people who are too busy or don't know how to do things themselves.

The Hooks's move was a corporate relocation. Annette's husband took a new job in a different state with an employer who paid for the move. But corporate transfers are less common in these days of corporate belt-tightening.

Moves in general are less common. The number of U.S. households making long-distance moves declined from 5.7 million in 1988–89 to 5.4 million in 1991–92. Yet those who move long-distance remain the cream of the crop for the moving industry. They are a lucrative market for moving companies, realtors, and corporate relocation specialists.

While households that make long-distance moves spend the most, most household moves are local, made within the same county. But even short-distance movers need to move their household goods, and they also create business, although on a smaller scale, for the moving industry.

Movers, both short- and long-distance, tend to be young. One-third of Americans in their 20s move in a given year, compared with less than 10 percent of those aged 45 and older. Those who move long-distance are somewhat older and more affluent than those who move locally.

One in four households buys the home it moves into. This creates business for real-estate agents, home-mortgage lenders, and home inspectors. Builders and architects profit when people buy new homes. Almost one in five homes sold are brand-new.

But most homes people move into (74 percent) are rental properties. Two-thirds of these are multi-family units. The apartment market has been a difficult one in recent years because of overbuilding combined with a shrinking supply of young people, although better times may be ahead as the young-adult population begins to grow again toward the turn of the century.

TRENDS IN THE MARKET

Sixteen million American households containing 43 million people moved between March 1991 and March 1992, according to the Census Bureau, accounting for 17.3 percent of the total population aged one and older. In 1950 and 1960, the mobility rate was closer to 21 percent. Although it has fluctuated somewhat since that time, overall it has declined.

The long-term decline in American mobility is partly due to the fact that moving tends to be a transition of the young, and the population is aging. In 1980, 41 percent of U.S. adults were under age 35. The share declined to 35 percent in 1994, and it will fall to 31 percent by 2000.

Mobility Rates

Americans are less likely to move than they used to be, but the numbers of movers have continued to grow.

(number in thousands and percent of population aged one and older who moved in 12-month period ending in March, by type of move, selected years, 1951–92)

	number moved	percent moved	within same county	to different county, same state	to different state	moved from abroad
1991–92	42,800	17.3%	10.7%	3.2%	2.9%	0.5%
1990–91	41,539	17.0	10.3	3.2	2.9	0.6
1988–89	42,620	17.8	10.9	3.3	3.0	0.6
1985–86	43,237	18.6	11.3	3.7	3.0	0.5
1980–81	38,200	17.2	10.4	3.4	2.8	0.6
1970–71	37,705	18.7	11.4	3.1	3.4	0.8
1965–66	37,586	19.8	12.7	3.3	3.3	0.5
1960–61	36,533	20.6	13.7	3.1	3.2	0.6
1950–51	31,464	21.2	13.9	3.6	3.5	0.2

Source: U.S. Census Bureau

One-third of people in their 20s move during the course of a year. The mobility rate declines steadily with age, to 20 percent for those in their 30s, 12 percent for those in their 40s, 9 percent for those in their 50s, 6 percent for those in their 60s, and just 5 percent for those aged 70 and older.

Other factors related to the likelihood of moving include homeownership status, changes in marital and employment status, income, and ethnicity. Renters are much more likely than home-owners to move, 34 percent compared with 9 percent in 1991–92, possibly because they tend to be younger and have fewer financial or family commitments to consider.

When marriages end, at least one person has to move. One-fourth of divorced persons moved between 1991 and 1992. The divorced are followed by the never-married—who tend to be young—with a mobility rate of 21 percent. Married people have a mobility rate of 15 percent, and widowed people (the oldest group) are least likely to move—8 percent did so in 1991–92.

Who Moves

People most likely to move are those in the Armed Forces, those in their 20s, renters, and Hispanics.

(population in thousands as of March 1992 and percent who moved between March 1991 and March 1992, by selected characteristics)

	number	percent who moved
total aged one and older:	247,380	17.3%
1 to 9	34,115	20.0%
10 to 14	18,021	15.4
15 to 19	16,568	17.5
20 to 24	17,848	36.6
25 to 29	20,132	33.1
30 to 44	61,932	17.9
45 to 64	48,173	9.2
65 and older	30,590	5.4
sex:		
men	120,436	17.7%
women	126,944	16.9
race/ethnicity:		
white	207,030	16.7%
black	30,773	20.0
Hispanic*	21,544	23.5
tenure:		
in owner-occupied unit	165,612	8.9%
in renter-occupied unit	81,768	34.3
labor force status, aged 16 or older:		
employed in civilian labor force	115,724	18.5%
unemployed in civilian labor force	9,728	28.7
not in labor force	65,568	12.4
in Armed Forces	841	46.8

* Hispanics may be of any race.

Source: U.S. Census Bureau

People who were unemployed in March 1992 were more likely to have made a move during the previous year than those who were employed, 29 percent versus 18 percent. It is not clear, however, whether the moves were precipitated by unemployment or whether they caused it (as when a man or woman follows a transferred spouse). Military personnel are, by definition, employed, but they are the most mobile Americans of all—47 percent moved between March 1991 and March 1992.

Households with annual incomes of $50,000 or more are less likely to move than those with incomes below $20,000 or those with incomes between $20,000 and $49,999, 12 percent versus 21 percent and 17 percent, respectively. Again, this is at least partially due to age, because income tends to rise with age.

Both age and income may explain why 23 percent of Hispanics move during the course of a year. "You have in that group recent immigrants from Central and South America who have very low incomes," says Kristin Hansen, a Census Bureau analyst. "Hispanics also have a younger age structure than non-Hispanics."

Long-Distance vs. Local Moves

Long-distance moves, defined as those between states or between counties within states, account for one-third of all household moves. Fifteen million people in five million households made long-distance moves within the U.S. in 1991–92. Three percent of the population moved from one state to another, and another 3 percent to a different county in the same state.

Two-thirds of household moves are local—i.e., within the same county. Twenty-seven million Americans in ten million households, or 11 percent of the population, made local moves between 1991 and 1992.

Long-distance movers are older and more affluent than local movers. Those aged 45 and older accounted for 17 percent of long-distance moves, versus 13 percent of local moves. Median household income for those who made interstate moves was $27,100, compared with $25,900 for those who moved to a different county within the same state, and $24,000 for those who moved within the same county.

Married-couple families make up a greater proportion of long-distance movers than they do of local movers. Married-couple families comprise 40 percent of households who move long-distance but just 35 percent of those who move short distances. Single-parent families, on the other hand, comprise 14 percent of households who move long-distance, but make up 22 percent of those who move locally.

The Seasons and Regions for Moving

Almost one-third of moves occur during June, July, and August, according to John L. Goodman of the Federal Reserve Board. This is nearly twice the share that takes place during the winter months of December, January, and February. The monthly distribution of moves has been fairly stable over a 25-year period.

June graduations and weddings might seem the impetus for summer moves because they often result in new households. It also makes sense for families with children to relocate during summer vacations. But Judith Waldrop of *American Demographics* says that "Goodman's analysis of the American Housing Survey finds that newlyweds and parents of school-aged children make up only one-third of all adult movers. People with no obvious incentive to move in summer, such as the elderly and parents of preschoolers, also choose this time of year to relocate."

Goodman suggests that the seasonality of moves may have originated around weddings and school calendars and gradually became a firmly established habit, a cycle to which consumers, realtors, and home builders are accustomed. As Waldrop puts it, "Americans tend to move during the summer because this is when the greatest selection of housing is available."

Americans also seem to have acquired the habit of going West. Those whose moves end in Western states have the highest annual mobility rate (21 percent in 1991–92), followed by the South (19 percent), the Midwest (16 percent), and the Northeast (12 percent).

For a long time, more Americans have moved out of the Northeast than moved into it. But until 1990–91, this net outmigration was compensated for by immigrants from abroad. In 1990–91, the Northeast saw a significant net outflow for the first time—376,000 more persons moved out than moved in. In 1991–92, however,

Moving Motivations

Becoming a homeowner is one of the biggest reasons for moving.

(percent of homeowners and renters who moved in past 12 months, by reason* for move, 1991)

	owners	renters
private/government displacement	4%	7%
new job/transfer	10	12
to be closer to work/school/other	6	13
other, financial/employment-related	5	6
needed larger home	16	12
to establish own household	14	14
married	4	2
widowed/divorced/separated	3	6
other, family/person-related	10	11
wanted better home	15	12
change from owner to renter	—	1
change from renter to owner	23	—
wanted lower rent or maintenance	3	9
other housing-related reasons	7	8
other	15	14
not reported	3	2

* *Reasons add up to more than 100 percent because people could list more than one.*

Source: U.S. Department of Housing and Urban Development/U.S. Census Bureau

fewer residents left the region, and immigrants once again compensated for them.

The South and West, in contrast, see more people moving in than moving out. Overall, 607,000 more people entered the South than exited the region in 1991–92. Two-thirds were immigrants. The West saw net inmigration of 571,000 people in 1991–92; three-quarters were immigrants. The Midwest had similar numbers of U.S. residents moving in and out of the region, but immigration provided a net gain of 113,000 people.

Future Movers

Young people will continue to dominate the moving market, in spite of the fact that their numbers are declining. Diane Crispell of *American Demographics* projects that the number of movers in their early 20s will fall by 5 percent between 1992 and 2000, but still make up the largest segment of the market at 13 percent, down from 15 percent in 1991–92. The number of movers aged 30 to 34 could decline 12 percent, but will still account for 9 percent of all movers, down from 12 percent in 1991–92.

Baby boomers may be less likely to move as they grow older, but they will also be more likely to pay for moving-related services than they were in their youth, which means that professional moving services could gain business at the expense of the do-it-yourself rental industry. On the other hand, the number of young movers will start to pick up after 2005 as the children of baby boomers grow up and head out on their own.

GETTING THERE—MOVING COMPANIES AND RELOCATION SERVICES

Most movers are young renters who move locally. To get to their destination, they often rent or borrow trucks, line up friends, and do it themselves. Other local movers just can't face the prospect and hire professional movers like the aptly named Lansing, Michigan company, Two Men and a Truck.

Two Men is owned by Mary Ellen Sheets, whose teenaged sons started it as a summer business in the mid-1980s. When the boys went away to college, Sheets continued to receive customer inquiries, so she bought a used truck, hired two movers, and went to work. In 1989, she franchised the business; by 1993, she had 32 franchises in 15 states. "A lot of our customers are the people who used to move themselves," says Sheets. "But now baby boomers are older, and their friends don't want to help them anymore." Indeed, much of the baby boom has outgrown apartments and moved up to single-family homes. Only about one-third of Sheets' residential business involves moves into or out of apartments.

Gail Kelley operates the Columbus, Ohio franchise of Two Men and a Truck. Kelley says that half of her moves involve young couples with no children, and another one-third are families with children. The remainder are single young adults, older couples, and single elderly people. "We move more single women than single men," notes Kelley. This makes sense; men are less likely than women to live alone. Men are also more likely to go out and borrow or rent a truck and move themselves, says Kelley. Again, this makes sense; men who live alone tend to be younger than women who live alone.

When couples move, the wife is usually the one who calls for information or to book the move. She may or may not make the final decision, however. "If they're both working, we don't usually hear, 'I need to check with my husband.' They just do the deal," says Kelley. But if women are not working, "they say they'll call back after they talk to their husband."

For those who move long distances, professional moving services are more important. While fewer people make long-distance than local moves, more employ professionals to do the job. At least half of households making interstate moves use professional carriers, according to John Mehalic at the American Movers Conference (AMC) in Alexandria, Virginia.

AMC data reflect the decline in moving rates. In 1987, 52 of the largest interstate carriers reported a total of just over one million shipments of household goods. In 1992, 62 of the largest carriers reported 937,000 shipments. That year, 38 percent of shipments were corporate relocations and 41 percent were households paying for their own moves. The rest were government and military moves.

Corporate relocations are definitely down. "Corporations seem to be in a frenzy to downsize and cut staff," says Steve Mumma, a senior vice president at Atlas Van Lines in Evansville, Indiana. "They're also cutting back on moving people around." Because of this trend, Atlas has tried to attract more business from households paying their own way. In 1988, such households accounted for just 17 percent of Atlas' business. By 1993, the share increased to 22 percent. But corporate relocations are still the company's specialty, and they provide the lion's share of the business, at 60 percent.

Corporate relocation is a $15 billion industry in the U.S., according to the Employee Relocation Council (ERC) in Washington, D.C. It generally includes payment for shipment of household goods, as well as temporary living accommodations, house-hunting trips, payment of closing costs, and real-estate assistance. The average cost to relocate a homeowning employee grew from $15,800 in 1979 to $46,700 in 1991, then dropped slightly in 1992, to $45,300.

The majority of transferred employees are middle managers, according to the ERC. Three-fourths are married, and 60 percent have dependent children. Most are baby boomers in their late 30s, with salaries ranging from $40,000 to $60,000. Women make up an increasing portion of the ranks. In 1980, they comprised just 5 percent of corporate transfers. By 1991, the share tripled to 15 percent.

Whether transferees are men or women, most have spouses, many of whom also work. The majority of transfers include what the industry calls a "trailing spouse." Career counselors and job-placement agencies help these spouses find jobs. As of 1993, 54 percent of relocation specialists surveyed by Runzheimer International of Rochester, Wisconsin, provided spousal job assistance to transferees, up from 20 percent in 1984. Twenty-two percent extend this assistance to unmarried partners. The average cost of such services is $1,200, and they include résumé writing, access to job networks, and career counseling.

International transfers comprise a growing area of the relocation industry. In 1993, the ERC surveyed 180 corporate members who transfer employees to other countries and found almost half had increased their international assignments over the past three years. These companies averaged 68 U.S. employees on foreign assignments, just 6 percent of whom were women.

Overseas assignments require major adjustments by employees and their families, and companies prepare them in a number of ways. Most offer foreign-language training (87 percent), 57 percent provide cultural orientation, and 31 percent provide "repatriation" programs for returning employees. Companies often contract these services out to firms specializing in international relocation services.

Chicago resident Rebecca Rolfes has worked as a consultant for two companies specializing in international relocation. Rolfes counseled couples moving to Belgium, where she lived for several years when her husband was relocated there. People who relocate worry that they will feel isolated in a foreign country, says Rolfes. This fear is justified, she notes, especially for those who don't speak the language. Isolation can be hardest on the employee's spouse, typically the wife, because she doesn't have colleagues who speak English. "She will usually be the one who learns the new language, if anyone in the family does," says Rolfes.

THE HOUSING MARKET

One-fourth of people buy the home they are moving into, according to the 1991 American Housing Survey. With the historically low interest rates of recent years, consumers have become especially optimistic about the ability of people to afford the "American Dream." The share of people saying this is a "very good time to buy a home" increased from 38 percent in 1992 to 50 percent in 1993, according to the 1993 Fannie Mae National Housing Survey. The proportion who feel that "homeownership is within reach for most young people age 30 to 35" increased from 47 percent in 1992 to 74 percent in 1993.

Although the fortunes of the housing industry depend on economic factors such as interest rates, they also depend enormously on demographic change. In the early 1970s, as the first wave of baby boomers hit their 20s, housing starts increased from 1.5 million units in 1965 to nearly 2.4 million in 1972.

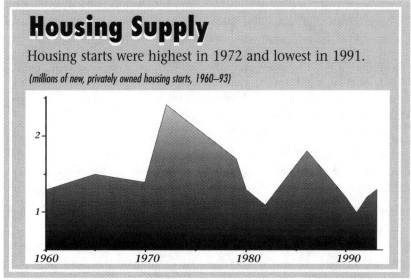

Housing Supply

Housing starts were highest in 1972 and lowest in 1991.

(millions of new, privately owned housing starts, 1960–93)

Source: U.S. Census Bureau

"A lot of those additional units were multi-family units," says Steve Berman, a Census Bureau analyst. "[Baby boomers] were getting out of school, and they needed apartments." The percent of new housing starts that were multi-family rose from 35 percent in 1965 to 44 percent in 1972. Then baby boomers entered their home-buying years in the late 1970s, and the share of single-family units grew. By 1979, just 32 percent of the 1.7 million homes built were multi-family units.

The recession of the early 1980s was difficult for the housing industry, which saw fewer than 1.1 million housing starts in 1982. Mid-decade prosperity resulted in an increase to 1.8 million in 1986. Although baby boomers were about to be replaced by the smaller baby-bust group in the apartment market, builders increased the share of multi-family housing starts that year to 35 percent. They later would suffer for this overbuilding, but in the "go-go" 1980s, housing of any type seemed a sure winner. Increasing housing prices kept homeowners feeling secure about their investments.

But as the decade came to a close, things changed. As James W. Hughes and Todd Zimmerman observe in *American Demographics*: "In 1989, the unthinkable happened. In many markets, home prices plunged . . . baby boomers, who had led demographic trends all their lives, were forced to confront a new demographic reality. The housing pyramid beneath them began to shrink as the smaller baby-bust generation entered the market. The tide of new buyers was receding, and the trade-up process began to melt down."

Housing starts numbered just over 1 million in 1991, the lowest since World War II. In 1992, they recovered to 1.2 million, and in 1993, to 1.3 million. In 1993, just 13 percent of new housing starts were multi-family units.

Housing starts are not the only indicator of housing-market activity. Housing sales are another. At least 80 percent of single-family housing sales are of existing, not new, homes. In 1981, when interest rates averaged over 16 percent, Americans bought 2.9 million homes, according to the National Association of Realtors and the Census Bureau. By 1986, interest rates had dropped to about 10 percent, and Americans bought 4.2 million homes. They also bought 4.2 million in 1992 when interest rates averaged 8.4 per-

Housing Demand

Almost one in five homes sold in the U.S. is new.

(thousands of new and existing homes sold, and mortgage interest rates, 1980–93)

	new homes sold	existing homes sold	average mortgage interest rate (fixed)
1993	670	3,799	7.3%
1992	610	3,520	8.4
1991	509	3,220	9.3
1990	534	3,211	10.1
1989	650	3,346	10.3
1988	676	3,513	10.3
1987	671	3,436	10.2
1986	750	3,474	10.2
1985	688	3,134	12.4
1984	639	2,829	13.9
1983	623	2,697	13.2
1982	412	1,991	16.1
1981	436	2,419	16.6
1980	545	2,973	13.8

Source: U.S. Census Bureau, National Association of Realtors, Federal Home Loan Mortgage Corporation

cent, and 4.5 million in 1993 when interest rates averaged a low 7.3 percent.

Housing values are another indicator of the industry's health. Homes appreciated at a slower rate in the early 1990s than in previous years. According to the National Association of Realtors, the average price of an existing home increased 17 percent between 1985 and 1987—from $90,800 to $106,300. Between 1990 and 1992, the average price grew just 10 percent—from $118,600 to $130,900. The average price for a new home increased 26 percent between 1985 and 1987—from $100,800 to $127,200, according to the Census Bureau. But it actually declined 4 percent between 1990 and 1992—from $149,800 to $144,000.

Not all areas of the country have suffered equally from declining prices, and some have not suffered at all. According to the National Association of Home Builders, the average sales price of all homes (both new and existing) declined less than 1 percent between 1990 and 1992. But they fell 14 percent in Maine, 11 percent in New Hampshire, 8 percent in Connecticut, 6 percent in Vermont, and 4 percent in California. During the same time period, they grew 26 percent in Washington state, 23 percent in Washington, D.C., 16 percent in Texas, 14 percent in Oregon, and 13 percent in Oklahoma.

The Future Housing Market

What are prospects for housing sales in the future? Not nearly what they were in the late 1960s, because the number of new households will grow more slowly than in the past. During the 1970s, the number of households grew 27 percent, as young baby boomers moved out on their own.

Household growth slowed to 14 percent in the 1980s. According to projections by *American Demographics*, the number of U.S. households will increase just 6 percent between 1990 and 1995—from 93 million to 99 million. Between 1995 and 2000, they will increase 11 percent, to 110 million. Between 2000 and 2005, they will grow just 1 percent to 111 million, as the small tail-end of the baby bust begins forming its households. The children of baby boomers will begin moving out on their own by 2005, causing households to increase 6 percent between 2005 and 2010, to 118 million.

Some analysts predict that because of the aging baby boom and the current decreased demand for housing, housing prices may decline as we head into the 21st century. Decreased demand will make it even more important to offer consumers what they want.

FINDING AND BUYING THE DREAM HOUSE

The building industry has responded to changing consumer tastes by altering the size, style, and amenities of housing. In 1970, new privately owned single-family homes had an average of 1,610 square feet of living space. By 1992, average size had increased to 2,095 square feet. "People want more space today," says Alice Moore Weaver, a Nashville real-estate agent with more than 20 years of experience. "We've all acquired more things. Twenty years ago, no one had a personal computer. Now, more and more people are working out of their homes."

Americans want more space for everything, not just their computers. Just 58 percent of new homes had garages in 1970, but by

Dream Homes

New homes are larger than they used to be. They are also more likely to have central air conditioning, garage, fireplace, and at least two bathrooms.

(thousands of new privately owned single-family homes, average square footage, and percent distribution by selected characteristics, 1970, 1980, and 1992)

	1992	1980	1970
total units	964	852	813
average square footage	2,095	1,700	1,610
stories:			
one	48%	60%	74%
two or more	47	31	17
split-level	5	8	10
parking:			
garage	83%	69%	58%
carport	2	7	17
bedrooms:			
two or fewer	12%	17%	13%
three	59	63	63
four or more	29	20	24
bathrooms:			
1-$1/2$ or fewer	13%	28%	52%
two	40	48	32
2-$1/2$ or more	47	25	16
central air-conditioning	77%	63%	34%
fireplace(s)	63%	56%	35%

Source: U.S. Census Bureau

1992, 83 percent did. Only 48 percent of new homes had two or more bathrooms in 1970. By 1992, 87 percent did. "People really like to have a bathroom for each bedroom, if it's possible," says Weaver. Americans want other comforts, too. Only 35 percent of new homes had fireplaces in 1970, compared with 63 percent in 1992. Central air-conditioning came with 34 percent of new homes in 1970, but 77 percent in 1992.

Consumer preferences have changed in other ways as well. In 1991, the National Association of Home Builders (NAHB) surveyed potential homebuyers about their preferences for first homes. In years gone by, a lot of living was done in living rooms. But the NAHB survey found that most people today prefer a large "family room" to a large living or dining room.

Kitchens used to be separate from other areas of the home, but today only 30 percent want this type of layout. Two-thirds prefer a more open floor plan. Alice Moore Weaver says this has been influenced by the increase in dual-earner families: "When parents are making dinner, they want access to the kids who are sitting in the den. It's an opportunity for family time together."

The NAHB survey found that several amenities were of particular importance to potential homebuyers, including washers and dryers, linen closets, additional bathrooms, central air-conditioning, walk-in closets, microwave ovens, dishwashers, pantries, and security systems.

The study also found that renters intending to buy currently lived in a home with a median of 1,000 square feet of living space. They wanted almost twice as much room when they bought a home, 1,900 square feet.

The need for more living space is a common reason for moving. But people have many others, and they often cite more than one. According to the 1991 American Housing Survey (AHS), of the 4.2 million homeowners who moved during the previous year, 23 percent said they did so to change their status from renter to owner. Sixteen percent said they needed a larger home; 15 percent wanted a better home; and 14 percent moved to establish their own household. Ten percent moved because of a new job, 6 percent to be closer to work or school, 4 percent because they got married, and 3 percent because they became widowed, divorced, or separated.

The AHS found that the most important reason for choosing a particular home is financial. Nearly half (45 percent) cited this as an important factor in their decision. Other factors were room layout and design, mentioned by 32 percent; size, mentioned by 19 percent; yard/trees/view, mentioned by 16 percent; and exterior appearance and quality of construction, each cited by 13 percent. Sixty-three percent looked at homes in more than one neighborhood before making their final selection.

Homeowners who have recently moved are substantially different from all homeowners. Recent movers are younger, more affluent, and more likely to have children than the average homeowning household. The median age of the householder in owner-occupied housing where a move occurred during the previous year is 37 years, according to the 1991 AHS. The median age of householders in all owner-occupied homes is considerably higher—51 years. Median household income of recent movers was $40,600, compared with $35,600 for all homeowners. And 46 percent of recent-mover homeowning households have children, compared with 37 percent of all homeowners.

When people are ready to buy a home, they are likely to turn to real-estate agents for general information. According to the 1993 Fannie Mae National Housing Survey, 65 percent of people say they would go to a real-estate agency for general information about home prices, neighborhoods, and interest rates. Twenty-one percent would turn to banks, 14 percent to newspapers, magazines, and publications, 11 percent to friends and family, and 9 percent to books.

But for specific information about mortgages, consumers more often turn to banks. Over half (57 percent) say they would go to banks for this purpose. One-third (31 percent) would turn to real-estate agents, 13 percent to mortgage lenders or mortgage brokers, and 13 percent to friends or relatives.

Most homeowners have mortgages. Of those who have moved during the past year, 79 percent have mortgages, according to the 1991 AHS. Nine in ten are new, rather than assumed, mortgages. Seventy-eight percent are fixed, rather than adjustable, rate. One-fourth are government—FHA or VA—loans.

Six in ten recently moved homeowners report a mortgage term

of 28 to 32 years. The next most frequent term is 13 to 17 years, held by 11 percent. For half, savings or cash on hand was the major source of the downpayment. For 28 percent, selling a previously owned home provided the major source of downpayment funds.

Sometimes people find their dream house, only to discover hidden problems. This was the plot of a 1986 comedy, The Money Pit, in which a hapless couple played by Tom Hanks and Shelley Long sank huge sums of borrowed money into a beautiful, but deeply flawed home.

Since this scenario is the nightmare of every potential homeowner, home inspectors have been doing a brisk business. They are employed by prospective buyers to assess the condition of a property prior to purchase. The number of members and candidates for membership in the American Society of Home Inspectors tripled to 4,300 between 1989 and 1994, says spokeswoman Vera Hollander Wadler. Nationally, about 35 to 45 percent of homes receive inspections prior to purchase, says Wadler, but that share varies by market. Although resale homes are most likely to be inspected, some buyers also have new homes inspected, she notes.

Davis Drewry, a home inspector in the high-income Washington suburb of Fairfax, Virginia, says that 75 to 80 percent of resale homes in his area undergo inspections. "The more educated the consumers are and the more expensive the property is, the more people are concerned about what they're getting," says Drewry. Real-estate agents are important sources of referral for home inspectors, he adds.

Needless to say, mortgage lenders are wary of money pits, too. They want to know that a home is worth the selling price, so most require property appraisals. This provides business for the country's 75,000 real-estate appraisers, most of whom are small independent operators who contract with lending institutions, says Ronald Beckham, director of national affairs at the National Association of Real Estate Appraisers.

Mortgage lenders typically require homeowners' insurance as well. Indeed, nine in ten recently-moved homeowners say they possess such insurance, according to the 1991 American Housing Survey.

HOME IMPROVEMENT

People improve their homes for two reasons: to sell them and to make them look the way they want. Many such changes tend to be cosmetic, including interior and exterior painting, wallpapering, carpeting, refinishing floors, and window treatments. These are particularly important when putting a house on the market. "Most people are interested in buying a house that looks like it's in good condition," says Nashville real-estate agent Alice Moore Weaver.

Once they move in, buyers often make additional adjustments to suit their tastes and lifestyles. "The things that happen in the first 18 months tend to be fairly cosmetic," says Ann Marie Moriarty, a senior editor at *Remodeling* magazine. "They usually wait till they've been in the house about five years before they do anything major, like add a room or remodel the kitchen. Most people stretch themselves fairly thin to purchase a house, and oftentimes don't have the extra cash that it takes to do a major project right away."

Data from the 1991 American Housing Survey appear to support Moriarty's contention. Owner-occupied homes that changed hands during the previous year were no more likely than all owned homes to have had recent major remodeling work. In fact, they were often less likely. Sixteen percent of all owner-occupied homes had a roof fully or partially replaced during the past two years, compared with just 9 percent that changed hands. Six percent of all owner-occupied homes had siding installed, compared with 3 percent where a recent move took place. Thirteen percent of owner-occupied homes had storm doors or windows installed, but just 7 percent where there had been a recent move. It is unclear whether the work done in homes that change hands is more often done by the seller or buyer.

Not surprisingly, people in new homes are less likely to make major improvements than those in older homes. Fewer than 2 percent of homes less than five years of age had a roof fully or partially replaced during the past two years. Just 1 percent had siding installed, and 4 percent had storm doors or windows installed. Similar numbers of homebuyers move into very old or very new homes. One in five moved into a home that was less than two years old, according to the 1991 AHS. About one in five moved into a home over 40 years old.

Fixing Up

Recent-mover homeowners are less likely than all homeowners to live in homes with new roofs, storm doors, windows, siding, bathrooms, or additions.

(percent of homeowner households and recent-mover households with selected home improvements in past two years, 1991)

	all homeowner households	recent-mover* homeowner households
replaced roof	16%	9%
built addition	4	3
added/remodeled kitchen	8	9
added/replaced bathroom	10	9
added/replaced siding	6	3
installed storm doors/windows	13	7
added insulation	7	7

*In past 12 months

Source: U.S. Department of Housing and Urban Development/U.S. Census Bureau

Although they may hold off on big projects for a while, consumers are willing to spend for small jobs like painting, carpeting, wallpapering, and minor replacements and fix-ups immediately after their move. Recent movers are an important market for the home-improvement industry, says Judy Riggs, executive director of the Home Improvement Research Institute.

Large home-center chains like Lowe's appeal to people who can do some home improvements on their own. At one time, these centers were just big warehouses that offered good selection and prices, but minimal help from sales associates. If people wanted customer service, they went to their local hardware store. But now the warehouse stores have caught on and are embracing customer service as well. This change in orientation could hurt independent hardware stores. A lot of money is at stake. Industry revenues for the nation's 22,100 individual hardware stores and 10,600 home-center units were estimated at $66 billion in 1993, according to Ellen Hackney of the Indianapolis-based National Retail Hardware Association.

Do-It-Yourself vs. Buy-It-Yourself

In 1990, 78 percent of U.S. households took part in a "do-it-yourself" home-improvement activity, according to a study by the Retail Hardware Research Foundation in Indianapolis. Thirty percent of these households could be considered "heavy" do-it-yourselfers, accounting for nearly 60 percent of all do-it-yourself activity. This group is most likely to own fairly new single-family homes and to consist of upper-middle- to lower-upper-income two-parent families with adults aged 30 to 55.

Painting is a frequent do-it-yourself activity. A 1993 study by the St. Louis–based National Decorating Products Association found that one in five American households does inside or outside painting each year. Of these, 75 percent buy the paint and do the painting themselves. Fourteen percent hire a painter who purchases the paint and does the work.

Yet another segment (11 percent) buys the paint but hires a painter to do the work. The home-improvement market has seen a growing trend toward "buy it yourself" and have someone else do it. "This is largely because there are so many working couples," explains Hackney of the National Retail Hardware Association. "They have enough income that they can afford to have at least part of the job installed. They have less time at home to do it themselves."

As baby boomers age, the "buy-it-yourself" trend will probably increase. What is easy to do for someone in their 20s and 30s may be more difficult in their 40s and 50s. Another factor behind the "buy-it-yourself" trend is that many people simply do not have the required expertise. Painting is one thing, but remodeling a bathroom is quite another. According to a 1992 Maritz Marketing Research study reported in *American Demographics*, the most important reason for contracting out is not a lack of time, but a lack of knowledge.

Women are important to the home-improvement industry. They don't do much of the work itself, but they frequently decide what to buy and buy it. A 1992 survey by the Home Improvement Research Institute found that women were the primary brand influencers and buyers of wallpaper and window blinds. They were more likely than men to put up the wallpaper, but less likely than men to install the blinds.

"We've done focus groups with women where we've asked them how they participated in do-it-yourself projects," says Hackney of the National Retail Hardware Association. "Women are very much involved in deciding what projects are going to be done and what products are going to be used, even to the point of making the purchase. Once it all gets home, though, in many cases it is the men who actually do the job." The Home Improvement Research Institute study found that women selected 35 percent of paint sold in 1991, but applied just 26 percent of it themselves.

Most consumers figure out colors, styles, and furniture layouts on their own. But some hire help when moving into a new residence. According to the Maritz Marketing Research survey, 64 percent of American adults usually do their own decorating, 20 percent have friends or relatives help them, and 10 percent say they don't do any home decorating.

The remaining 6 percent hire professional decorators. That 6 percent keeps Gary Aretz in business. He and his wife own Aretz Interiors in Mishawaka, Indiana. Most of their clients are over the age of 35, in dual-career households with incomes exceeding $50,000. The homes they decorate are rarely under 2,000 square feet. "Women usually start the process [of hiring an interior designer]," says Aretz. "The older men are interested in the bottom line. Younger men are usually a little more interested in design."

Appliances and Utilities

Like furniture, appliances are often tied to residential moves. Homes that have acquired new owners in the past year are much more likely than other homes to have relatively new appliances. Obviously, newly built homes have new appliances. But even existing homes often get new appliances either right before or right after they change hands. Homeowners may purchase new appliances to replace worn-out machines before they put a house on the market. New owners may purchase them because former owners took the appliances when they left. "The major appliances people often move are refrigerators, washers, and dryers," notes Nashville real-estate agent Alice Moore Weaver. New homeowners may also buy appliances because they want to upgrade.

According to the 1991 American Housing Survey, 56 percent of owner-occupied homes that changed hands during the previous year have a refrigerator less than five years old, compared with 35 percent of all owner-occupied homes. Fifty percent of homes that changed hands have ovens less than five years old, compared with 29 percent of all owner-occupied homes. In homes that changed hands during the previous year, 50 percent have washers less than five years old, compared with 33 percent of those in all owner-occupied homes. And in homes where there has been a move during the past year, 46 percent have dryers under five years old, versus 27 percent of those in all owner-occupied homes.

Utility companies also vie for the business of recent movers. Over half (56 percent) of owner-occupied homes that have changed hands during the past year are heated by gas, and one-third are heated by electricity. But 63 percent use electricity for cooking, compared with 36 percent that use gas.

Homebuyers keep telephone companies busy since 94 percent of recently moved homeowners have their phones connected within one year of the move. Movers must also decide whether they want to subscribe to cable television. More and more are deciding that they do. The share of households with cable increased from 23 percent in 1980 to 63 percent in 1993, according to A.C. Nielsen Company.

Reaching the Lucrative Homeowner Market

Although new homeowners are a profitable market, they are also on the move. Fortunately, a variety of businesses provide ways to reach recent movers, and even potential future ones.

The traditional way to contact recent movers has been through the "Welcome Wagon" concept. For years, Welcome Wagon hostesses have paid calls on new homeowners and "gifted" them with coupons from local merchants. Businesses also play a variation on this theme by marketing directly to new homeowners. They may find them listed in the local newspaper, or by using the Post Office's National Change-of-Address file or other recent-mover databases available from commercial vendors.

The only problem is that by the time a move has been made, so have many moving-related purchases—those involving real-estate agents, moving companies, mortgages, appliances, home inspections, and homeowners' insurance to name a few. But INPHO, a media company in Cambridge, Massachusetts, has devised a way of contacting the mover market during the "pre-move" stage. Consumers interested in the sales price of homes in a particular area can call a home-sales service. When they do so, their names and addresses are obtained (with their knowledge), providing a direct-mail list of potential movers. The service is available in California, Massachusetts, and several other states.

THE RENTAL MARKET

Despite Americans' desire for homeownership, 74 percent of households that moved during the previous year ended up in rental units, according to the 1991 American Housing Survey. Two-thirds of these renter households moved to multi-family units. Many such households may live in rental housing a long time. According to the Census Bureau, just 9 percent of renter families qualified for a median-priced mortgage under 1991 conditions.

Because of overbuilding during the 1980s and a smaller pool of young people—traditionally the best customers for apartment complexes—competition for renters will be intense for the rest of the 1990s. Real-estate analyst Kenneth Danter suggests that the industry look toward nontraditional niches, such as renters with children.

Recent-mover renter households are somewhat more likely to have children than the general population of renting households. Forty-one percent of renter households that experienced a recent move have children, more than the 38 percent for all renter households and almost as high as the 46 percent for homeowners who recently moved. But recent-mover renters are more likely than recent-mover homeowners to be single parents, 22 percent versus 9 percent. The median household income of recent-mover renters is also far lower than that of recent-mover owners, $20,700 versus $40,600. Even so, it's slightly higher than that of all renters ($20,300).

Danter notes that renters with children have special needs. They appear to prefer townhouse units over garden units. Programs such as on-site day care and after-school activities can also make apartment housing more appealing to families.

As with homeowners, renters who move tend to be younger than the general population of renters. According to an analysis of the 1991 American Housing Survey in *Apartment Resources*, a Danter Company publication, 46 percent of recent-mover renters were headed by someone under the age of 30, compared with 20 percent in renter households that did not move. Danter also found that nearly one-fourth of moves to rental units create newly formed households caused by such transitions as moving out of the parental home and the break-up of marriages.

The 1991 AHS found that 44 percent of renter households that recently moved ended up in units with two bedrooms, 30 percent in units with one bedroom, and 23 percent in units with three or more bedrooms. Median size was 1,233 square feet, and median monthly rent was $483.

Certain amenities are more important to renters at different times in their lives. According to a Danter Company survey of shoppers at upscale apartment complexes across the country, 70 percent of those aged 25 to 34 felt obtaining a larger unit was very important, compared with just 33 percent of those aged 65 or older. But only 26 percent of those aged 25 to 34 felt it was very important to be closer to shopping, compared with 52 percent of those aged 65 or older. "Better schools" were very important to 40 percent of those aged 35 to 44, but just 10 percent of those aged 65 or older. A garage was very important to 67 percent of those aged 55 to 64, but only 36 percent of those aged 18 to 24. At least two-thirds of each age group wanted a balcony or patio, however.

Like movers in general, most renters choose late spring and summer to make their moves. Eighteen percent of people in the apartment market who move do so in June, according to Danter Company research. That's followed by July (17 percent), August (16 percent), and May (14 percent).

Many factors impact those shares in particular markets, says Kenneth Danter. "In very hot areas, you get very little movement in July and August." The arrival of college students in college towns and "snowbird" retirees in states like Florida create their own patterns. But that pattern is different in Orlando, says Danter, due to seasonal hiring at Walt Disney World.

"In coastal areas where there are military bases, especially bases with aircraft carriers, move-ins and -outs correspond to when the carrier is in dock," says Danter. He says there is also a cycle in Washington, D.C. that goes with a change in administrations.

These patterns have a great impact on utility companies called upon to "hook up" movers. Who gets the business depends on the nature of the local housing market. Rental units that change hands are somewhat less likely than owner-occupied units to be heated by gas (48 percent versus 56 percent) and more likely to be heated by electricity (38 percent versus 32 percent). Recent-mover renters are less likely than owners to have telephone service (83 percent versus 94 percent).

There is an even greater divergence in the percentages with certain appliances. A far smaller share of recent-mover renters than owners have washers (40 percent versus 90 percent), dryers (35 percent versus 85 percent), or central air-conditioning (40 percent versus 56 percent). The median age of such renter-occupied units is 23 years, compared with 14 years for owner-occupied units, according to the 1991 American Housing Survey. This makes renters a good market for laundromats and stores that sell fans and window-unit air-conditioners.

People move to new rental units for reasons similar to those who buy homes. Both owners and renters frequently move to get a better, larger home, or to establish their own household. But there are differences between the two groups of movers. Twice as many renters as owners say they moved to be closer to work or school (13 percent versus 6 percent) or because they became widowed, divorced, or separated (6 percent versus 3 percent). And the top reason homeowners give—to change their status from renter to owner—does not apply to those who remain or become renters.

PRODUCTS AND SERVICES FOR
The Moving Transition

Moving Services

Moving vans—interstate and local
Do-it-yourself truck rentals
Relocation services—domestic and foreign

Home Buying

Services of real-estate agents
Real-estate appraisers
Home mortgages
Home inspections
Homeowner's insurance
Existing homes
Contractors/developers for new homes

Home Improvement

Draperies, blinds, and other window treatments
Wallpaper
Carpeting and flooring
Paint and painting
"Handyman" services
Appliances
Utility service: fuel, water, sewer, phone
Cable TV service
Lawn mowers and lawn service
Interior decorating services
Security products

Rental Market

Apartments
Renters' insurance
Furnishings

SOURCES

Adkins, Mark A., Bradley T. Farnsworth, and Hal R. Marsolais. *Positioning to the DIY Consumer: Success Requirements for Superior Performance in the 1990s*. Indianapolis, IN: Russell R. Mueller Retail Hardware Research Foundation, 1990.

American Movers Conference. *Moving Industry Financial and Economic Statistics*, Alexandria, VA: American Movers Conference, 1993.

American Movers Conference. *Moving Industry Financial Annual 1993*, Alexandria, VA: American Movers Conference, 1993.

American Movers Conference. *Quarterly Marketing Study*, Alexandria, VA: American Moves Conference, 1992.

Crispell, Diane. "**Movers of Tomorrow.**" *American Demographics*, Ithaca, NY, June 1993, p. 59.

Danter Company. "**Recent-mover Renters: The American Housing Survey of 1991.**" *Apartment Resources,* Danter Company, Columbus OH, July 1993, pp. 2–6.

Danter, Kenneth F. "**Apartment Lending After the Boom.**" *Mortgage Banking*, Washington, DC, July 1991, pp. 41–48.

Danter, Kenneth F. "**Understanding Multifamily Markets.**" *Mortgage Banking*, Washington, DC, July 1993, pp. 18–29.

DeAre, Diana. *Geographical Mobility: March 1990 to March 1991*, Washington, DC: U.S. Bureau of the Census, 1992.

Editors of *American Demographics*. "**The Future of Households.**" *American Demographics*, Ithaca, NY, December 1993, pp. 27–40.

Employee Relocation Council. *1993 International Survey*, Washington, DC: Employee Relocation Council, 1993.

Employee Relocation Council. *1993 Relocation Trends Survey*, Washington, DC: Employee Relocation Council, 1993.

Fannie Mae. *National Housing Survey 1993*, Washington, DC: Fannie Mae, 1993.

Goodman, John L. "**A Housing Market Matching Model of the Seasonality in Geographic Mobility.**" *The Journal of Real Estate Research* 8, pp. 117–137.

Hansen, Kristin A. *Geographical Mobility: March 1991 to March 1992*, Washington, DC: U.S. Bureau of the Census, 1993.

Home Improvement Research Institute. *1992 Product Purchase Tracking Study*, Lincolnshire, IL: Home Improvement Research Institute, 1992.

Hughes, James W. and Todd Zimmerman. "**The Dream is Alive.**" *American Demographics*, Ithaca, NY, August 1993, pp. 32–37.

Krafft, Susan. "**Reaching Movers Before the Big Day.**" *American Demographics*, Ithaca, NY, December 1993, p. 14.

Larson, Jan. "**Getting Professional Help.**" *American Demographics*, Ithaca, NY, July 1993, pp. 34–38.

National Association of Home Builders. *Housing Backgrounder*, Washington, DC: 1993.

National Association of Home Builders. *Housing Market Statistics*, Washington, DC: 1993.

National Asssociation of Home Builders. *What First Time Home Buyers Want, Executive Summary*, Washington, DC: National Association of Home Builders, 1992.

National Cable Television Association. *Cable Television Developments*. Washington, DC: National Cable Television Association, 1994.

National Decorating Products Association. *Consumer Paint Study*, St. Louis, MO: National Decorating Products Association, 1993.

Runzheimer International. *Runzheimer Reports on Relocation*, Rochester, WI: 1994.

Speer, Tibbett. **"Helping Renters Make the Down Payment."** *American Demographics*, Ithaca, NY, December 1993, pp. 21–22.

U.S. Bureau of the Census. *Current Construction Reports*, Series C25, *Characteristics of New Housing: 1992*, Washington, DC: U.S. Department of Commerce, 1993.

U.S. Bureau of the Census. **New Privately Owned Housing Units Started: 1959 to 1993** [unpublished data]. Washington, DC: U.S. Department of Commerce, 1993.

U.S. Bureau of the Census/U.S. Department of Housing and Urban Development. **American Housing Survey for the United States in 1991**, Washington, DC: U.S. Government Printing Office, 1993.

Waldrop, Judith. **"Movers Today."** *American Demographics*, Ithaca, NY, June 1993, p. 4.

OTHER RESOURCES

Fannie Mae. *Housing America*. Washington, DC: Fannie Mae, 1993.

Long, Larry. *Migration and Residential Mobility in the United States*, New York, NY: Russell Sage Foundation, 1988.

McCollum, Audrey. *The Trauma of Moving*, Newbury Park, CA: Sage Publications, 1990.

National Association of Realtors. *The Effect of Demographics on Future Housing Prices*, Washington, DC: National Association of Realtors, 1993.

CONCLUSION
Life Changes Mean Business

AT THIS POINT, it should be apparent that life transitions make for good business opportunities. Changes in the timing and frequency of transitions have greatly increased the potential demand for a wide variety of products and services. Demographic change, specifically an aging population, is creating a bigger market for transitions of mid- and later-life, but a temporarily smaller market for transitions of youth. Women's changing roles have affected the nature of both family- and job-related transitions.

The time crunch and stress that men and women experience during transitions opens the door to business opportunities galore, both those directly aimed at consumers and those purchased on their behalf by employers. Serving the customer well during transitions could mean the beginning of a beautiful and long-lasting relationship.

1. Transitions previously considered one-time events now occur more than once.

When people were asked by a 1988 CBS News/*New York Times* poll to recall their most memorable day, the number-one answer, cited by

23 percent of adults, was their wedding day. If this poll had been conducted in 1960, it would have been obvious which wedding they meant—their first and only. But in 1988, an appropriate follow-up question would have been, "Which one?" because marriage is no longer a once-in-a-lifetime transition for many people. Neither is first parenthood, if its definition includes stepparenthood.

The fact that family-related transitions now happen more than once means more marketing opportunities—more weddings to cater, more divorces to settle. The same is true for work-related transitions. Schooling used to continue serenely from the age of about six to 18 (or 22 for those who went to college). If an individual dropped out along the way, tough luck. The "once-in-a-lifetime" opportunity for learning was over. But today, people can and do go back to school at any age. Likewise, women have more opportunities in the work force, and they are taking advantage of them.

Retirement still conjures up images of rocking chairs and golf games. But these images are out-of-date. As many as one-third of those who retire re-enter the paid labor force to some extent and many others volunteer their services, suggesting that many people now experience multiple and varied phases of retirement.

In a multi-transition environment, good customer service is critical, because it opens opportunities to serve the same customer again and again. Take a real-estate agent who helps a young couple find a suitable home. If the couple divorces a few years later, and if they had a positive experience with the agent, they may once again knock on her door to help them sell the house. Down the road, they may also be in the market for new homes with new spouses.

2. Ages at which "transitions of youth" occur have shifted upward.

Many life transitions happen to young people. But "young" is older than it used to be. It once referred to those in their teens and early 20s. Now it is more likely to mean those in their late 20s and early 30s. Indeed, people most frequently enter first marriages and become parents for the first time in their mid- to late 20s, and an increasing number do so at even greater ages.

Most Americans still graduate from high school at 18, but a

smaller share move directly into the "real world" of work; a growing share delay this transition by going to college. Furthermore, people take longer to finish college than they used to, not because they are less intelligent, but because many work and attend school at the same time or go back and forth between work and school. This extends the time it takes to earn a degree. Less than one-third of those receiving bachelor's degrees in 1990 did so within four years of graduating from high school, compared with close to half of those who received their sheepskins in 1977.

This makes for an older student population. In 1970, 28 percent of students enrolled in higher education were aged 25 or older. In 1991, almost half were. Older consumers have greater purchasing power. They are also savvy consumers with greater life experience, which should be taken into account when designing products and services. For example, older students prefer learning through group discussion and may be less tolerant than 20-year-olds of standard professorial lectures.

This aging process has affected other transitional markets, too. When older people have a baby, they are likely to be more interested than their younger counterparts in the medical and social aspects of childbirth. And couples who marry or remarry at greater ages are less likely than young first-timers to be in the market for traditional wedding gifts.

3. Markets for "transitions of youth" will (temporarily) decline.

Every silver lining has a cloud attached to it, and transitional markets are no exception. Since most transitions still occur to young people (albeit "older" young people), and this age group is currently shrinking, the number of consumers to whom these transitions occur is declining. The baby boom is quickly moving past the ages at which most graduations, weddings, job changes, and divorces occur. In 1994, 35 percent of the adult population in the U.S. is under age 35. By 2000, the share will decline to 31 percent.

Of course, the fact that many consumers will experience certain life transitions more than once will help to cushion the blow. Other encouraging news is that the market for some youth transitions will pick up a bit when the children of baby boomers begin dominating the 18-to-24 age group around the turn of the century.

Nevertheless, in the short term, the U.S. will have fewer young adults. *American Demographics* editor Judith Waldrop discusses several ways to cope with slow-growing markets. The basic idea is to increase share of the existing market. Here are a few examples of transition-related businesses already following some of Waldrop's suggestions:

Find a Fast-Growing and Underserved Niche

Boston's First Step, ltd. markets baby products to child-care centers through a mail-order catalog. Although the number of births in the U.S. may decline slightly during the late 1990s, the need for infant care will probably grow. First Step has identified day-care providers as an underserved market with special needs.

Adapt to the Future

When cloth diapers went out of vogue in the early 1990s, Atlanta's Lullaby Diaper Service adapted by offering disposables, too, thereby attracting mothers who were interested in using a combination of the two. In the same way, many colleges have adapted to the needs of older, part-time students by offering classes at nights and on weekends.

Create Incentives to Buy

To increase its share of the young newlywed market, ARBOR National Mortgage of Uniondale, New York set up a bridal registry program so wedding guests can contribute to the downpayment on a couple's home. This provides couples with an incentive to obtain a home mortgage from ARBOR.

Each year, the baby-furniture industry develops products with added safety features. This encourages parents who are not first-timers to buy new models instead of using hand-me-downs.

4. Markets for "transitions of maturity" will grow.

Retirement and caregiving are transitions that occur to people in middle age and later life. The average caregiver is a woman in her mid-40s. The average retiree is a man in his mid-60s. In 1994, 32 percent of the adult population in the U.S. is aged 45 to 69. The share will increase to 35 percent by 2000 and 40 percent by 2010.

While both transitions occur to mature individuals, from a marketing perspective the dynamics of retirement and caregiving couldn't be more different. Caregiving conflicts with the time people need for other activities, like work. The challenge is to show caregivers how products or services will help them conserve time yet still provide quality care for aging relatives. The elder-care management business has grown rapidly because it meets these needs.

Retirement, on the other hand, frees up time. The challenge here is to convince people that a product or service will fill their time in a meaningful way. Boston-based Elderhostel has succeeded in this regard by combining travel with learning experiences.

5. Women have been affected more than men by changes in life transitions, and women more often make the buying decisions surrounding transitions.

Family life has traditionally been associated with women, so it comes as no surprise that they are more involved with and affected by family-related transitions. In addition, for all family transitions with the possible exception of divorce, women are a more important target market than men because they make the bulk of purchase decisions.

Mothers remain more involved than fathers in childrearing, starting well before the baby's birth. Women make most of the decisions concerning prenatal care and childbirth, as well as baby-care products and services. They also make most of the decisions about caregiving services for elderly parents, since they provide the majority of that care. Although men are more involved in weddings than they were in the past, women largely run the show. There is no male equivalent of *Modern Bride*.

The increased likelihood of divorce over the past quarter century has had a greater impact on women because they usually get custody of the children. The rise in single-parent families is essentially a rise in single-mother families. This has important implications for marketers because households headed by single mothers are far less affluent than those headed by couples or single or noncustodial fathers.

Women have dominated most of the changes in work-related transitions, too. In 1960, 40 percent of women aged 25 to 44 were in the paid labor force. By 1993, three-fourths were. The variety of jobs open to women today is much greater than in the past. As a result, employed men are somewhat less likely today to change occupations than they were in the mid-1960s, but employed women are over 50 percent more likely.

In the future, women will dramatically change the face of the retirement market, too. Currently, both men and women retire at age 63 on average. There is no clear consensus on whether retirement age will rise or fall when baby boomers begin entering their retirement years at the turn of the century. But it is abundantly clear that the share of women retirees who have spent their entire adult lives in the labor force will grow substantially.

Marketers would do well to anticipate the economic power of tomorrow's retired baby-boom women. They will need the same types of financial and legal retirement-related services that men have been using for some years. Women's economic power should also make them more important decision-makers when it comes to couples' post-retirement lifestyle and purchasing behavior.

6. Transitions occur over a period of time and often have two or three different stages.

Life transitions do not occur instantaneously. They typically involve two or three stages, all of which present business opportunities.

In the "pre-transition" period, consumers do a great deal of preparatory research, planning, and decision-making. If the transition involves a tangible event or ceremony, as with weddings, graduations, births, and moves, consumers buy things to help them get ready for it—the services of wedding consultants, childbirth education classes, and realtor services. Even when no formal event (or a perfunctory one) marks the transition, as in divorce, caregiving, and career change, people still need preparatory products and services, such as legal and other expert help for divorce, counseling for career change, and home modification for caregiving.

The ceremony or event itself produces the immediate opportunities most readily associated with transitions—cakes, dresses, and flowers for weddings; caps, gowns, and photographs for graduations; moving companies for moving day; gifts for almost everything.

Finally, during "post-transition" life, consumers adjust to their new status and role. This stage may yield the most important and long-term opportunities for the widest variety of products and services, many of which are not unique to a specific transition or to transitions in general. For instance, both new graduates and newly-weds may set up new households; homebuyers may be more likely than average to buy paint, draperies, and wallpaper, but new parents and divorcing couples trying to sell a home buy them, too.

It is important to remember that adjustment to post-transition life can last quite a while. Homeowners frequently make initial changes to their dwelling over a period of one or two years. The effects of divorce can last several years. Caregiving may require on-going adjustment, including the final one that occurs when a loved one dies.

7. Consumers are often highly stressed during periods of transition.

People develop patterns in their daily lives that are comfortable because they are familiar. The lives of college students come to revolve around semesters, spring breaks, and exam weeks. As graduation day approaches, many students experience anxiety. There will be no more nights studying in the library, no more summer vacations.

Life transitions are stressful because they replace the known and familiar with the unknown and unfamiliar. In a 1993 survey by Roper Starch Worldwide, adults who had been through various transitions were asked if they experienced difficulty adjusting to their new roles. Other than the death of a spouse, which almost nine in ten people found difficult, getting divorced was the hardest transition. Seven in ten respondents said they had difficulty when their marriage ended. About four in ten found retiring hard; the share was higher among younger retirees, many of whom probably retired involuntarily. More than one-third of those who made long-distance moves had trouble adjusting.

Challenging Changes

Losing a spouse through either death or divorce is the most traumatic change for people who have been through the experience.

*(percent of adults aged 18 and older who find selected life transitions difficult,*1993)*

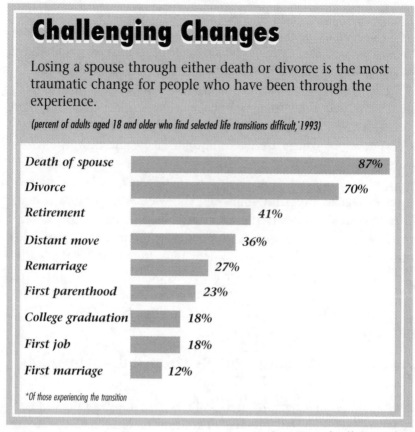

Death of spouse	87%
Divorce	70%
Retirement	41%
Distant move	36%
Remarriage	27%
First parenthood	23%
College graduation	18%
First job	18%
First marriage	12%

*Of those experiencing the transition

Source: Roper Starch Worldwide, New York, NY

Even supposedly joyful transitions are stressful. Nearly one-fourth of respondents told Roper that becoming a parent for the first time was difficult—27 percent of women and 19 percent of men. Almost 20 percent said that college graduation and a first job were hard transitions to make. Interestingly, more than one in four adults said that remarriage was difficult, but just 12 percent felt this way about a first marriage. Perhaps the presence of children and bad memories from a previous marriage make the remarriage transition a rockier one.

Businesses that market to people in transition are frequently dealing with people under stress. The opportunity lies in alleviating consumers' anxiety; the challenge is to do so in a sensitive way. For example, perhaps at no time is the desire for reassurance and a sense of mastery greater than before, during, and after the essentially un-controllable event of childbirth. This is one of the reasons why pregnancy and childbirth books, childbirth education classes, birthing rooms, and midwives have become so popular (along with the fact that parents are older and better-educated than they used to be).

But people consider retirement and moving even more difficult than becoming a parent. Retirement usually marks the end of several decades in the labor force and a loss of structure in daily activities. Long-distance moves mean the loss of a familiar community and all it contains, from grocery stores and schools to family, friends, and neighbors. Marriage, parenthood, and graduation are, in this day and age, largely voluntary events, but retiring and moving may or may not be. Retirement and outplacement counselors, health-care providers, those in the travel industry, and others who serve retirees can allay their anxieties. Moving companies, realtors, mortgage lenders, and others who make their business by relocating people can do the same.

8. Consumers often lack the time to handle transition-related tasks.

It used to be that when a woman married, she went straight from her parents' home to her husband's home. In 1960, the median age at first marriage for a woman was 20, and many wed right out of high school. Others worked until they got married, then left the labor force to become full-time homemakers. A bride and her mother—who was also at home—had plenty of time and energy to plan the festivities.

Today, the median age at first marriage for an American woman has increased to 24. Many brides have been to college—perhaps far from home—and lived on their own in dormitories and apartments. Many are no longer living in the towns and cities where they grew up. Most are employed as of their wedding day and have no plans to give up their jobs after throwing the bouquet. But planning a wedding while concentrating on a career can be difficult, not to mention the fact that mom may not be available to help with the details. This is where the surrogate mother of the bride—a wedding consultant—steps in.

Many businesses have emerged or expanded to serve busy people going through life transitions. They perform the tasks that consumers have no time for, including child- and elder-care, house-cleaning, interior decorating, catering, and moving. The time crunch has also helped drive growth in the direct-mail industry because it allows people to shop from home. New homeowners receive catalogs selling linens and domestics, as well as furniture and gardening supplies. New and expectant parents are deluged with catalogs featuring infant furniture and clothing, maternity wear, and child-proofing products.

9. Consumer transitions provide business-to-business opportunities, too.

Life transitions also present many opportunities for business-to-business marketing. Much of this interchange takes place between large employers and independent contractors. Just as consumers are buying more transition-related services, so are employers.

Large companies once retained staff to conduct employee training sessions and even produced their own training films. But more and more are hiring out training-related tasks. Independent consultants also produce many of the retirement planning seminars, tapes, and brochures that employers offer. Companies that may have maintained in-house employee assistance programs in the past now outsource information and referral services for those who need elder- and child-care assistance.

Schools are another example of transition-related organizations that outsource products and services. Outside suppliers provide many of the items that surround graduation—caps and gowns, yearbooks, class rings, and senior pictures. As competition for students became more intense during the 1980s, colleges and universities began to hire outside consultants to market to potential students.

10. Businesses can use transitions to develop lifelong relationships with customers.

Consumers typically re-evaluate their needs for products and services at several transition points in their lives. For example, a college freshman may acquire a bank credit-card. The same customer may return to open a joint checking account after getting married. He or she may even come back a few years later to look into a mortgage or open a retirement account. People also frequently reconsider their insurance needs when they marry, become parents, divorce, or remarry. They modify wills and other legal documents at these times, too. The bankers, financial planners, and lawyers who serve these customers well may keep them a lifetime.

Likewise, the hotel, reception hall, or catering service that successfully hosts a high school prom may be in the running for future wedding business. The newlywed couple who enjoyed their honeymoon cruise may buy an anniversary trip for their parents. Schools with satisfied graduates can look forward to alumni contributions.

The value of easing a consumer through one of life's big changes may extend even beyond that individual's lifelong loyalty. The truly satisfied customer will provide additional business by spreading the word. The new mother who has had a good experience with a nurse-midwife is likely to tell her pregnant friends about it. And so the chain of life continues, from transition to transition, from person to person.

Index

by Carol Roberts

Note: Tables are indicated by italics.

AMERICAN
DEMOGRAPHICSBOOKS®

EVERYBODY EATS: SUPERMARKET CONSUMERS IN THE 1990S

This is the first book to focus exclusively on supermarket shoppers and the factors that influence their food purchasing decisions. It divides shoppers into four age segments and further defines them in terms of region, race and ethnicity, and economic groups.

THE AMERICAN FORECASTER ALMANAC: 1994 BUSINESS EDITION

A fascinating compendium tracking key trends in almost every aspect of American culture, this book covers technology, consumer goods, business, health, education, fashion, entertainment, travel, and leisure.

THE INSIDER'S GUIDE TO DEMOGRAPHIC KNOW-HOW: EVERYTHING YOU NEED TO FIND, ANALYZE, AND USE INFORMATION ABOUT YOUR CUSTOMERS

Now in its third edition, this useful sourcebook covers federal, state, local, private, and international sources of demographic data. It directs you to the right source of information and explains how to ask for the numbers you need.

HEALTH CARE CONSUMERS IN THE 1990S: A HANDBOOK OF TRENDS, TECHNIQUES, AND INFORMATION SOURCES FOR HEALTH CARE EXECUTIVES

This handbook makes the connection between demographic realities and related health care issues. It will help you define your target market and carve out a niche that you can serve profitably and effectively.

THE BABY BUST: A GENERATION COMES OF AGE

As a generation, busters are unique in their experiences, beliefs, politics, and preferences. This is the first statistical biography of this generation. It tells their story through demographics, opinion polls, expert analysis, anecdotes, and the indispensable comments and experiences of busters themselves.

TARGETING FAMILIES: MARKETING TO AND THROUGH THE NEW FAMILY

Word-of-mouth product recommendations made from one family member to another are significantly more effective than those made between friends or colleagues. Learn how to get family members on your sales force and how to implement a "Full Family Marketing" approach that attracts youths, spouses, and seniors.

CAPTURING CUSTOMERS: HOW TO TARGET THE HOTTEST MARKETS OF THE '90S

Find out how to combine demographics with geographic, psychographic, and media preference data, and how to use consumer information to identify opportunities in nearly every market niche.

BEYOND MIND GAMES: THE MARKETING POWER OF PSYCHOGRAPHICS

The first book that details what psychographics is, where it came from, and how you can use it.

SELLING THE STORY: THE LAYMAN'S GUIDE TO COLLECTING AND COMMUNICATING DEMOGRAPHIC INFORMATION

A handbook offering a crash course in demography and solid instruction in writing about numbers. Learn how to use numbers carefully, how to avoid misusing them, and how to bring cold numbers to life by relating them to real people.

THE SEASONS OF BUSINESS: THE MARKETER'S GUIDE TO CONSUMER BEHAVIOR

Learn which demographic groups are the principle players and which consumer concerns are most pressing in each marketing season.

DESKTOP MARKETING: LESSONS FROM AMERICA'S BEST

Dozens of case studies show you how top corporations in all types of industries use today's technology to find tomorrow's customers.

About the Author

PAULA MERGENHAGEN is a regular writer for *American Demographics,* a monthly business magazine published by Dow Jones & Company, Inc. She frequently writes on life transitions and the business opportunities they provide.

Dr. Mergenhagen has a Ph.D. in Sociology from Vanderbilt University. She has taught there and at the University of Tennessee. She has held research positions with the Vanderbilt Institute for Public Policy Studies, the United Way, and Demographic Data Consultants, a market research firm in Nashville, Tennessee.

Her articles have appeared in a wide variety of publications, including the *Journal of the American Medical Association, Sociology and Social Research,* and *Urban Affairs Quarterly.*

She and her husband live in Nashville, Tennessee.